THE CAMBRIDGE CO
TO SENSATION F]

CW00548236

In 1859 the popular novelist Wilkie Collins w
from head to toe in white garments, laying her cold, thin hand on the snouɪucɪ ʋ. ·
young man as he walked home late one evening. His novel *The Woman in White*
became hugely successful and popularised a style of writing that came to be
known as sensation fiction. This *Companion* highlights the energy, the impact
and the inventiveness of the novels that were written in 'sensational' style,
including the work of Mary Elizabeth Braddon, Mrs Henry Wood and Florence
Marryat. It contains fifteen specially commissioned essays and includes a chron-
ology and a guide to further reading. Accessible yet rigorous, this *Companion*
questions what influenced the shape and texture of the sensation novel, and what
its repercussions were both in the nineteenth century and up to the present day.

ANDREW MANGHAM is Associate Professor in Victorian Literature and Culture
at the University of Reading. He is the author of *Violent Women and Sensation
Fiction: Crime, Medicine and Victorian Popular Culture* (2007).

A complete list of books in the series is at the back of the book

THE CAMBRIDGE
COMPANION TO
SENSATION FICTION

EDITED BY
ANDREW MANGHAM

CAMBRIDGE
UNIVERSITY PRESS

CAMBRIDGE
UNIVERSITY PRESS

University Printing House, Cambridge CB2 8BS, United Kingdom

Published in the United States of America by Cambridge University Press, New York

Cambridge University Press is part of the University of Cambridge.

It furthers the University's mission by disseminating knowledge in the pursuit of education, learning, and research at the highest international levels of excellence.

www.cambridge.org
Information on this title: www.cambridge.org/9780521157094

© Cambridge University Press 2013

First published 2013

Printed in the United Kingdom by TJ International Ltd. Padstow Cornwall

A catalogue record for this publication is available from the British Library

Library of Congress Cataloguing in Publication data
The Cambridge companion to sensation fiction / edited by Andrew Mangham.
pages   cm
ISBN 978-0-521-76074-4
1. English fiction – 19th century – History and criticism.   2. Sensationalism in literature.   3. Literature and society – Great Britain – History – 19th century.
I. Mangham, Andrew, 1979 – editor of compilation.
PR878.S44C36   2013
823'.809353–dc23
2013013364

ISBN 978-0-521-76074-4 Hardback
ISBN 978-0-521-15709-4 Paperback

CONTENTS

CONTENTS

ILLUSTRATIONS

CONTRIBUTORS

JANICE M. ALLAN is Senior Lecturer in English at the University of Salford. She has edited *Bleak House: A Sourcebook* (2004) and has written a number of articles and chapters on the sensation genre and deviant femininities. She is the executive editor of *Clues: A Journal of Detection* and is currently working on a reader of contemporary sources relating to sensation fiction.

ANNE-MARIE BELLER is Lecturer in English at Loughborough University. She is the author of *Mary Elizabeth Braddon: Writing in the Margins* (2014) and *Mary Elizabeth Braddon: A Companion to the Mystery Fiction* (2012). She is the co-editor of a special edition of *Women's Writing* on lesser-known female sensationalists and has published journal articles and chapters on Braddon, Wilkie Collins, Ellen Wood and Amelia B. Edwards.

MARIACONCETTA COSTANTINI is Professor of English literature at G. d'Annunzio University of Chieti-Pescara, Italy. She has published monographs, articles and book chapters on Victorian literature and culture. Her recent publications include the book *Venturing into Unknown Waters: Wilkie Collins and the Challenge of Modernity* (2008) and the edited collection *Armadale: Wilkie Collins and the Dark Threads of Life* (2009).

GRETA DEPLEDGE is Visiting Lecturer at Royal Holloway, University of London and Associate Lecturer for the Open University. She is the co-editor of *The Female Body in Medicine and Literature* (2011), is currently finishing a monograph entitled *Woman Pathologised: Medical Practice, Surgery and Literary Culture in the Nineteenth Century* and has published various articles on Florence Marryat and edited three of Marryat's novels. She is the co-founder of the Victorian Popular Fiction Association.

PAMELA K. GILBERT is the Albert Brick Professor of English at the University of Florida. She has published widely in the areas of Victorian literature, cultural studies and the history of medicine. Her books are *Disease, Desire and the Body in Victorian Women's Popular Novels* (1997), *Mapping the Victorian Social Body* (2004), *The Citizen's Body* (2007) and *Cholera and Nation* (2008). She has edited the *Blackwell Companion to Sensation Fiction* (2011) and *Imagined Londons* (2002), and co-edited *Beyond Sensation: Mary Elizabeth Braddon in Context* (1999). She has also edited an edition of Rhoda Broughton's novel, *Cometh Up as a Flower* (2010).

TATIANA KONTOU is Senior Lecturer in nineteenth-century literature at Oxford Brookes University. She is the author of *Spiritualism and Women's Writing: From the Fin de Siècle to the neo-Victorian* (2009) and editor of *Women and the Victorian Occult* (2010). She has recently co-edited *The Ashgate Research Companion to Nineteenth-Century Spiritualism and the Occult* (2012) and is working on a forthcoming monograph titled '*Her Father's Name': Gender, Theatricality and Spiritualism in Florence Marryat's Fiction*.

GRAHAM LAW is Professor in media history, Waseda University, Tokyo, and the author of *Serializing Fiction in the Victorian Press* (2000). He has edited several Victorian sensation novels, including David Pae's *Lucy the Factory Girl* (2001) and Dora Russell's *Beneath the Wave* (2004). He is also the co-editor of *The Public Face of Wilkie Collins: The Collected Letters* (2005), and the co-author of *Wilkie Collins: A Literary Life* (2008).

MARY ELIZABETH LEIGHTON and LISA SURRIDGE specialise in Victorian litera-ture, especially illustration studies. Leighton's work appears in *Victorian Periodicals Review*, *Essays on Canadian Writing* and *English Studies in Canada*. Surridge is the author of *Bleak Houses: Marital Violence in Victorian Fiction* (2005) and the co-editor of *Aurora Floyd* (1998). Their joint work appears in *Victorian Studies*, *Victorian Periodicals Review*, *The Blackwell Companion to Sensation Fiction* (2011), *Victorian Literature and Culture* and *Charles Dickens in Context* (2011). Together, Leighton and Surridge edit *Victorian Review*, Canada's only Victorian studies journal, and are co-writing a book on Victorian illustrated serial fiction. Their co-edited *Broadview Anthology of Victorian Prose* was published in 2012.

TARA MACDONALD is Assistant Professor of English at the University of Amsterdam. She is completing a monograph on the New Man and the marriage plot in the late Victorian novel, portions of which have been published in *Critical Survey* and *Women's Writing*. More recently, she has begun a project on sensation novels and modes of self-consciousness. Work based on this project appears in *Critical Survey* and *Economic Women: Desire and Dispossession in Nineteenth-Century British Culture* (2013). In addition, she has co-edited a special issue of *Women's Writing* entitled *Beyond Braddon: Forgotten Female Sensationalists*.

ANDREW MANGHAM is Associate Professor in Victorian literature at the University of Reading. He is the author of *Violent Women and Sensation Fiction* (2007), and editor of several books including *Wilkie Collins: Interdisciplinary Essays* (2007) and *The Female Body in Medicine in Literature* (2011).

ANDREW MAUNDER is Reader in Victorian Literature at the University of Hertfordshire. He is the author of *Bram Stoker* (2005) and the co-author of *Wilkie Collins: A Literary Life* (2010). He has edited *East Lynne* (2000) and two anthologies: *Varieties of Women's Sensation Fiction* (2004) and *British Literature of World War I* (2011).

LILLIAN NAYDER is Professor and Chair of English at Bates College, Maine. Her books include *Wilkie Collins* (1997), *Unequal Partners: Charles Dickens, Wilkie Collins, and Victorian Authorship* (2002) and *The Other Dickens: A Life of Catherine Hogarth* (2010).

RICHARD NEMESVARI is Professor of English and Dean of Arts at St Francis Xavier University, Canada. His monograph *Thomas Hardy, Sensationalism, and the Melodramatic Mode* was published in 2011. His most recent articles were published in *A Companion to Sensation Fiction* (2011), and *The Ashgate Research Companion to Thomas Hardy* (2010). He is a Vice-President of The Thomas Hardy Association and General Editor of the forthcoming Cambridge University Press edition of the novels and stories of Thomas Hardy.

LYN PYKETT is Professor Emerita at Aberystwyth University. A former editor of the *Journal of Victorian Culture*, she has published widely on nineteenth- and early twentieth-century literature and culture. Her books include *Emily Brontë* (1989), *The Improper Feminine: The Women's Sensation Novel and the New Woman Writing* (1992), *The Sensation Novel from The Woman in White to The Moonstone* (1994), *Engendering Fictions: The English Novel in the Early Twentieth Century* (1995), *Charles Dickens* (2002) and *Wilkie Collins* (2005). Recent publications include *The Nineteenth-Century Sensation Novel* (2012, an expanded version of her 1994 book), a chapter in the nineteenth-century volume of the *Oxford History of the Novel in English* (2012) and a new Oxford World's Classics edition of *Lady Audley's Secret* (2012).

LAURENCE TALAIRACH-VIELMAS is Professor of English at the University of Toulouse. She is the author of *Wilkie Collins, Medicine and the Gothic* (2009) and *Moulding the Female Body in Victorian Fairy Tales and Sensation Novels* (2007), and the editor of Braddon's *Thou Art the Man* (2008). She has also edited a collection of articles on the popularisation of science in children's literature (*Science in the Nursery: The Popularisation of Science in France and Britain, 1761–1901* (2011)).

SAVERIO TOMAIUOLO is Lecturer in English literature and language at Cassino University, Italy. He has written a monograph on Alfred Tennyson's narrative poems, a book on translation theory and articles and essays on postmodernism and Victorian literature. He is the author of *In Lady Audley's Shadow: Mary Elizabeth Braddon and Victorian Literary Genres* (2010) and *Victorian Unfinished Novels: The Imperfect Page* (2012).

ACKNOWLEDGEMENT

The editor would like to thank Verity Burke for her kind, enthusiastic and hard-working help with getting this book ready.

CHRONOLOGY

1850   Wilkie Collins's first novel *Antonina* is published

1851   Ellen Wood, 'Seven Years in the Wedded Life of a Roman Catholic' published in *New Monthly Magazine* and *Bentley's Miscellany*

1852   Wilkie Collins, *Basil*

1853   Charles Reade, *Peg Woffington*

1854   Wilkie Collins, *Hide and Seek*

1855   Wilkie Collins's play *The Lighthouse* is performed by Charles Dickens's theatre company at Tavistock House

1856   Wilkie Collins, *After Dark* and *A Rogue's Life*
        Charles Reade, *It's Never Too Late to Mend*

1857   Wilkie Collins, *The Dead Secret*
        Wilkie Collins's play *The Frozen Deep* is performed by Dickens's theatre company at Tavistock House
        Wilkie Collins collaborates with Dickens on *The Lazy Tour of Two Idle Apprentices* and *The Perils of Certain English Prisoners*

1858   Wilkie Collins's play *The Red Vial* is produced at the Olympic Theatre

1859   Wilkie Collins, *The Queen of Hearts*
        Wilkie Collins's *The Woman in White* begins serialisation in *All the Year Round* and *Harper's Weekly*
        Charles Reade's *A Good Fight* is serialised in *Once a Week*

1860   Mary Elizabeth Braddon, *Three Times Dead*
        Wilkie Collins's *The Woman in White* completes serialisation in *All the Year Round* and is published in volume form
        Ellen Wood, *Danebury House* written for a competition by the Scottish Temperance League; wins £100

Ellen Wood, *East Lynne* begins serialisation in *Colburn's New Monthly Magazine*

1861   Mary Elizabeth Braddon, *Garibaldi and Other Poems*
    Mary Elizabeth Braddon's *Lady Lisle* and *Ralph the Bailiff* serialised, respectively, in *Welcome Guest* and *St James's Magazine*
    Mary Elizabeth Braddon, *Lady Audley's Secret* begins serialisation, first in *Robin Goodfellow*, then in the *Sixpenny Magazine*
    Mary Elizabeth Braddon, *The Black Band* begins serialisation in *The Halfpenny Journal*
    Charles Reade, *The Cloister and the Hearth*
    Ellen Wood, *East Lynne* published in volume form

1862   Mary Elizabeth Braddon, *Lady Audley's Secret* and *Ralph the Bailiff and Other Tales* published in volume form
    Mary Elizabeth Braddon, *The White Phantom* serialised in *The Halfpenny Magazine*
    Mary Elizabeth Braddon, *Aurora Floyd* is serialised in *Temple Bar*
    Wilkie Collins, *No Name* begins serialisation in *All the Year Round*; published in volume form in December 1862
    Ellen Wood, *Mrs Halliburton's Troubles* and *The Channings*

1863   Mary Elizabeth Braddon, *Aurora Floyd*, *Eleanor's Victory* and *John Marchmont's Legacy* all published in volume form
    Wilkie Collins, *No Name* completes serialisation in *All the Year Round*
    Charles Reade, *Hard Cash*
    Ellen Wood, *The Shadow of Ashlydyat* and *Verner's Pride*

1864   Mary Elizabeth Braddon, *Henry Dunbar* and *The Doctor's Wife*
    Wilkie Collins, *Armadale* begins serialisation in the *Cornhill Magazine*
    Ellen Wood, *Lord Oakburn's Daughters*

1865   Mary Elizabeth Braddon, *Only a Clod* and *Sir Jasper's Tenant*
    Florence Marryat, *Love's Conflict*
    Ellen Wood, *Mildred Arkell*

1866   Mary Elizabeth Braddon, *The Lady's Mile*
    Mary Elizabeth Braddon begins to edit the family periodical *Belgravia*

Wilkie Collins, *Armadale* completes serialisation in the *Cornhill* and is published in volume form

Charles Reade, *Griffith Gaunt* is published in volume form

Ellen Wood, *St Martin's Eve*

1867   Mary Elizabeth Braddon, *Rupert Godwin* and *Birds of Prey*

Rhoda Broughton, *Not Wisely But Too Well* and *Cometh Up as a Flower*

Wilkie Collins and Charles Dickens collaborate on *No Thoroughfare*, which is published in the Christmas number of *All the Year Round*; dramatic adaptation is performed at the Adelphi Theatre on Christmas Eve

Ouida, *Under Two Flags*

Ellen Wood becomes editor of *Argosy* magazine

Ellen Wood, *Lady Adelaide's Oath*

1868   Mary Elizabeth Braddon, *Charlotte's Inheritance*, *Dead Sea Fruit* and *Run to Earth*

Wilkie Collins, *The Moonstone* is serialised in *All the Year Round* and then published in volume form

Ellen Wood begins to write her 'Johnny Ludlow' stories in the *Argosy*

1869   Wilkie Collins's play *Black and White* is produced at the Adelphi Theatre

1870   Wilkie Collins, *Man and Wife*

Charles Dickens dies

1871   Mary Elizabeth Braddon, *Fenton's Quest* and *The Lovels of Arden*

Wilkie Collins, *Poor Miss Finch* serialised in *Cassell's Magazine*

Wilkie Collins's adaptation of *The Woman in White* is produced at the Olympic Theatre

1872   Wilkie Collins, *The New Magdalen* is serialised in *Temple Bar*

Wilkie Collins, *Poor Miss Finch* is published in volume form

Florence Marryat begins editing *London Society*

1873   Mary Elizabeth Braddon, *Milly Darrell*

1874   Wilkie Collins, *The Law and the Lady* is serialised in *The Graphic*

Wilkie Collins, *The Frozen Deep and Other Stories*

1875   Mary Elizabeth Braddon, *Hostages to Fortune*

Wilkie Collins, *The Law and the Lady* is published in volume form

1876 Mary Elizabeth Braddon, *Joshua Haggard's Daughter*
   Mary Elizabeth Braddon retires as editor of *Belgravia*
   Wilkie Collins's adaptation of *Armadale*, entitled *Miss Gwilt*, is
performed at the Globe Theatre

   Wilkie Collins, *The Two Destinies*
   Florence Marryat retires as editor of *London Society*
   Florence Marryat, *Her Father's Name*
   Ellen Wood, *Parkwater*

1877 Wilkie Collins's dramatic version of *The Moonstone* is performed
at the Olympic Theatre

1878 Wilkie Collins, *The Haunted Hotel*
   Wilkie Collins, *The Fallen Leaves* is serialised in both *The World*
and *Canadian Monthly*

1879 Mary Elizabeth Braddon, *Vixen* and *The Cloven Foot*
   Rhoda Broughton, republication of *Tales for Christmas Eve* as
Twilight Stories
   Wilkie Collins, *The Fallen Leaves* is published in volume form
   Wilkie Collins, *A Rogue's Life*

1880 Wilkie Collins, *Jezebel's Daughter*

REFERENCES AND ABBREVIATIONS

The following short references will be used for frequently cited critical material and letters:

BGLL   William Baker, Andrew Gasson, Graham Law and Paul Lewis (eds.), *The Public Face of Wilkie Collins*, 4 vols. (London: Pickering and Chatto, 1999)

Mansel   H. L. Mansel, 'Sensation Novels', *Quarterly Review* 113 (1863), 251–68 and 482–514

ON   Margaret Oliphant, 'Novels', *Blackwood's Edinburgh Magazine* 94 (1867), 257–80

OSN   Margaret Oliphant, 'Sensation Novels', *Blackwood's Edinburgh Magazine* 91 (1862), 564–84

Rae   W. Fraser Rae, 'Sensation Novelists: Miss Braddon', *North British Review* 43 (1865), 180–204

1

ANDREW MANGHAM

Introduction

What is sensation fiction? The truth is, it is difficult to say with any certainty. Literary scholars agree generally that, in or about November 1859, Victorian literature changed and that the definitive moment came when a ghostly woman, dressed from head to foot in white garments, laid a cold, thin hand on the shoulder of a young man as he walked home late one evening. The incident takes place in the opening section of Wilkie Collins's *The Woman in White* (1859–60), a novel that had been commissioned by Charles Dickens to build on the success of his new magazine *All the Year Round*. Following the triumph of Collins's novel, other writers (most notably Mary Elizabeth Braddon and Ellen Wood) emulated *The Woman in White*'s style; critical responses to the resulting vogue of writing referred to the emerging genre as 'sensation fiction'. The more we look into this genre with an eye to noticing patterns and discernible boundaries, however, the more we notice those patterns and consistencies fade away. On a basic chronological level, it is difficult to know where sensation fiction begins and ends. Anne-Marie Beller's chapter in this Companion, 'Sensation Fiction in the 1850s', demonstrates how the style we have come to associate with the sensation school was being used much earlier than 1860. What is more, Lyn Pykett's closing chapter, 'The sensation legacy' shows, with a quotation from Phillip Waller, that 'the sensation novel did not so much die as "burst apart into subspecies"'. These subspecies included the detective novel, New Woman fiction and science fiction.

There is a risk, then, when we talk about sensation fiction, of overstating the suddenness with which it came and went. That the form's emergence was sudden and dramatic is something we see from the strongly flavoured reactions that Janice M. Allan discusses in chapter 7 of this book. Yet literary genres do not emerge in a vacuum. The novel's evolution has not been, in the words of G. K. Chesterton, a road on which 'man leav[es] his home behind him', but rather a building in which 'improvement means a man exalting the towers and extending the gardens of his home'.[1] The hieroglyphs of influence are inscribed indelibly into the foundations of every literary development, and such is true of the sensation novel. This Companion opens with two chapters that aim to chart two of the most important origins of the sensation style. Secondary criticism has shown how, in many ways, it was a hybrid of popular forms that had gone before it: melodrama and penny dreadful literature stand out as being two of the most obvious examples. In chapter 2 of this Companion, however, Anne-Marie Beller demonstrates how many of the themes and narrative idiosyncrasies of the genre were first explored in shorter sensational pieces written in the 1850s. 'While the 1860s was in many respects the decade of sensation', she writes, 'the genre's "infancy" is clearly perceptible in the 1850s, in terms of the work already being produced by many of the authors later connected to sensationalism; in the emergence of key tropes and techniques of sensation fiction; and also in broader social developments which frequently served as the raw material for the sensational plots and thematic concerns of the genre throughout the following decade.'

It has been acknowledged by a number of studies that the popularity of the gothic mode, at the beginning of the nineteenth century, had a significant impact on the shape and texture of the sensation novel. In chapter 3 of this Companion, Laurence Talairach-Vielmas discusses how sensation fiction drew upon the gothic's representation of women as beleaguered and margin-alised in order to thematise women's roles and power (or lack of it) in mid-century popular literature. Gothicism in the sensation novel, according to Talairach-Vielmas, became a powerful method of expressing radical yet deep-seated ambivalences towards traditional views of female sexuality and gen-dered bodies.

The sensation novel was a visual genre. In their chapter 'Illustrating the sensation novel', Mary Elizabeth Leighton and Lisa Surridge highlight how the form took advantage of new printing technologies in order to present visual image and written word side by side. Their chapter illustrates how images added to the sensational effect of these stories, and contributed, also, to the profusion of detail that sensation fiction became (in)famous for. The image of the artist becomes, according to Leighton and Surridge, a particular feature of the sensation plot itself which adds an element of complex self-reflexivity to these works' trajectories.

Another aspect of the sensation novel's 'visual' life was its representation on the stage. As Andrew Maunder illustrates in chapter 5, many of the landmark sensation texts were adapted, often without authors' consent, for the popular stage. As with the figure of the artist, the character of the actor, and the stage more generally, became a staple part of the genre's development. Jennifer Carnell's biography of Braddon, *The Literary Lives of M. E. Braddon* (2000), does an excellent job of reconstructing the life that Braddon had as an actress prior to becoming an author. Wilkie Collins had a fancy for treading the boards too, and he first met Dickens during their participation in an amateur production of Bulwer's *Not So Bad as We Seem* (1851). Another sensation novelist, Florence Marryat, participated in theatre for much of her life – she became an opera singer and was well known for staging theatrical séances. Maunder discusses how sensation fiction, indeed, took on another life for the stage; theatre adaptations, plus the fact that the novelists themselves were able to straddle the boundary between literary and dramatic form, resulted in the story of the Victorian theatre becoming a crucial chapter in the biography of the sensation novel. There was, Maunder notes, some ambivalence and concern over the cheapening of literature and theatre – caused predominantly by the popularisation of both forms in sensation and melodrama – but 'stage adaptations did not damage novels', he adds, 'but transformed them, affecting the audience's interpretation of them – an experience which even we can appreciate. After all, who, nowadays, does not think of *Oliver Twist* without also recalling to mind *Oliver!*?'

There is something about the sensation novel's methodological scepticism (or, in plainer words, its unwillingness to leave anything undoubted and unquestioned) that led to a powerful ability to question fixed traditions and ideologies in complex and radical ways. Richard Nemesvari, in chapter 6 of this volume, discusses how the genre developed a sophisticated means of questioning that most explosive of topics: sexuality. The queering of characters such as Marian Halcombe (who has the spirit and resolve of a man, plus feelings for her half-sister Laura Fairlie that do not appear to be entirely Platonic) and Lady Audley (again, a character whose strength of personality surpasses that of any of the male characters, and whose sisterly relationship with Phoebe Marks develops into a bond that seems 'queer'), is a means of demonstrating how 'queerness' exposed tensions and injustices at the heart of Victorian idealism. Indeed, Janice M. Allan's chapter on 'The contemporary response to sensation fiction' is, in essence, about the 'queering' of sensation fiction. Concentrating on the critical reaction to the form, Allan demonstrates how the term 'sensation' has always been 'slippery, elusive, and able to resist classification' and how, moreover, it was created by critics as a means of getting to grips with something that was 'other' or that was impossible to compartmentalise in ways that were typically Victorian. This polyvalence is what makes the sensation novel such a significant and powerful form, according to Allan. The way in which it has outlived the boxes and compartments created for it by nineteenth-century commentators is testament to how it cannot be bound by conclusions, agreements and collusions.

Hence, what sensation fiction has to say about a range of important topics is worth paying attention to; unfettered by some rigid formative strictures, deliberately provocative and polemic, the sensation text says searching things about some rather tense issues. In this Companion, Mariaconcetta Costantini, Saverio Tomaiuolo and Tara MacDonald each show, respectively, how the sensation format's knack of questioning and probing beneath surfaces leads to important representations of class, race and gender. In chapter 8, Costantini focuses on the representations of class identity and how the sensation genre contributed to discussions of the 'rising professional'. This quintessentially Victorian figure was a man whose work ethic is shown, by its place in sensation novels, to pose new challenges for the emerging middle class while suggesting new reforms, roles and ideologies for established professions (such as law and medicine). Tomaiuolo's chapter illustrates how the Indian Mutiny of 1857–8 became an adaptable image of rebellion – an image, moreover, that allowed Braddon to articulate narratives of struggle and conflict within the British domestic setting. He notes how 'colonial questions' represent sensation's 'attempt to find a middle ground and an "in-between space" to articulate "hybrid" strategies of social renewal'. Quoting the post-colonial critic Homi Bhabha, he adds: 'these "in-between" spaces provide the terrain for elaborating strategies of selfhood – singular and communal – that initiate new signs of identity, and innovate sites of collaboration and contestation in the act of defining the idea of society itself'. It seems to me that, call it what we may – queer, other, liminal, uncanny – the sensation novel is obsessed with 'in-between' spaces that provide a no-holds-barred area for asking controversial questions. Tara MacDonald's contribution on 'Sensation fiction, gender and identity' highlights how the form's obsession with masquerade and questions of identity disrupts the narrative in a way that raises questions about what is considered to be 'normal', and how we recognise it. Pykett has noted that the sensation novel was seen, during the nineteenth century, as a female form. 'One of the genre's most distinctive features was the way in which it displayed women and made a spectacle of femininity.'[2] Yet, as MacDonald demonstrates in chapter 10, the form also made spectacles of masculinity and androgyny. Strong and 'masculine' women such as Marian Halcombe and Cornelia Carlyle (*East Lynne*) are matched in number by weak and 'feminine' men (Frederick Fairlie, Noel Vanstone (*No Name*), Paul Marchmont (*Marchmont's Legacy*) and characters whose gender is not entirely definitive. One of the most striking examples of the latter is Miserrimus Dexter in Collins's *The Law and the Lady* (1875), whose long hair, beautiful face and lack of anatomy below the waist, all point to a questioning of his gender role. 'The sensation novel's playful engagement with human complications and misconceptions', observes MacDonald, 'made it an ideal form in which to disrupt gender conventions and challenge stable notions of identity'.

Sensation fiction was uniquely modern and of its time. As a product of the age of newspapers and new print technologies, the genre was ideally suited to comment on contemporaneous developments by incorporating them into its novels. In the eleventh chapter of this book, Tatiana Kontou demonstrates how, in spite of a strict naturalism that seemingly precluded any representations of the supernatural, the sensation form drew upon the themes and images associated with spiritualism. In both sensation novels and spiritualist practice, she argues, staged and domestic performances blurred the boundaries of the 'natural' and the 'supernatural'. Lillian Nayder continues the theme in chapter 12 by beginning her discussion with *Frankenstein* (1818) – a book that was pivotal to a shift from supernaturalism to 'gothic science' in literature. She observes how science was an important component in sensation's search for a unique vocabulary of modernity. Science, she adds, became 'gendered' in the popular novel. Images and languages derived from physiology, chemistry and physics were employed by sensation novelists in a way that can be viewed as 'reactionary as it is radical'. Interdisciplinary appropriations highlight, for Nayder, the complexity of the sensation form and, importantly, there is nothing simple, univocal or 'even' about ideas that moved between science and literature.

Graham Law's chapter on 'Sensation fiction and the publishing industry' charts the rise of the sensation genre, both as an idea and as a symptom of Victorian modernity. He traces the literary use of the term 'sensation' to stage melodrama in America, yet also demonstrates how the specific mid-nineteenth-century rise of cheap periodicals, circulating libraries and railway bookstalls fuelled the rise of a class of literature that some critics dismissed as 'so many yards of printed stuff'. What Law highlights is the 'fast' nature of sensation novel consumption, a fact which led critics to censure the form as ephemeral, hastily produced and suited to a mass market which preferred literature to be sugary and strong rather than worthy intellectual roughage. Yet, because sensation fiction was serialised in magazines, and because it was printed alongside articles and reports of world events, it was uniquely placed to comment on contemporaneous developments and to incorporate news and buzzwords into its spicy narratives. Tomaiuolo has shown, for instance, how images and languages drawn from the Indian Mutiny infiltrated into the sensation narratives of Mary Braddon. Kontou demonstrates how images of spiritualist practice also shaped the look and texture of the sensation novel. In chapter 14, Pamela K. Gilbert looks into the ways that developments in medicine had a hand in shaping the sensation style. She focuses on the professionalisation of medicine, the rise of the nineteenth-century 'mad doctor' and the red stain of vivisection. All of these burning issues found a platform in the sensation novel, and the medical figure provided, according to Gilbert, the impetus to discuss larger issues relating to the role of 'humanness' in the Victorian period.

Finally, this collection concludes with two chapters that focus on the legacies of the sensation novel. As I noted at the start of my introduction, Waller suggested, rather persuasively, that 'the sensation novel did not so much die as "burst apart into subspecies"'. In chapter 15, Greta Depledge follows the lead of Pykett's *The Improper Feminine* (1992) in suggesting that one the most important of those ramifications was the New Woman novel of the *fin de siècle*. I have suggested elsewhere that one aspect that *fin-de-siècle* literature inherited from sensation fiction was the obsession with dangerous female characters.[3] Depledge adds that in introducing what was often the dangerous woman's nemesis, the female sleuth, the sensation novel became crucial to the development of the New Woman genre. The latter, itself a significant foundation of the Modernist Age, is well known for its introduction of strong female characters, and for raising questions of gender equality, sexual freedom and rights for women. Female detectives, who had inhabited sensation narratives such as Braddon's *Eleanor's Victory* (1863) and Collins's *The Law and the Lady*, looked 'to moderate a path through ideas of feminity, womanhood and gender constructions. They negotiate[d] a new role for themselves' and, in doing so, uttered a war cry that inspired the New Women of the late nineteenth century. In the last chapter, Lyn Pykett explores an idea that Allan raises in chapter 7: namely the durability of the sensation form – its ability to break out of its Victorian chrysalis and to take flight as other methods and styles. Arguing with the nineteenth-century idea that the genre was a 'short-lived . . . phenomenon', Pykett demonstrates how sensation developed into (or, at least, influenced the shape of) later genres such as *fin-de-siècle* horror, science fiction, film, television serials and, most recently, the neo-Victorianism of authors like Michael Faber and Sarah Waters. 'The numerous developments, adaptations, mediations and appropriations of sensation novels', she concludes, 'suggest not only the continuing appeal of sensation fiction, but also its adaptive capacity as it is reworked for the cultural imaginary and social and ethical concerns of the twentieth and twenty-first centuries'. The sensation novel's narratorial style was a powerful and significant moment in the Victorian literary tradition; its capacity for asking important questions continues.

NOTES

1. G. K. Chesterton, *The Victorian Age in Literature* (London: Williams and Norgate, 1913), 12.
2. Lyn Pykett, *The Sensation Novel: from The Woman in White to The Moonstone* (Plymouth: Northcote House, 1994), 6–7.
3. Andrew Mangham, *Violent Women and Sensation Fiction: Crime, Medicine and Victorian Popular Culture* (Basingstoke: Palgrave Macmillan, 2007), 209–11.

2

ANNE-MARIE BELLER

Sensation fiction in the 1850s

> That bitter term of reproach, 'sensation', had not been invented for the
> terror of romancers in the fifty-second year of this present century; but the
> thing existed nevertheless in divers forms, and people wrote sensation
> novels as unconsciously as Monsieur Jourdain talked prose.[1]

The sensation novel is invariably associated with the 1860s and is frequently seen as commencing with the publication of the three genre-defining novels, *The Woman in White* (1859–60), *East Lynne* (1861) and *Lady Audley's Secret* (1862). Margaret Oliphant, in her review essay of 1862, credited Collins with 'originating a new school in fiction' and discussions of the 'new' vogue for sensation novels proliferated in periodicals as diverse as the *Christian Remembrancer* and the *The Medical Critic and Psychological Journal*.[2] Modern scholarship on sensation fiction, since its inception in the 1970s, has tended to reproduce this assumption regarding the newness of the form at the beginning of the sixties. Winifred Hughes, for example, in her important recovery of sensation fiction in 1980, suggested that the sub-genre 'had no perceptible infancy ... it sprang, full-blown, nearly simultaneously, from the minds of Wilkie Collins, Mrs Henry Wood, and M. E. Braddon'.[3] Although this 'genesis myth' has not gone unchallenged in the significant body of scholarship on the sensation novel produced over the last thirty years, the idea of the early 1860s as a point of origin has continued to hold currency, despite the fact that it is an unsatisfactory account on a number of levels.

While several critics have acknowledged that in many ways sensation fiction was not precisely new at the beginning of the 1860s, and have pointed variously to influences which include sensational penny fiction, Edward Bulwer Lytton's *Eugene Aram* (1832), the fiction of the Brontës, Newgate novels of the thirties and forties and earlier gothic fiction, there has been no sustained examination of the roots of sensationalism in the decade immediately preceding the widespread cultural discussion of the phenomenon. Andrew Maunder's six-volume collection of lesser-known sensation novels, which includes a bibliography of fiction from 1855 onwards, has made a significant contribution towards encouraging us to think beyond the usual parameters and, as he writes in the introduction to the series, '[i]t is slightly questionable whether 1860s Victorian readers and critics were struck by the newness of these novels as forcefully as recent critics like to think'.[4] In this chapter, I aim to further the idea that it was not so much the case that 'the sensation novel *exploded* onto the literary scene at the start of the 1860s',[5] but that it was more a dawning recognition on the part of critical commentators and the middle-class press that this type of fiction had gradually been gaining momentum for several years and was now popular to a worrying degree. While the 1860s was in many respects the decade of sensation, the genre's 'infancy' is clearly perceptible in the 1850s, in terms of the work already being produced by many of the authors later connected to sensationalism; in the emergence of key tropes and techniques of sensation fiction; and also in broader social developments which frequently served as the raw material for the sensational plots and thematic concerns of the genre throughout the following decade.

Scholars such as Andrew King and Graham Law have meticulously demonstrated how sensationalism permeated popular print culture throughout the earlier decades of the Victorian period, in penny fiction and in the proliferation of new periodicals catering to the working classes.[6] Indeed, many detractors of the sensation novel in the early 1860s explicitly identified these 'low' productions as the source of the 'contagion' infecting the three-decker and thereby 'making the literature of the Kitchen the favourite reading of the Drawing-room'.[7] There have, however, been relatively few studies of those middle-brow novels published during the 1850s which might be seen as recognisable precursors of the sensation novel as it was defined in the early 1860s in the prominent reviews by Margaret Oliphant, Henry Mansel and W. Fraser Rae. My aim here, then, is to trace the emergence of the sub-genre in the middle-class fiction market of the 1850s, with a view to re-emphasising how far the public perception of a newly created 'sensation genre' at the beginning of the following decade was dependent on, and shaped by, the review press.

The 1850s began with the publication of novels, on both sides of the Atlantic, which arguably contained clear sensational elements: in England Charles Dickens's *David Copperfield* (1849–50) and, in America, Nathaniel Hawthorne's *The Scarlet Letter* (1850). Neither, of course, was a sensation novel in the purest sense (although precise definition remains a moot point), yet their deployment of several of the tropes which came to characterise sensation fiction in the 1860s belies the idea that literary sensationalism erupted out of nowhere with the publication of *The Woman in White*. In their blending of realism and melodrama, their interest in sexually transgressive women, the inclusion of seduction, adultery and dramatic 'sensation scenes', these works anticipated the dominant mode of popular fiction for the next couple of decades.

Dickens, of course, was a key figure in the development of literary sensationalism, both as an important influence on the main practitioners and also as an author who provided a blueprint for sensationalising everyday life and domestic relations. Dickens's often-quoted statement in the preface to *Bleak House* (1852–3) that he had 'purposely dwelt on the romantic side of familiar things' could be applied with equal validity to any later sensation novel and might indeed be taken almost as a *modus operandi* for the later sub-genre.[8] For some critics in the early years of the debates of the 1860s he was the leader of the 'sensation school'. One of the earliest uses of the term appeared in a *Sixpenny Journal* review essay, which included *A Tale of Two Cities* (1859) and *Great Expectations* (1860–1) as examples of 'sensation novels', while Margaret Oliphant also included Dickens in her 1862 survey of the trend, comparing *Great Expectations* unfavourably with *The Woman in White*.[9] However, as the critical campaign hardened, Dickens became conspicuously absent from the attacks levelled at sensation fiction, causing George Augustus Sala to comment in 1868: '[t]he only wonder is that the charitable souls [critics] have failed to discover that among modern "sensational" writers Mr Charles Dickens is perhaps the most thoroughly, and has been from the very outset of his career the most persistently, "sensational" writer of the age'.[10] The early critics had indeed noticed but, as the sensation phenomenon grew, the attacks focused increasingly on less established writers than Dickens and, significantly, on women writers predominantly.

Unease about the increasing tendency towards sensationalism in literature was being voiced throughout the 1850s, contrary to the tendency to locate these anxieties exclusively in the following decade. Richard D. Altick notes that '[t]he rate at which sensational fiction was selling around 1850 gave deep concern to all public-spirited citizens'.[11] Altick, of course, is referring to such productions as the penny bloods aimed at the lower classes, but elsewhere there is evidence of more general concern for the status of literature at all levels. In an 1856 essay, Walter Bagehot noted the propensity for sensationalism and predicted its increasing exploitation in mainstream fiction: 'Exaggerated emotions, violent incidents, monstrous characters crowd our canvas; they are the resource of a weakness which would obtain the fame of strength. Reading is about to become a series of collisions against aggravated breakers, of beatings with imaginary surf.'[12] Bagehot's prescient complaints closely anticipate those of Mansel, Rae and Oliphant a decade later, and they are echoed in other contemporaneous essays in relation to 1850s fiction.

In one lengthy review essay entitled 'Literature of 1856', the anonymous critic comes to the exasperated conclusion that the novels of the year are 'for the most part, utter and unmitigated rubbish'.[13] Like Bagehot, who pinpoints exaggeration, violence of plot and 'monstrous' characterisation as the chief elements affecting the deterioration of fiction, the writer here also appears to diagnose the problem as a failure of realism, or at least the verisimilitude commonly evoked by Victorian reviewers as the measure of success: 'Where these writers pick up their ideas about nature and life we know not; but this we know, that the personages who live and move and have their being in these books are not to be met with anywhere but in these books. They are not flesh and blood ... there is no truth in them.'[14] These comments closely prefigure criticisms levelled at sensation novelists in the following decade, such as Rae's attack on Braddon's characterisation skills, which he claims demonstrate her 'entire ignorance of human nature and mental processes'.[15] Reviewers during the 1850s also anticipated the later opponents of sensation fiction in their implicit hostility to the increased presence and commercial success of female novelists: 'And who are the writers of fiction? For the most part ladies, who think that a ream of paper, a bottle of ink, and a bundle of crow-quills are all that is necessary to write a book with.'[16] Despite these misgivings about trends in fiction writing during the 1850s, many of the novels which notably pre-empt the sensation fiction of the following decades did receive favourable reviews. Before considering some of the lesser-known novels that deserve to be reinserted in to the literary-historical account of sensation fiction, it is important first to acknowledge the early work of one of the central figures of Victorian sensation and his role in the development of, arguably, the most popular fictional mode of the mid-century.

Basil (1852) and the sensation of modern life

It is interesting that Braddon's narrator, in the excerpt from *The Doctor's Wife* (1864) heading this chapter, alludes specifically to the 'fifty-second year of this present century' because it was in 1852 that Wilkie Collins published *Basil*, a work which employs many of the key themes and characteristics that would later come to define the sensation novel. It was Collins's first novel to place a sensational tale of crime, treachery and emotional turmoil into a contemporary middle-class setting, leading more than one modern critic to posit *Basil* as a credible prototype for sensation fiction or even as the first true sensation novel.

Basil constitutes a distinct departure from Collins's first published novel, the historical romance *Antonina, or the Fall of Rome* (1850), and its subtitle 'A Story of Modern Life' anticipates later sensation fiction's focus on modernity and its domestication of the gothic. At its most fundamental level, *Basil* is a novel about identity and class, and it also offers a remarkably frank examination of mid-Victorian sexual mores. *Basil* relates 'the history of little more than the events of one year' in the life of a well-born and affluent young man, whose life is abruptly overturned when he contracts a secret marriage with a linen draper's daughter whom he meets on an omnibus.[17] Forced to keep the knowledge of this *mésalliance* from his proud and autocratic father, Basil is cast into a nexus of secrecy, deception and complex intrigue wholly typical of the 1860s sensation novel. The episode where Basil overhears Margaret Sherwin's betrayal of him with Mannion, a man seeking vengeance for the death of his father, was found eminently distasteful by more than one reviewer: '*I heard and I knew* – knew my degradation in all its infamy, knew my wrongs in all their nameless horror' (160, emphasis in original). This brazen acknowledgement of the unspeakable was the primary reason that many reviewers of *Basil* condemned the novel with such pronounced loathing. The *Athenaeum* lamented its 'vicious atmosphere' and a writer for the *Westminster Review* objected to '[t]he incident which forms the foundation of the whole', describing this as 'absolutely disgusting'.[18]

If *Basil* pre-empts sensation fiction in terms of its subject matter and methods, it does so too at the level of language. There is a notable insistence on the word 'sensation' itself, which is obsessively repeated throughout the opening chapters: 'The first reckless luxury of a new *sensation*' (38); 'a cold faint *sensation* came over me' (38); 'my heart's dearest *sensations*' (41); 'this giant *sensation* of a day's growth' (42); 'the *sensations* which now influence me' (54). The novel's recurrent use of the word serves to emphasise the way in which psychological effects in *Basil* are inseparable from the physiological, whereby emotion and feeling are consistently foregrounded as the primary conduits through which meaning is relayed. Collins's emphasis on 'sensation', lexically as well as thematically, also serves as a reminder that the word already had an established place within Victorian cultural discourse by the 1850s; Oliphant in fact uses the term 'sensation' to describe Collins's fictional effects as early as 1855, several years before the label had properly taken hold.[19] One might argue that it was this shift to the narrative thematisation of 'sensation' in *Basil*, and the suspense for the reader generated by this approach, which most clearly anticipated the tone and effects of sensation fiction. As a reviewer for *Bentley's Miscellany* recognised, 'the intense everywhere predominates', leading to the interesting suggestion that '[t]o write effectively of *Basil* we ought to have another vocabulary at command'.[20]

Arguably, it is Collins's treatment of sexuality that both condemns the novel for many Victorian reviewers and at the same time rescues *Basil* from a rather hackneyed mediocrity. Certainly, the story of seduction and betrayal is a familiar staple of traditional melodrama. Yet, not only does Collins reverse the conventional gender dynamics in making his hero (rather than heroine) the victim of seduction and deception, but his explicit treatment of the subject transforms a predictable theme, infusing it with new complexity.

While many critics recognised *Basil*'s power, others were exercised over the morality of treating such subjects in fiction. As one reviewer put it: 'much occurs daily – as any one may see who reads the police reports in *The Times* – about which the less that is said the better'.[21]

Mannion's many references to Margaret's sexual appetite were a key reason for the largely shocked response to *Basil*, and in his 1862 revised edition Collins deleted several of the more controversial passages. When Mannion informs Basil, for example, that 'Margaret Sherwin was not a pure-minded girl, not a maidenly girl' (245), he continues in the original text with the words, 'She was fit to be any man's mistress, no man's wife.' Collins had already been forced to make significant revisions to the original 1852 text at the behest of the publisher, all aimed at toning down the sexual explicitness. Most of these cuts related to the central episode of Basil listening to his betrayal by Margaret, which in Collins's original conception was to have been set in a brothel.

Basil's emphasis on modernity and its contemporary setting, the preoccupations with class and gender, identity and sexual transgression, its use of crime, mystery, doubling and melodramatic incidents are all characteristic features of the 1860s sensation novel. However, as Tim Dolan and Lucy Dougan have pointed out, 'in the early 1850s Collins was not experimenting in isolation with a narrative mode that would await its proper definition for years to come', and they convincingly argue that a number of texts produced in these years 'belong to the moment of modern life, which can be legitimately claimed as an important, and overlooked, point of departure for the sensation novel'.[22] In the immediate years after the publication of *Basil*, a short story and two novels appeared which similarly explored the sensationalism of contemporary life and, if Collins's novel was notable for its violence, this was to be taken to the next level as murder – that favoured resource of the sensation novelist – took centre stage.

Murder and sensation in *My Brother's Wife* (1855), *Paul Ferroll* (1855) and 'St Martin's Eve' (1853)

Amelia B. Edwards and Caroline Clive both embarked on their careers as novelists in 1855 and their first published works arguably deserve recognition as important precursors of the sensation novel. Indeed, both writers are worthy of more critical attention than they have hitherto received, and not merely for their role in promulgating early versions of literary sensationalism. Edwards's relationship to the sensation genre is a complicated one. Her plots habitually involve murder, secret identities, adultery or bigamy, yet critics in the 1860s insistently distinguished Edwards from other 'sensation authors', claiming that her work was 'far above the Miss Braddon school'.[23]

Edwards's first novel, *My Brother's Wife*, is a sensational tale of treachery and murder, narrated in the first person by Paul Latour, a well-born young Frenchman who falls in love with his orphaned cousin, Adrienne. Unfortunately for Paul, who describes himself as 'decidedly plain' and afflicted with a limp, Adrienne prefers the more obvious attractions of his handsome and dissipated younger brother, Théophile.[24] The ensuing marriage soon runs into trouble when Théophile becomes entangled with a beautiful opera singer called Thérèse Vogelsang. Despite the efforts of Paul and Thérèse's formerly abandoned husband to rescue Théophile from the singer's clutches, the couple elope, though not before Thérèse has persuaded her lover to sell his newly acquired country estate and hand over the proceeds. Théophile never makes it to Paris; he is murdered *en route* by Thérèse's co-conspirator and sometime lover, the sinister theatre manager Alphonse Lemaire. Paul brings his brother's murderer to justice and, although Thérèse evades the clutches of the law, she cannot escape the inexorable justice exacted by Edwards's narrative. On a trip to London, Paul gives a shilling to a starving, ragged street singer, whereupon this desperate wretch proceeds to throw herself off a bridge into the Thames and, when her body is pulled out of the water, Paul recognises her as Thérèse Vogelsang.

Despite its inclusion of adultery, elopement, murder and suicide, *My Brother's Wife* avoids the ambiguous moral tone that provoked many critics of sensation fiction in the early 1860s. However, if reviewers were appeased by the clear moral viewpoint, other aspects of the narration did offer cause for uneasiness. The fact that the narrator is a young Frenchman, and that Edwards's convincing ventriloquising of the male viewpoint arguably leads to some ambiguous moments in the text, led one reviewer to ponder: 'This author, were it not for the name of Amelia B. Edwards on the title page, we should pronounce to be a young man who has travelled, read, and experienced more of life in its widest sense, than the generality.'[25] One might read these comments as an early example of the discomfort with women's writing that enters sensational territory, an uneasiness which would intensify in the following decade, leading to the notable attacks on female sensationalists by W. Fraser Rae and Francis Paget.

If Edwards's narration in *My Brother's Wife* largely eschewed moral ambiguity in its portrayal of transgression, no such claim could be made about Caroline Clive's debut novel, *Paul Ferroll*, in which the eponymous central character, a respected author and landowner, calculatedly murders his wife in order to marry the woman he truly loves. Clive's novel anticipates 1860s sensation fiction in presenting a murderer as the protagonist, but more importantly by employing a detached, almost clinical, narrative voice, which refuses to condemn either the murderer or his crime. This absence of authorial judgement troubled many critics, even those who praised the originality and power of the novel: 'We can find no fault in it as a work of art; but the interest and sympathy excited in favour of the murderer, proves how false is the morality, and how greatly abused has been the gift of authorship.'[26] Perhaps surprisingly, given his later defence of Braddon against similar charges of immorality, even George Augustus Sala called it a 'remarkable and eminently disagreeable fiction'.[27]

Just as shocking as the neutral tone of the narrative for some readers was Clive's decision to allow her protagonist to evade justice. Finally found guilty after confessing his crime, Ferroll is rescued by his daughter and escapes abroad, leading a reviewer for the *Examiner* to object that 'the author can[not] bring herself to exhibit this wife-killing hero in his proper attitude at Tyburn'.[28] In a similar vein, a writer for *The Times* indignantly requested to know 'To what account is Paul Ferroll's crime so forcibly represented if unaccompanied by punishment?'[29] Presumably as a concession to such censure, Clive added a subsequent resolution to the third edition, in which Ferroll contracts a fever and dies, although, as Adrienne Gavin notes in her excellent introduction to the Valancourt edition, 'the new ending is a very light sop to criticism rather than any real moral condemnation of the hero'.[30]

Like many later sensation novels, *Paul Ferroll* is interested in the potential lack of congruity between outward semblance and ulterior criminality. The opening of the novel evokes a serene pastoral idyll, only to immediately demolish the associations conjured. 'Nothing looks more peaceful and secure than a country house seen at early morning', the narrator informs us, yet by the end of this first chapter Paul Ferroll's wife has been stabbed to death in her own bed.[31] Clive's protagonist is similarly not what he seems, and the inability of other characters to perceive Ferroll's true nature beyond his gentlemanly exterior owes as much to their assumptions about class as it does to the murderer's concealments. Adeline Sergeant speculated that *Paul Ferroll* was 'successful, most of all, because it introduced its readers to a new sensation. Hitherto they had been taught to look on the hero of a novel as necessarily a noble and virtuous being, endowed with heroic, not to say angelic qualities; but this conviction was now to be reversed'.[32] Arguably, this was a distinctly mid-Victorian view of what a novel's protagonist should be. English picaresque novels in the eighteenth century, influenced by the sixteenth-century Spanish *picaresca* narratives, and perhaps more directly by Miguel de Cervantes's *Don Quixote* (1605, 1615), focused on roguish pro-tagonists, though in an episodic form distinct from the plots of sensational fiction of the 1850s and 1860s. Sergeant's comments also overlook the

Newgate novel of the 1830s and 1840s, which had also centred on the criminal outsider, provoking similar criticisms to those levelled at *Paul Ferroll* about the glorification of murder and immorality. However, the focus on domestic and middle-class criminality in *Paul Ferroll* aligns it more closely with the sensation novels of Collins, Wood and Braddon in the following decade.

Clive's novel is in fact structured almost symmetrically around two murders and two trials. In addition to murdering his first wife, Ferroll later shoots a man in cold blood during a working-class riot, a man moreover whom he has previously befriended. Though the strength of public feeling necessitates a trial at which Ferroll is found guilty of murder, his wealth, influence and esteemed position in society soon ensure his full pardon. Ferroll's life is, therefore, shaped by two violent crimes, the respective natures of which emphasise the novel's dichotomy between the public and the private. Ferroll's highly public shooting of a lower-class man, in front of a group of his own peers, contrasts sharply with the secret, hidden, domestic murder of his unwanted wife, raising interesting questions about class privilege and Victorian assumptions regarding criminality, as well as about the nature of the public/private divide.

Both *My Brother's Wife* and *Paul Ferroll* also anticipate the experimentation with narrative form found in some sensation novels, notably those by Collins. Clive intersperses her narrative with diary entries written alternately by Ferroll and his second wife as a way of allowing the reader more intimate access to the psychology of these characters and also offering multiplicity of perspective. In *My Brother's Wife*, Edwards makes frequent use of letters to disrupt the monologism of the first-person narrative and, in one chapter, abandons the conventional novel form entirely to present the action as a scene from a play, complete with stage directions. A later chapter recounting the trial of Théophile's murderer mimics a court transcript, and the section ends with an article about the trial from a 'leading journal' (276). In these ways, both novels also foreshadow the documentary-style narratives of many 1860s sensation novels, particularly those of Collins and Charles Reade. Clive's habit of saving newspaper cuttings of murder reports, including the case of the poisoner William Palmer which came to trial the year following the publication of *Paul Ferroll*, is similarly reminiscent of Reade's methods of research, whereby the author would obsessively collect, in a series of voluminous notebooks, articles and editorials from newspapers and periodicals as sources for his plots and characters.

If Clive's novel shocked Victorian readers by representing a respectable English gentleman as a cold-blooded killer, then the idea of a middle-class female murderer was more appalling still. Nearly a decade before the critical furore over the fiendish Lady Audley, Braddon's rival, Mrs Henry Wood, was already unleashing a murderous woman on the world in 'St Martin's Eve', an early *New Monthly Magazine* story that would later be expanded into her 1866 novel of the same title. Wood was a prolific contributor to the *New Monthly* from 1851 until the serial publication of her novel *The Shadow of Ashlydyat* ended in November 1863, and she also contributed fiction to *Bentley's Miscellany* from 1854 to 1858. Many of these stories were early versions of her later novels so that, in a very literal sense, the sensation fiction produced by Wood in the 1860s was often not new at all. In a number of ways, the murder in 'St Martin's Eve' published in 1853 is decidedly more disturbing than any of the fictional crimes of the following decade.

Wood's story is morbid and, in places, unpleasantly sadistic in its representations of violence against children. Death, violence and madness shape the narrative, causing a reviewer for *Bell's Life* to warn that it 'is one of those sad tales that freeze the blood with horror, and we cannot recommend its perusal to any of our delicately-nerved readers'.[33] The plot centres on Charlotte Norris, a proud and imperious young woman, who marries George Carlton within a year of his first wife's death following childbirth. Charlotte has always 'been subject to fits of ungovernable rage, so violent, that they seemed to fall little short of insanity'[34] and inevitably becomes intensely jealous of her stepson, Benja, whom she ultimately murders.

The earlier short story version of 'St Martin's Eve' is arguably more sensational than the later novel. In the novel, Charlotte's character is more nuanced and she frequently acts kindly to Benja, which does not happen in the story; her beatings of the boy are also toned down for the novel, and the murder itself is more graphically violent in the earlier version. Instead of simply locking Benja in a burning room, as she does in the novel, Charlotte's actions in the original story are far more sadistic: 'Instinct caused Benja to endeavour to spring away from the flames, but Mrs Carlton held him with a firm, revengeful hand, beating him about the head and ears, and the blaze caught his pinafore.' Charlotte then locks the door on him, 'leaving the ill-fated child to burn slowly away to death' (337). Driven utterly insane by her crime, Charlotte Carlton shares the fate of Lady Audley, ending her days in a lunatic asylum. Arguably though, Charlotte's crimes are more heinous than those of Braddon's character, raising interesting questions about the respective responses to them. While the different mode of publication is a relevant factor here, it is surely also the case that Wood escaped the extreme hostility that some reviewers exhibited towards Braddon's representation of female monstrosity simply because the critical backlash against sensation had not yet begun.

The 'Woman Question' in *My Lady* (1858)

A central aspect both of sensation novels and the critical discourse which accompanied them in the 1860s concerned the nature, role and legal position of women, or what the Victorians themselves termed 'the Woman Question'. The 1850s saw the real emergence of organised feminist activity and, not only was there a sustained attempt through campaigning and petitioning to challenge various aspects of the laws pertaining to women, but key legislation was also passed. A Royal Commission was appointed in 1850 to look into the question of reforms in matrimonial law and in 1857 the Matrimonial Causes Act led to the establishment of the divorce courts. Journalists' reports of the proceedings fuelled debate and provided plentiful source material for those novelists intent on representing 'modern life'. As an example, the scandalous and much-publicised Yelverton Case captured the public attention from 1857 and the press coverage of Theresa Longworth's attempts to sue Major Charles Yelverton for bigamy highlighted problematic areas of the law in relation to marriage and property, which in turn were picked up and exploited by novelists.

An early novel to respond to the debates about women's shifting positions within society was the anonymously penned *My Lady* in 1858. My Lady Umphraville's comfortable life is overturned when Sir Philip, her husband of twenty years, elopes with another man's wife. The ensuing narrative of the wronged wife's trials presents a detailed critique of the double standard entrenched within the existing marriage laws and marshals, through its sympathetic heroine Eleanor Umphraville, an effective case for the need for reform. As one character highlights the inequity in an embittered speech to the guilty husband: 'There's that other poor man could cast himself free of the woman you ruined; why can't my lady, the purest wife in England, cast off you and your dishonourable name, a viler sinner?'[35] Not only does my lady have to deal with the shame of the public scandal, with the case widely discussed in the national newspapers, but she has to bear far worse when Sir Philip decides to return to the family home and reclaim his position as husband. Unwilling to tolerate this situation, Eleanor demands a separation and moves out with her daughters; Sir Philip refuses to allow her to take her beloved sons with her. The husband's behaviour towards his estranged wife becomes increasingly unreasonable, culminating in his taking out a court order to sue for the restitution of his conjugal rights. Yet before this can come to anything, my lady contracts a fever and dies in a tragic denouement.

My Lady carried a similar subtitle to *Basil* – 'A Tale of Modern Life' – emphasising the way in which these novels anticipated the vogue for tackling (and sensationalising) contemporary issues and concerns. For some critics, however, the examination of the divorce laws and the sexual double standard offered by *My Lady* was not an appropriate topic for fiction: 'This is a novel which never should have been written. The subject matter of the tale is one which could in no way be dilated upon with advantage to readers of light literature; but here we have it treated of in the most objectionable manner.'[36] Perhaps the indignant reviewer objected to the forthright acknowledgement of the double standard as much as the inclusion of adultery. One character outlines a man's 'privileges' to my lady's son in no uncertain terms:

> you may forsake your wife; you may go ... and make some other man's wife a pest and nuisance, too vile for honest folk to look upon; ... and then you can come home ... and take possession of your own property, your goods and chattels, maybe a woman worth a hundred such as you, and keep her bound to your pleasure. If she flies from you, you can drag her back again; you can spend her money; you can take away her children; you can shut her up from every comfort under heaven. (204)

My Lady provides a fascinating commentary on the new divorce laws precisely at the time that their implications were first beginning to be understood and reflected on. A few years later, Ellen Wood propelled the debate further by presenting the upper-middle-class wife as the adulterer in her best-selling *East Lynne*.

The novels I have briefly discussed here were not isolated instances of an emergent sensationalism. Charles Reade was already publishing novels in the decade preceding his association with sensation fiction and *It is Never Too Late to Mend* (1856), his fervent critique of the English prison system, is essentially the first of the sensationalist 'novels with a purpose' for which he would become renowned. Joseph Sheridan Le Fanu's short fiction of the fifties contains sensational techniques and, in addition to *My Brother's Wife*, Edwards's *The Ladder of Life* (1857) and *Hand and Glove* (1858) are both recognisably in the sensation mould. Certain works by Mrs Gordon Smythies (Harriette Maria Gordon) and Mrs C. J. Newby (Emma Warburton) also exhibit nascent sensational qualities, with Smythies in particular anticipating classic sensation fiction tropes as early as 1840 in her *Cousin Geoffrey, the Old Bachelor*, a full two decades before Mansel included her novel *The Daily Governess* (1861) in his 1863 *Quarterly Review* essay. All these authors bear out Braddon's claim that sensation fiction 'existed ... in divers forms' within the middle-class fiction market, long before the 'bitter term of reproach' had been invented.

NOTES

1. Mary Elizabeth Braddon, *The Doctor's Wife*, ed. Lyn Pykett (Oxford University Press, 1998), 11.
2. OSN, 565.

3. Winifred Hughes, *The Maniac in the Cellar: Sensation Novels of the 1860s* (Princeton University Press, 1980), 6.

4. Andrew Maunder, 'Introduction', *Varieties of Women's Sensation Fiction: 1855–1890* (London: Pickering and Chatto, 2004), xii.

5. Hughes, *Maniac in the Cellar*, 5. Emphasis added.

6. See, for example, Andrew King, *The London Journal 1845–1883: Periodicals, Production and Gender* (Aldershot: Ashgate, 2004) and ' "Literature of the Kitchen": Cheap Serial Fiction of the 1840s and 1850s', in *A Companion to Sensation Fiction*, ed. Pamela K. Gilbert (Oxford: Blackwell, 2011), 38–53; Graham Law, *Serializing Fiction in the Victorian Press* (London and New York: Palgrave Macmillan, 2000).

7. Rae, 105.

8. Charles Dickens, 'Preface', *Bleak House* (1852–3; London: Penguin, 1994), vi.

9. Cited in Kathleen Tillotson, 'The Lighter Reading of the 1860s', introduction to Wilkie Collins, *The Woman in White* (1859; Boston: Riverside, 1969), xi–xii.

10. G. A. Sala, 'On the "Sensational" in Literature and Art', *Belgravia* 9 (1868), 449–58 (454).

11. Richard D. Altick, *The English Common Reader: A Social History of the Mass Reading Public, 1800–1900* (1957; Chicago and London: University of Chicago Press, 1983), 293.

12. Walter Bagehot, 'Essay on Mr Macaulay', *National Review* 2 (1856), 381.

13. Unsigned, 'Literature of 1856', *The Critic* (2 February 1857), 603.

14. *Ibid.*

15. Rae, 195.

16. Unsigned, 'Literature of 1856', 603.

17. Wilkie Collins, *Basil*, ed. Dorothy Goldman (1852; Oxford University Press, 1990), 1. Further references to this edition will be given in the text.

18. D. O. Maddyn, Review of Wilkie Collins, *Basil*, *Athenaeum* (4 December 1852), quoted in *Wilkie Collins: The Critical Heritage*, ed. Norman Page (London: Routledge and Kegan Paul, 1974), 48; Anon., Review of Wilkie Collins, *Basil*, *Westminster Review* (October 1853), quoted in Page, *Critical Heritage*, 52.

19. Margaret Oliphant, 'Modern Novelists – Great and Small', *Blackwood's Edinburgh Magazine* 77 (1855), 554–68 (566).

20. Unsigned review of Wilkie Collins, *Basil* and William Makepeace Thackeray, *The History of Henry Esmond*, *Bentley's Miscellany* 32 (1852), 576–86 (584).

21. Unsigned, 'A Trio of Novels: *Esmond*, *Reuben Medlicot*, and *Basil*', *Dublin University Magazine* 41 (1853), 70–9 (78).

22. Tim Dolan and Lucy Dougan, 'Fatal Newness: *Basil*, Art, and the Origins of Sensation Fiction', in *Reality's Dark Light: The Sensational Wilkie Collins*, ed. Don Richard Cox and Maria K. Bachman (Knoxville: University of Tennessee Press, 2003), 21–2.

23. Unsigned review of Amelia B. Edwards, *Half a Million of Money*, *The Standard* (4 April 1866), 6.

24. Amelia B. Edwards, *My Brother's Wife* (London: G. Routledge, 1855), 6. A further reference to this edition wil be given in the text.

25. Quoted in Brenda Moon, *More Usefully Employed: Amelia B. Edwards, Writer, Traveller and Campaigner for Ancient Egypt* (London: Egypt Exploration Society, 2006), 27.

26. Unsigned review of Caroline Clive, *Paul Ferroll: A Tale*, *New Quarterly Review* (4 October 1855), 422.

27. G. A. Sala, 'How I Went to Court: A Proud Confession', *Belgravia: A London Magazine* 3 (1874), 304.

28. Unsigned, 'The Literary Examiner', *Examiner* (8 September 1855), 564–6 (565).

29. Unsigned, 'New Novelettes', *The Times* (2 February 1856), 7.

30. Adrienne E. Gavin, 'Introduction', *Paul Ferroll* (Kansas City: Valancourt, 2008), xvi.

31. Caroline Clive, *Paul Ferroll: A Tale*, ed. Adrienne E. Gavin (1855; Kansas City: Valancourt, 2008), 3.

32. Adeline Sergeant, 'Mrs Archer Clive', in Sergeant, *Women Novelists of Queen Victoria's Reign* (London: Hurst and Blackett, 1897), 172.

33. Unsigned 'Literature', *Bell's Life in London and Sporting Chronicle* (13 November 1853), 8.

34. Ellen Wood, 'St Martin's Eve', *New Monthly Magazine* 99 (1853), 327–42 (331–2). A further reference to this edition will be given in the text.

35. Anon., *My Lady: A Tale of Modern Life* (1858; London: Smith, Elder, 1862), 203. A further reference to this edition will be given in the text.

36. Unsigned, *The Morning Post* (9 October 1858), 3.

3

LAURENCE TALAIRACH-VIELMAS

Sensation fiction and the gothic

Sensation writers' debt to the gothic probably explains the genre's popularity from the publication of Wilkie Collins's *The Woman in White* in 1859 to the end of the 1860s. Secrets and mysteries abound, villains and villainesses plot murders, and characters are resurrected as if by magic. The new 'spectrality' of sensational characters, moreover, re-adapts gothic conventions to a secular and materialistic modern world, using multiple identities, fake death and science to re-animate the dead. The burying of women's secrets and bodies is undoubtedly what made the genre so sensational, starting with the spectral woman in white, who has 'sprung out of the earth or dropped from the heaven'[1] to thrill Walter Hartright's nerves in the middle of the night. As in Mary Elizabeth Braddon's *Henry Dunbar* (1864), in which the 'dark chapter in the criminal romance of life, never to be revealed upon earth' is 'hidden in [the hero's and heroine's] own breasts',[2] the secret of the woman in white remains unknown, just as readers are never certain of what the eponymous Lady Audley's secret is exactly. Female characters are more often than not buried alive when they threaten the Victorian status quo, even if only symbolically, and images of unsafely or unlawfully interred secrets and bodies haunt the seminal sensation novels. Collins's Anne Catherick or Braddon's Lady Audley, unclassifiable, unknowable, half mad, threatening though harmless-looking, are emblematic of the genre. None of the gothic ingredients is missing. Collins's woman in white is simultaneously a distressed damsel and spectral figure, linked to a place of seclusion. She haunts churchyards and dismal lakes, has clairvoyant dreams, claims she knows what lies in the manuscript of the past – the marriage register which Sir Percival Glyde has forged – is subjected to nervous shocks and ultimately buried under Laura's name, illustrating how '[t]he sins of the fathers [are] visited on the children' (568). For Lady Audley, who ends up like her mother in a mental home, the repetition of the past and the way in which the mother's fate is visited on the daughter epitomise the significance of feminine identity in sensation novels, bringing up to date the images of incarcerated women found in Radcliffean gothic.[3]

More significantly still, in order to resurrect the past, these two seminal sensation narratives from Collins and Braddon respectively play more than any other sensation novel upon churchyard scenes: characters meet in church-yards or dream they visit them, they decipher inscriptions on tombstones and their investigations systematically lead them back to graves and headstones. If potentially hair-raising, these scenes yet signal the ways in which churchyard scenes help sensation writers relate secrecy to earthly depths, as if the detec-tives must literally excavate, in order to exhume, the skeletons of the past. As this chapter will show, *The Woman in White* and *Lady Audley's Secret* use gothic sites and stereotypes to play upon fears related to women's corpore-ality. To do so, they revisit churchyards, charnel houses, coffins or images of the dead body to mediate between the Radcliffean romance and the sensa-tional narrative, suggesting that the quest always implies a probing of women's concealed depths, and often using medical exploration to revamp gothic images of exhumation. Such a displacement of the genre's fascination for depths is, I would argue, the most sensational feature of this popular literary form.

Rewriting the gothic romance

Sensation novels recurrently seem to stage fears related to the marital institu-tion. Most sensation narratives link female identity and marriage, thereby recalling prototypical gothic tales which explore women's nightmarish domestic lives. In Ann Radcliffe's stories, the naïve female character usually falls prey to a male villain and experiences the violence of a male-dominated world. Metaphors of entrapment and literal imprisonment frame the her-oine's experience through powerlessness. The legal disqualifications that women faced in nineteenth-century England, especially their loss of legal identity through marriage, turned women into ghostly figures, who, in Lenora Ledwon's terms, 'not only haunt the legal system but haunt the social order, challenging that order to name [them]'.[4] Through marriage, women become blanks – white women, socially spectral since their marriage con-demns them to a 'symbolic "civil death"'.[5] Ledwon's gothic terminology is significant to this discussion. Sensation novels frequently stage the threat that marriage represents for female identity: the most significant sensation novels of the 1860s all play on female characters' multiple identities, from Wilkie Collins's *The Woman in White*, *Armadale* and *No Name* to Mary Elizabeth Braddon's *Lady Audley's Secret*, *Eleanor's Victory* and *Henry Dunbar*, and even Ellen Wood's *East Lynne*. The spectral women or female doubles revamp the gothic romance, showing how, if tombstones erase their identity, the way in which the narratives represent 'spectrality' reveals fears related to women's bodies and their unruly physiology.

The image of the limitation of woman's freedom and the dramatisation of man's superior position appears at the opening of *The Woman in White*. The novel is presented as 'the story of what a Woman's patience can endure, and what a Man's resolution can achieve' (5), and the plot is grounded upon the burial of Anne Catherick under Laura Fairlie's name. Yet, if *The Woman in White* places many key scenes in churchyards as prototypical gothic and hair-raising sites, the characters cannot solve the mystery of the replacement of Laura's body by Anne Catherick's by exhuming the body interred in Limmeridge Churchyard. Interestingly enough, the narrative's missing exhumation scene figures in a film adaptation of the novel, a choice which suggests even more the significance of buried female bodies in sensation novels. Indeed, Tim Fywell's 1997 BBC adaptation, drawing on Dante Gabriel Rossetti's exhumation of Elizabeth Siddal's body, plays upon the exhumation of Laura and Anne's father's tomb. The opening of the tomb is not simply gothic: it becomes sensational through the secret that Walter Hartright and Marian Halcombe discover. The tomb contains a body part (a lock of Anne's hair) and a sexual secret (Anne's revelation of her marriage to Percival). Fywell's unfaithfulness to the original script reveals the essence of sensationalism, recalling Braddon's Pre-Raphaelite representation of her villainess when her portrait discloses her sensual/sexual nature, hinting thereby at her guilt. In both Fywell's adaptation and Braddon's sensation novel, the gothic and its representation of woman's spectrality in marriage is associated with Pre-Raphaelitism, an aesthetic movement which sexualised women, often by fetishising their hair, making them both fearful and desirable while simultaneously sexual and virginal, as in J. E. Millais's *The Bridesmaid* (1859), where the hair, framing the face of the young female subject, has erotic undertones. This example shows that the fear concealed behind the derelict castles and labyrinthine passageways of gothic fiction changed as the gothic was rewritten and reworked throughout the nineteenth century. Related to 'women's psychology and social status',[6] the gothic sites that incarcerate women gradually lost their symbolic resonances. Instead, fears related to physical intrusion and violation appeared, shaping the (sexualised) female body as a new gothic castle, and using body parts or organs to rework clichés that prototypically partake of the gothic romance. For instance, the discovery of Laura's feelings for the romantic hero is presented through metaphors of physical penetration, almost suggestive of dissection: 'I shrank then – I shrink still – from invading the innermost sanctuary of her heart, and laying it open to others' (65). The heroine's heart oscillates between metaphor and reality, turning her body into a sanctuary with doors and chambers, concealed pathologies replacing ghosts and other supernatural creatures, and paving the way for the secluded and spectral distressed damsel's experience of the first symptoms of cardiac disease right after the news of Laura Fairlie's marriage to Sir Percival Glyde.

The manuscript in the chest

In *The Woman in White*, Sir Percival's Blackwater Park propels the gothic atmosphere: Blackwater Park is almost a replica of prototypical gothic castles, with a ruined wing dating from the fourteenth century and a more modern one which is inhabited. An impression of architectural chaos and a sense of seclusion inform the setting and construct it as a dangerous and violent place. The house is 'shut in – almost suffocated by trees' (199), 'stifled by them' (206), locked up like a prison. Blackwater Park is enclosed in a series of concentric circles – a 'great square which is formed by the three sides of the house' (206) and 'which had a moat round it once' (199) with 'a large circular fishpond with stone sides and an allegorical leaden monster in the middle, occup[ying] the centre of the square'; the pond itself is 'encircled by a broad belt of turf' (206). With its two wings and two galleries potentially symbolising splintered personalities, all the more so as the building is reflected by a nearby lake as another shadowy double, the building becomes almost self-reflexive, a place of confinement for the characters locking the text itself in a gothic frame.

Yet the amateur detective refuses to investigate the place further, out of regard for her 'petticoats and stockings' (205). Tellingly, the old wing and the Elizabethan bedrooms only become of interest when Marian is hidden away there, as she suffers from typhus fever and is subjected to medical supervision. Count Fosco's description of the scene, though deriding the gothic, rewrites fear by connecting it indirectly with the medical:

> [W]e concealed our interesting invalid in one of the uninhabited bedrooms at Blackwater. At the dead of night, Madame Fosco, Madame Rubelle, and myself (Percival not being cool enough to be trusted), accomplished the concealment. The scene was picturesque, mysterious, dramatic, in the highest degree. By my directions, the bed had been made, in the morning, on a strong moveable framework of wood. We had only to lift the framework gently at the head and foot, and to transport our patient where we pleased, without disturbing herself or her bed. No chemical assistance was needed, or used, in this case. We placed the candles and opened the doors, beforehand. I, in right of my great personal strength, took the head of the framework – my wife and Madame Rubelle took the foot. I bore my share of that inestimable precious burden with a manly tenderness, with a fatherly care. Where is the modern Rembrandt who

could depict our midnight procession? Alas for the Arts! alas for this most pictorial of subjects! the modern Rembrandt is nowhere to be found. (622)

The reference to the baroque painter does not simply call to mind his dramatic contrasts between light and darkness. Highly realistic and emotionally intense, Rembrandt's paintings also played upon secret passages and depths, and Fosco's depiction of the bed with the sleeping Marian can but evoke Rembrandt's images of the anatomy lessons of Professor Deyman (1656) or Dr Nicolaes Tulp (1632). Thus, Fosco's dismissal of the gothic atmosphere gives the scene much more macabre hues through hints at the medical, allusions that are strengthened by the aptly named Madame Rubelle, recalling the disease rubella.

Likewise, around Blackwater Lake chaos is sustained by damp, overgrown reeds and rushes, reinforcing the resemblance with Radcliffe's Udolpho. However, as Fosco makes explicit, the place could be no sensational crime scene:

'Some people call that picturesque,' said Sir Percival, pointing over the wide prospect with his half-finished walking-stick. 'I call it a blot on a gentleman's property. In my great-grandfather's time, the lake flowed to this place. Look at it now! It is not four feet deep anywhere, and it is all puddles and pools. I wish I could afford to drain it, and plant it all over. My bailiff (a superstitious idiot) says he is quite sure the lake has a curse on it, like the Dead Sea. What do you think, Fosco? It looks just the place for a murder, doesn't it?'

'My good Percival!' remonstrated the Count. 'What is your solid English sense thinking of? The water is too shallow to hide the body, and there is sand everywhere to print off the murderer's footsteps. It is, upon the whole, the very worst place for a murder that I ever set my eyes on.'

'Humbug!' said Sir Percival, cutting away fiercely at his stick. 'You know what I mean. The dreary scenery – the lonely situation ...' (234)

The gothic conventions to which Percival refers, the 'dreary scenery' and the 'lonely situation', are too clichéd to be of any use, and certainly do not pay homage to the modern science of forensics, well trained in reading the body. Still, death permeates the scene all the more through linking the site with contagious diseases. Indeed, the conversation between Fosco and Percival around the Lake and the mention of the curse, manifestly a hint at cholera, plaguing England in 1849–50 and making all pools of stagnant waters suspicious in the eyes of medical authorities, foreshadows Marian's typhus fever (680), due perhaps to the poisonous waters of Blackwater lake. The 'curse', just like Marian's later premonitory dream, in which contamination is symbolised by white wreaths of smoke touching and killing the members of Hartright's expedition, rework the gothic framework. The role played by pathology, shaping the contagious agents as the real villains of the narrative, relates mystery and uncertainty to the medical. Little by little, gothic sites are linked to ailments or symptoms which reveal the novel's epistemological framework. Chest disorders need to be decoded, signalling secrecy and guilt, like Sir Percival's cough, and symptoms must be traced, as when the weak-hearted asylum inmate's footsteps are printed in the sand.

'She's dead and buried; and you are alive and hearty'

When Anne Catherick dies, her death is not medically assisted, and the spectral woman is merely given a stimulant by the Count so that she may travel to London. But her heart weakness and her 'knowledge' of Sir Percival Glyde's secret are conflated through the gothic plot, since her cardiac disease originates from the news of his marriage to Laura Fairlie. Thus, her chest, as a physical container, becomes highly symbolic, completely revamping old gothic trunks and chests. As a matter of fact, physical pain in the chest and mental fright become indissociable when Laura 'presse[s] her hand over her heart, as if some sudden pain or fright had overcome her at that moment' (397). Through the motif of the heart, the scene anticipates the exchange of identity and Laura's live burial. Anne's cardiac disease is further caught within the novel's gothic framework when Laura is locked up in the lunatic asylum under Anne's name. The nurse ironically contrasts the burial of the false Lady Glyde with the 'hearty' Anne Catherick (436). The contrast reactivates the connections between the burial of the woman's body and her cardiac pathology, while images of depths permeate the text through references to medical technology, such as the stethoscope, when Hester Pinhorn remembers the doctor ausculting Anne with 'a bit of hollow mahogany wood … shaped like a kind of trumpet' (409).

Consequently, the heart not only conveys the romantic discourse of the novel, but concurrently illustrates women's victimisation, confinement and burial. In fact, the heart epitomises the discourse on woman's corporeality which the narrative and the characters try to bury. Asking Mr Fairlie to offer Laura 'the hospitality of [his] house (and heart)' (362), Fosco, with his 'infectious breast' (362), makes the term slip from metaphor to physical reality, revealing the organ as potentially flooded with unhealthy waters and recalling both the shallow waters of Blackwater Park and typhus fever. Similarly, when the Count's unfathomable eyes mesmerise Marian, her clairvoyant dream, showing a veiled woman rising out of a white tomb, makes the 'thought of Laura [well] up like a spring in the depths of [her] heart, and [filled] with waters of bitterness' (293). Marian's dream, with its churchyard scene and spectral apparition, echoes Anne Catherick's dream and her reading of Sir Percival's 'inmost heart' (78). In the first premonitory dream, the text, warning Laura of her fate as Sir Percival's wife, matches gothic conventions by associating the villain with a dark manuscript containing the crimes of the past. In the second clairvoyant vision, however, the female spectre reveals Marian's own depths, constructing the female body through circulation of fluids and a language of ebb and flow, and pointing to the laws of hydraulics.[7]

This mechanistic view of emotions is important because, as Helen Small has shown, such slippages between an organic construction of the heart and the novel's romantic quest and characters, participate in the construction of sensationalism. They highlight the characters' physiological responses to stimuli, as when Hartright hears of Laura's marriage, the word going 'like a bullet to [his] heart', his 'arm los[ing] all sensation', making him unable to move or speak (71), as if experiencing a stroke. For Small, such links between the language of romance and the discourse of physiology typify how many sensation writers used the romance 'as a vehicle for articulating their complaints against modern medicine', romance enabling writers to contrast 'a feeling hero or heroine and a heartless medical profession'.[8] Indeed, the heart is a representative organ in *The Woman in White*, 'central to sentimentalism but also to romance – and acutely vulnerable in the context of sensationalism'.[9] Aligned with violence, disease and death, whether Anne dies of heart disease, Percival is nearly 'wounded in the heart' (193) or Fosco stabbed 'over his heart' (640), the heart triggers sensationalism, ceasing to beat in the very first pages as soon as the woman in white first lays her hand on Hartright's shoulder. However, the physicality of the heart prevents closure: the happy ending depends upon 'restoring the possibility for romance ... [t]hrough returning the "broken heart" to the realm of metaphor'.[10] Thus, such images of characters probing depths or detecting heart sounds within a gothic framework reveal the narrative's fear of female corporeality, disturbing a hero who prefers looking at his beloved in watercolour paintings.

Hair-raising secrets

Mary Elizabeth Braddon implements a similar case in *Lady Audley's Secret*, which rewrites Collins's novel by highlighting tensions between painted surfaces and hidden depths. She continues to develop this connection in her yoking of Audley Court and her villainess's physiology, reworking images of depths in a sensational way. Because Lady Audley's victim has been pushed down a well, the well maps out the villainess's ultimate secret – her insanity – associated with 'the waters of a tideless pool putrefy[ing] by reason of their stagnation'.[11] The narrative's descent into the woman's mental processes and unruly physiology proposes a journey through passageways, showing the detective's attempt at sounding a spectral female body. Unlike Collins's narrative of female victimisation and male mercenary power, in Braddon's novel the female protagonist is neither locked up, exchanged, raped nor murdered. On the contrary, the female self, so much subjected to male power and violence in eighteenth-century gothic novels, is here independent and autonomous, playing upon the clichés of ideal femininity, capable of self-erasure and well versed in self-reproduction, fashioning a beautiful and seamless image which rarely betrays her criminal nature. Hence, while the heroine shifts from one identity to the next (from Helen Maldon and Helen Talboys to Lucy Graham and Lucy Audley), her spectral reflections continue to haunt the text, secularising the mysteries of the devilish woman whose face looks forever locked in childhood and innocence. Having faked her death in order to commit bigamy, Lady Audley becomes a living representation of death, a liminal figure hovering between the realm of the living and that of the dead. And yet, her innocent-looking appearance hardly ever betrays ghostly or vampiric features. As a result, Braddon's horror narrative is not simply concerned with discovering the rotting corpse of Lady Audley's first husband, which seemingly lies at the bottom of a well, and confounding the murderess. Rather, the spiral of crimes and secrets which the narrative gradually unravels takes us down to the horror of woman's degenerate physiology, down to the core of the heroine's insanity concealed beneath the artificial mask of beauty, beneath the 'pencilled eyebrows' (64) and velvet dresses which orchestrate her masquerade.

In fact, at the end of the novel, the omniscient narrator defines modern femininity as a collage of fashionable accessories and beauty aids, constructing the modern woman as much a gothic 'edifice' as Audley Court. In Audley Court doors are thick and locked. Metaphors of enclosure and images of imprisonment are scattered throughout the description of the former convent. Tropes of feminine repression pervade the setting, like the cliché of the nuns walled in and locked up. Time seems suspended, as the clock which has only one hand suggests. Mystery prevails throughout Audley Court, whether in the gardens, where the sheltering and shadowing over-arching trees remind the reader of the gothic arch, or where the tangled branches and the neglected weeds bury the unfathomable well – the most pregnant image of verticality and the site where the 'murder-scene' actually takes place – or in the house, a labyrinth with a secret chamber concealing a chest filled with Roman Catholic priests' vestments. Yet, for all its hints at gothicism, Audley Court is a monstrous collage made up of a series of rooms of various architectural styles added through the centuries and merely kept together by the ivy-covered façade which, firmly sealing its secrets, gives a picturesque, natural tinge to the multi-faced hybrid.

Likewise, the narrator suggests, the modern woman, for fear her hair may drop off as leaves fall from the trees at Audley Court (105), tries to deny the passing of time, fashioning herself into a macabre Cinderella, with wigs and false teeth:

> Amongst all privileged spies, a lady's-maid has the highest privileges ... She has a hundred methods for the finding out of her mistress's secrets ... That well-bred attendant knows how to interpret the most obscure diagnoses of all mental diseases that can afflict her mistress, she knows when the ivory complexion is bought and paid for – when the pearly teeth are foreign substances fashioned by the dentist – when the glossy plaits are the relics of the dead, rather than the property of the living; and she knows other and more sacred secrets than these. She knows when the sweet smile is more false than Madame Levison's enamel, and far less enduring – when the words that issue from between the gates of borrowed pearl are more disguised and painted than the lips which helped to shape them. When the lovely fairy of the ball-room re-enters her dressing-room after the night's long revelry, and throws aside the voluminous Burnous and her faded bouquet, and drops her mask; and like another Cinderella loses the glass-slipper, by whose glitter she has been distinguished, and falls back into her rags and dirt; the lady's-maid is by to see the transformation.   (336–7)

The passage is significant because the body parts which may be bought are linked to the gothic framework of the novel. If hair may drop off like leaves, as Lady Audley believes, turning the female body into a bleak picture of decay, hair can also be a 'relic of the dead', binding even more strikingly the artificial modern woman to the world of graveyards and corpses. Women's hair was sold for making wigs in the nineteenth century, and often taken from freshly buried corpses stolen by body-snatchers. So the 'relics of the dead' hint at the macabre commodification of women's hair. But these relics also indirectly point to the female body Lady Audley has buried under her name, that of a working-class consumptive girl, a tress of whose hair was cut off when she lay in her coffin and which the detective will use to incriminate the villainess.

Interestingly, another lock of hair reveals Lady Audley's past and is used by her maid to bribe her. In a secret drawer, a casket full of treasures contains 'hidden relics', as the title of the chapter points out: 'a lock of silky yellow hair, evidently taken from a baby's head' (30), imparting a fragrance of licentious sexuality to the narrative. And this embedded gothic locale, which echoes the secret chamber hiding Catholic clothes, is one of the many gothic conventions the novel uses, paving the way for Lady Audley's portrait. The latter is in Pre-Raphaelite style, the heroine's body covered by a crimson dress with folds that look like flames while her yellow hair is tinged with red gold hues. The glowing colours sexualise the villainess by fetishising her red gold hair. The painted Lady Audley becomes a passionate and sensuous creature, who strongly contrasts with the childish angel the text had so far presented. Double-locked in her apartment, the portrait is in fact a picture of the living dead, a representation of Helen Talboys which reveals the deception to Lady Audley's first husband. Positioned in the octagonal room among a series of twenty other paintings, the portrait marks a first stage in the novel's survey of the female self and woman's capacity to reinvent herself at will: the place is suffused with painted surfaces and mirroring devices functioning like so many tell-tale signs of the multi-faced heroine. Hinged upon a disruption of the boundaries of the self, the octagonal room triggers the narrative's quest into the liminal. Revealing the gothic double – the 'beautiful fiend' who looks like 'quaint mediæval monstrosities' (71) – the scene activates conventional gothic motifs, from the maze-like corridors and the threatening ghostlike family portraits, to the image of male invasion of female private rooms when Robert Audley and George Talboys access Lady Audley's apartments.

The portrait is, therefore, not simply a painted surface; it reveals hidden depths which the narrative capitalises on. Linked with her hidden child or with her faked death, Lady Audley's fair hair is closely associated with the character's power to transform herself and, of course, her bigamous exploits. This may be the reason why, as the headstone at Ventnor fails to reveal the real/sexual identity of the woman buried on the Isle of Wight,[12] the male characters start dreaming of earthly or watery depths in order to symbolically exhume the missing female body. In one of his dreams, Robert Audley finds the headstone gone in the churchyard; in another, he imagines Lady Audley as a mermaid. In one of the detective's dreams that appeared in the edition serialised in the *Sixpenny Magazine*, moreover, the hair plays once again a significant part in the representation of the *femme fatale*: Lady Audley appears as a Medusa tripping out of her grave. With her serpent-like locks creeping down her neck, the Medusa in Robert's nightmare, like the mermaid, stages the cycles of life and death and highlights femininity not only as dangerous but also as mysterious and secret:

> In another dream he saw the grave of Helen Talboys open, and while he waited, with a cold horror lifting up his hair, to see the dead woman arise and stand before him with her still, charnel-house drapery clinging about her frigid limbs, his uncle's wife tripped gaily out of the open grave, dressed in the crimson velvet robes in which the artist had painted her, and with her ringlets flashing like red gold in the unearthly light that shone about her.
>
> But into all these dreams the places he had last been in, and the people with whom he had last been concerned, were dimly interwoven – sometimes his uncle; sometimes Alicia; oftenest of all my lady; the trout stream in Essex; the lime-walk at the Court. Once he was walking in the black shadows of this long avenue, with Lady Audley hanging on his arm, when suddenly they heard a

great knocking in the distance, and his uncle's wife wound her slender arms about him, crying out that it was the day of judgment, and that all her wicked secrets must now be told. Looking at her as she shrieked this in his ear, he saw that her face had grown ghastly white, and that her beautiful golden ringlets were changing into serpents, and slowly creeping down her fair neck.[13]

As Elizabeth Bronfen's study of female bodies 'not safely interred beneath the earth' suggests, the female corpse unsettles semiotic meaning and disseminates ambiguity through the narrative.[14] Here, the female spectre is no trope of live burial, but the living dead creature that prevents both the closure of the grave and the story. While her appearance denies the marks of death and posits once again Robert's anxiety in terms of his horror of the liminal, the woman walking out of the womb-like grave reads like a reverse parturition – subversively giving birth to images of death. Animation (of the painted heroine in the gothic portrait) and metamorphosis, both subverting the usual passivity of the domestic angel, frame the male fantasy of female power. Lady Audley circulates from one image to the next, as she shifts from one identity to another, from one name to another or from one city to the next. Gliding, flowing or creeping, the heroine is associated with movement and circulation. The woman's endless recreation is what horrifies the detective who traces her steps via signs of her mobility: her bonnet-box on which railway labels are pasted, her letter telling her father about her departure, her book where a series of dedications indicates its circulation from owner to owner.

Drying up the flow of identities

Revealingly, the woman body parts play a key role in the investigation: a lock of hair makes Robert realise that the woman buried in Ventnor churchyard is not George's wife, described in a letter written almost immediately after George's marriage 'in which every feature was minutely catalogued, every grace of form or beauty of expression fondly dwelt upon, every charm of manner lovingly depicted' (209). It does not match either Lady Audley's 'hand', that is, her handwriting, in which Robert believes he can read 'the feathery, gold-shot, flaxen curls, the pencilled eyebrows, the tiny straight nose, the winning childish smile' in Lady Audley's 'graceful up-strokes and down-strokes' (64). In fact, the legibility of the female body which the narrative foregrounds shows how the investigation collects bodily parts, either literally or figuratively, in order to criminalise the female body. The detective turns, indeed, the female body into a text, recalling gothic hidden manuscripts recording the crimes of the past. As a result, Lady Audley merges more and more with the gothic setting. The portrait seems to become animated when the green and crimson shadows of the painted escutcheons in the mullioned window (recalling the contrast between the green cloth and the red Pre-Raphaelite model) colour Lady Audley's 'ghastly ashen grey' face (120). Cinderella's golden kingdom, with its caskets and costly mirrors, takes on the funereal hue of its inhabitant. Her 'wretchedness' (299) contaminates the objects about her and the delicate works of art that mark out her journey along a labyrinth of guilt appear as 'the mouldering adornments of some ruined castle' (299) defacing the 'shrine of her loveliness' (295). Through such macabre images of putrefaction, the gothic network constantly points to Lady Audley's crime: in the garden, which looks 'like an avenue in a churchyard' (66), the corpse of George Talboys may be rotting in the ruined well half choked up with leaves. But the leaves recall Lady Audley's Pre-Raphaelite hair and her fear that it may drop off like leaves, thus showing how the gothic depiction of the site is ultimately less linked with George Talboys's potential corpse than with female sexuality. Gradually, the images and metaphors the narrator uses to describe and define Lady Audley build up an 'edifice of horror' (254), paving the way for the narrative's focus on the villainess's physiology.

Indeed, when the murderous Lady Audley eventually sets fire to Castle Inn to get rid of the detective, her insanity is presented in physiological terms as 'some new and unnatural pulse in her heart' (310). Hence, when she is eventually brought to her 'living grave' (391), in 'the old world' (384), a former monastery in an 'old ecclesiastical town' (384) where she is to be locked up among other madwomen, the narrative merges the traditional gothic narrative of female incarceration with the modern Victorian scenario of medical control. Excess must be checked and unruly femininity curbed. The asylum, with its cellars peopled with 'legions of rats' (385), is the ultimate place where the 'dangerous' (379) creature will be confined. Imprisoned like the 'shivering flame struggl[ing] with the March wind [in] a great structure of iron and glass' (386), and thus subjected to panoptical surveillance, Lady Audley is left to melt into a landscape where 'the leafless branches [come and go] tremblingly, like the shadows of paralytic skeletons' (386), resembling the ghostlike shape behind the faded curtain, 'the shadow of a restless creature, who paced perpetually backwards and forwards' (386). The shadow shows how indirection has now replaced uninterrupted circulation, recalling earlier connections between the mind and the water at the bottom of the well. Now 'leafless', her flowing nature dried up, like Madame Fosco, 'as cold as a statue, and as impenetrable as the stone out of which it is cut' (219), Lady Audley becomes ultimately reduced to a black-edged letter when the news of her death is sent to her husband.

As these two examples have shown, sensation novels play upon the 'interchangeability of text and body',[15] the gothic revisions enabling sensation writers to deal with women's corporeality while remaining safely framed by the literary form. Consequently, the sensational women's bodies shaped as dangerous castles and concealing frightening depths suggest that beneath the surface of the text inscriptions on tombstones make the reader's flesh creep much more than the rattling bones buried beneath the earth. If Count Fosco's hand shows 'the bare bones' beneath the plump pasteboard (239), sensation writers, following in the footsteps of their gothic forefathers and foremothers, also tear off their society's mask to reveal women's condition.

NOTES

1. Wilkie Collins, *The Woman in White*, ed. John Sutherland (1859–60; Oxford University Press, 1996), 20. Further references to this edition will be given in the text.
2. Mary Elizabeth Braddon, *Henry Dunbar*, ed. Anne-Marie Beller (1864; Brighton: Victorian Secrets, 2010), 358.
3. Ann Radcliffe's gothic novels generally play upon frail virgins locked up in derelict castles by lustful and cruel villains.
4. Lenora Ledwon, 'Veiled Women, the Law of Coverture, and Wilkie Collins's *The Woman in White*', *Victorian Literature and Culture* 22 (1994), 1–22 (1).
5. *Ibid.*, 2.
6. Eugenia C. Delamotte, *Perils of the Night: A Feminist Study of Nineteenth-Century Gothic* (Oxford University Press, 1990), 5.
7. Mesmerism was based upon a manipulation of vital fluids, hence the images here.
8. Helen Small, *Love's Madness: Medicine, the Novel, and Female Insanity, 1800–1865* (Oxford University Press, 1996), 185.
9. *Ibid.*, 203.
10. *Ibid.*, 206.
11. Mary Elizabeth Braddon, *Lady Audley's Secret*, ed. David Skilton (1862; Oxford University Press, 1991), 287. Further references to this edition will be given in the text.
12. In the 1840s, Ventnor was a resort for the sick specialising in tuberculosis and cardiac care.
13. Mary Elizabeth Braddon, *Lady Audley's Secret*, *Sixpenny Magazine* 3 (1862), 65.
14. Elizabeth Bronfen, *Over Her Dead Body: Death, Femininity and the Aesthetic* (Manchester University Press, 1992), 291.
15. Chiara Briganti, 'Gothic Maidens and Sensation Women: Lady Audley's Journey from the Ruined Mansion to the Madhouse', *Victorian Literature and Culture* 19 (1991), 189–211 (204).

4

MARY ELIZABETH LEIGHTON AND LISA SURRIDGE

Illustrating the sensation novel

In 1865, *Beeton's Christmas Annual* published Thomas Hood's series of four parodic 'Illustrated Sensation Novels': 'Quintilia the Quadrigamist; or, The Heir and the Hounds'; 'Maurora Maudeley; or, Bigamy & Buttons'; 'Prinvilliers the Poisoner or, The Live Coal and the Deadly Cup'; and ''Arry the 'Eartless; or, A Bad Brother's Aim and End'.[1] Presented in a form resembling a modern comic strip, with minimal narration accompanying the illustrations, the series lampooned the sensation genre that had shot to popularity with Wilkie Collins's *The Woman in White* (1860). Hood mocked plot elements from contemporary novels such as Mary Elizabeth Braddon's *Lady Audley's Secret* (1862) and *Aurora Floyd* (1863); Ellen Wood's *East Lynne* (1861); and Wilkie Collins's *Armadale* (1866). Hood's heroine Quintilia (who pushes her brother into a river, her first husband into a dog pen and her second husband into an Alpine crevasse) recalls the murderous Lady Audley (who pushes her first husband into a well). Maurora Maudeley (whose name evokes both Aurora Floyd and Lady Audley) parodies the adulterous Isabel Vane of *East Lynne* when she appears as a bespectacled governess; her investigation by a detective also highlights a convention of the genre. Underscoring sensation fiction's focus on women and domestic crime, the adulterous Prinvilliers commits infanticide when she stabs her children and pushes them into the fire (see fig. 4.1). Importantly, the illustrations for Hood's parodic text emphasise the role of visual images in the sensation genre, a role that by 1865 was well established and readily available for parody. The heroine's abundant Pre-Raphaelite hair; the use of nocturnal scenes and white space; the visual representation of evidence such as buttons, poison bottles and documents; and the depiction of trial scenes all constitute common tropes of a genre whose visual elements contributed powerfully to its emphasis on realist detail and legal proof in combination with improbable plots and thrilling effects.

Since the 1970s, critics have explored sensation fiction's plot elements such as infanticide, bigamy, murder, adultery, domestic crime, female criminality, homoeroticism and disabled women's sexuality. They have also examined its

4.1 [Thomas Hood], *Prinvilliers the Poisoner: or, The Live Coal and the Deadly Cup*, 'Four Illustrated Sensation Novels'. *Beeton's Christmas Annual* (1865).

pseudo-documentary surface, debt to journalistic reportage, arousal of the reader's nervous system, affiliations with class anxiety and fusion of unlikely plot events with realist detail. However, few critics have explored the importance of visuality and illustration to the genre, even though many sensation novels were first published as illustrated serials, among them *Lady Audley's Secret* in the *London Journal* (1863); *Margaret Denzil's History* (1863–4) and *Armadale* (1864–6) in the *Cornhill*; and *Eleanor's Victory* (1863) and *The Notting Hill Mystery* (1862–3) in *Once a Week*. Furthermore, many novels that were serialised without illustrations in Britain were illustrated in their American serial versions: for example, *Great Expectations* (1860–1), *The Woman in White* (1859–60) and *The Moonstone* (1868) were unillustrated in *All The Year Round* but richly illustrated in *Harper's Weekly*, a journal that prided itself on the quality and number of its illustrations. As Hood's 'Four Illustrated Sensation Novels' suggests, therefore, sensation fiction was, in its serial version, often an illustrated form in which visual conventions and clues, flash forward or flash-back visual scenes, as well as page layout affected readers' emotional responses to and understanding of plot.

Sensation fiction and the study of book illustration

Sensation fiction participated in the golden age of book illustration, a period from 1859 to 1875 when artists such as George du Maurier, Luke Fildes, Arthur Hughes, Charles Keene, Frederic Leighton, John Everett Millais, John Tenniel and Frederick Walker provided memorable illustrations to the periodical press.[2] During this period, the book arts flourished, and fiction and poetry became inextricably linked to visual culture. The illustrated books of this golden age represent a richly dual reading experience in which readers encountered illustration as a key component of the novel. The illustrated Victorian novel thus combined visual and textual ways of perceiving and representing the world.

Readers, therefore, face the question of how to understand the relation between text and image in the illustrated serial sensation novel. A traditional way of viewing this relation emphasised the authority of the author, who was presumed to direct and possibly control the artist. In this model, illustration takes the back seat, echoing or supporting verbal meaning. Recently, however, scholars have emphasised instead the interplay of visual and verbal text, considering them as equal players in producing meaning. Under this new model, readers can recognise diverse possibilities of text/image relations: visual and verbal texts can complement, anticipate, undercut, elaborate upon or oppose one another, entering into a rich and complex dialogue. Such a model, relevant to all illustrated Victorian fiction, applies with particular force to serialised sensation novels, in which the placement and prominence of illustrations made images an essential part of the Victorian reading experience.

Sensation fiction and Victorian visual culture

Readers of the 1860s and 1870s expected visual and literary content to be packaged together, and journals such as *Once a Week*, the *Cornhill Magazine*, *Harper's Weekly*, *Good Words* and the *Graphic* aimed their literary products at such a market. Notably, William Makepeace Thackeray's editorship of the *Cornhill* exemplified this joint visual and verbal emphasis as he united in one person both author and illustrator, or (as they were represented in contemporary discourse) both pen and pencil. Illustrated sensation fiction appealed to middle-class periodical readers, but it also extended to more popular audiences: famously, W. Fraser Rae noted that the genre had made 'the literature of the Kitchen the favourite reading of the Drawing room',[3] appealing to a mass readership and appearing in periodicals from the *Cornhill* at a shilling to the *London Journal* at a penny per issue.

It was partly this mass popularity that prompted some critics to revile the genre as resembling an industrial product, 'so many yards of printed stuff, sensation-pattern, to be ready at the beginning of the season'.[4] Others worried that the genre would lead to female immorality: Margaret Oliphant derided its 'very fleshly and unlovely record' of female character. As she wrote, 'women driven wild with love ... women who marry their grooms in fits of sensual passion; women who pray their lovers to carry them off from husbands and homes they hate; women ... who give and receive burning kisses and frantic embraces ... such are the heroines who have been imported into modern fiction'.[5] Reviewers fretted that sensation novels focused on 'revolting topics', that they were 'mischievous in their tendency'[6] and that their provocation of bodily excitement would foster a 'diseased appetite'.[7] Importantly, the genre's mass appeal had its source in visual as much as textual content. This visual aspect included not only the illustrations that accompanied the serial text but also typographical effects that replicated pseudo-documents such as torn letters, marriage registry signatures, tombstone engravings, death certificates and the pages of the newspaper itself. The genre's thrilling effects emerge from the range of its documentary detail (often visual in form), which repeatedly brought the improbable into collision with the everyday.

As such, the sensation novel constituted an intrinsic part of a culture that experienced a fascination with, and rapid enlargement of, visual technologies such as the diorama, panorama, photograph, magic lantern show, illustrated newspaper and, ultimately, the cinema. The past decade's visual turn in Victorian studies has stressed the imbrication of Victorian literature in this emergent visual culture and demonstrated that Victorian readers' skills of visual interpretation became highly developed; they became readers of illustration, photography and painting as much as of text. As Théophile Gautier wrote on 22 May 1858, 'Our century does not always have the time to read, but it always has the time to see.'[8] Readers of sensation fiction thus became consumers of a visual/verbal genre that appealed to the eye as well as to the mind and emotions.

'Preaching to the nerves': illustration and sensational effect

As H. L. Mansel famously objected, sensation fiction 'preach[ed] to the nerves' rather than to the mind.[9] Illustration played a key role in the genre's generation of nervous excitement by representing atmospheric disturbance, streaming garments, women's unchaperoned nocturnal activity and figures starkly highlighted in white space against a dark background. Illustrations such as that for Part 1 of *Eleanor's Victory* (7 March 1863) evoked atmospheric unrest by depicting roiling smoke or clouds, as well as women's garments and hair disturbed by the wind. A parallel effect occurs in the illustration for Part 1 of *The Moonstone* (4 January 1868), which represents John Herncastle holding up a burning torch as he steals the diamond, the torch's smoke figuratively suggesting the social turbulence to be caused by the gemstone.

Similar suggestions of disturbance are evoked by images of young unchaperoned heroines, a visual trope appearing in a number of sensation novels. *Eleanor's Victory* participates in this visual theme of unrest with Part 3's representation of the heroine on the gaslit Paris streets (21 March 1863), as well as Part 23's nocturnal garden scene (8 August 1863), where Eleanor spies on the illicit burning of a will, the smoke from which suggests the social disturbances caused by her night-time activities and the interference with legal inheritance. The first illustration to Isa Blagden's *Santa, or A Woman's Tragedy* in *Once a Week* (23 August 1862) similarly features the unchaperoned heroine in the city at night, this time followed by a male stranger; the illustrator uses white space to contrast the male observer with the woman's dark and mysterious figure, which blends into the street scene behind her (fig. 4.2). That such tropes of illustration were recognised by contemporary artists and audiences as key aspects of the sensation genre is clear from F. C. Burnand's *Mokeanna; Or, The White Witness*, published in *Punch* from 21 February to 21 March 1863. This parodic sensation narrative included George du Maurier's image of

4.2 Isa Blagden, *Santa, or A Woman's Tragedy*, *Once a Week* (23 August 1862).

[THE WHITE WITNESS BACK-HAIRS THE LADY BETTINA.]

4.3 F. C. Burnand, *Mokeanna, Or The White Witness*, *Punch* (28 February 1863).

a woman in a night scene with tousled white garments and blowing hair; the exaggerated use of white space contrasts her figure starkly against the room's dark interior, suggesting mystery and suspense (fig. 4.3). Similarly, 'Prinvilliers the Poisoner' in Hood's 'Four Illustrated Sensation Novels' centres on images of the heroine in an ample white gown, swooning as her supposedly dead lover returns to her window at night. The white gown, the use of white space, the night scene: Hood's narrative draws on multiple well-known sensational tropes for its comic effect.

With its mysterious night-time encounter between the hero and an apparently crazed woman on the road to London, Collins's *The Woman in White* furnished what became perhaps the iconic image of the sensation genre: a mysterious woman in white clothing in a nocturnal scene. Collins's novel was unillustrated in Britain, but Part 1 of the American serial in *Harper's Weekly* (26 November 1859) features a memorable image of Anne Catherick in her white gown in the starlit London road. The illustrated serial novel repeats this image with significant variations, with Part 6 (31 December 1859) depicting Anne crouching on Mrs Fairlie's tombstone, the whiteness of her dress and the stone suggesting her affinity with death and the uncanny (fig. 4.4) and Part 26 (19 May 1860) representing Laura standing over her own tomb, her veiled white figure suggesting her affinity with this series of women in white. Frederick Walker's famous poster for the Olympic Theatre's adaptation of the novel crystallised this image: its nocturnal scene and starlit background frame a woman draped in white fabric, at night, apparently crossing a border or boundary into some other realm. It came to symbolise Collins's genius as well as the sensation craze he had initiated. Subsequent sensational illustrations implicitly alluded to this famous image, as in *Great Expectations* (also in *Harper's Weekly*), where Part 5's image of the gaunt Miss Havisham in her bridal gown (22 December 1860) appears as a horrifying version of the

"THE HAND HOLDING THE DAMP CLOTH WITH WHICH SHE HAD BEEN CLEANING
THE INSCRIPTION DROPPED TO HER SIDE; THE OTHER HAND GRASPED THE
MARBLE CROSS," ETC.

4.4 Wilkie Collins, *The Woman in White*, *Harper's Weekly* (31 December 1859).

"I SAW HER RUNNING AT ME, SHRIEKING, WITH A WHIRL OF FIRE BLAZING ALL ABOUT HER," ETC.

4.5 Charles Dickens, *Great Expectations*, *Harper's Weekly* (22 June 1861).

woman in white, and in *The Moonstone*, where Rosanna Spearman's supposed theft of the diamond in a white nightgown creates an imagined spectral
echo of Anne Catherick. *Great Expectations*'s image in Part 31 of Miss
Havisham on fire (22 June 1861) combines the powerful image of the
woman in white with the roiling smoke typical of sensational illustrations,
evoking her uncanniness and her potential for social destruction (fig. 4.5).
The image of the woman in white became widespread in Victorian culture,
with numerous manifestations in paintings by James Abbott McNeill
Whistler. Whistler denied that his *Symphony in White, No. 1: The White*

Girl referred to Collins's novel, but it was originally exhibited as *The Woman in White* in 1862, when 'it would have been hard to keep a painting of any white-clad female figure out of the powerful orbit of Collins's novel'.[10]

While sensational illustrations highlighted atmospheric and, by implication, social disturbances, they also suggested the genre's propensity for blurring social boundaries such as those of nation, class, gender and race; life vs. death; and human vs. non-human. This preoccupation with boundaries often took the form of threshold imagery: *The Moonstone*'s illustrations, for example, depict characters at the edge of the quicksand or the sea (Part 3, 18 January 1868), poised at doorways (Part 8, 22 February 1868) or crossing cultural boundaries. Such cultural crossings are exemplified by the chapter initial to Part 4 (25 January 1868), which shows the lurking shadows of the Indian jugglers in the Verinders' English garden at night (a scene that never occurs in the verbal text) (fig. 4.6).

In Collins's *No Name* (1862–3), the liminal position of the seashore offered illustrators rich possibilities for suggesting Magdalen Vanstone's position on the boundary between domesticity and revolt, stable and unstable identities, and life and death. John Everett Millais's frontispiece to the 1864 edition depicts Magdalen seated by a window ledge gazing at the sea, the poison bottle

4.6 Wilkie Collins, *The Moonstone, Harper's Weekly* (25 January 1868).

by her hand symbolising her suspension between life and death. E. Evans's illustration to Smith Elder's 1877 edition similarly positions Magdalen between land and sea, depicting her 'Alone on a Strange Shore', with an unsettled sky and disturbed sea behind her, and her garments and hair rent by the wind in a symbolic evocation of her inner turmoil. George du Maurier's illustration for Instalment 2 of Burnand's *Mokeanna* (28 February 1863) parodically invokes sensation fiction's preoccupation with such boundary crossings by placing the White Witness before an open window, with the outdoor air rushing through her voluminous hair and white garments.

Collins's *The Law and the Lady* (1874–5) similarly emphasises the transgression of boundaries because the character of Ariel is ambiguously gendered and Miserrimus Dexter identifies himself as part man, part wheelchair. The illustration to Part 12 (12 December 1874) starkly highlights Ariel's liminal gender identity (as well as the artist's role in depicting this): she is represented stepping through 'an invisible side-door ... masked by one of the pictures',[11] seemingly entering a frame alongside other framed images, and hence symbolically placed on the very boundary of artistic representation. Most strikingly, perhaps, Dexter seems to defeat categorisation altogether, with his missing legs, ambiguous genitalia, resemblance to animals and deliberate confusion with his own wheelchair ('My chair is Me', 494). The illustration to Part 13 captures Dexter's ambiguous status, showing him leaping from his wheelchair, a 'terrible creature', 'absolutely deprived of the lower limbs', landing on his hands 'as a monkey' (589). Emphasising his challenge to visual representation, a framed picture above the hearth shows a set of legs truncated at the waist, as if to represent other fragmentary bodies (fig. 4.7).

4.7 Wilkie Collins, *The Law and the Lady*, *The Graphic* (19 December 1874).

Page layout in *Harper's Weekly* (the American journal in which many British sensation novels were illustrated and serialised) enriched the capacity of illustrations to suggest sensational boundary crossings by allowing for multiple, sometimes contradictory, images on the same page. For example, Part 1 of the American serial version of *Great Expectations* (24 November 1860) encapsulates Pip's nightmarish sense of living between contradictory worlds: the top and bottom right illustrations on the instalment's second page show Pip conversing on the marshes with the convict Magwitch, their figures looming against a darkly lineated background, while the bottom left illustration shows him sharing the domestic hearth with the kindly Joe. At first, these images seem to contrast the dangers of the marshes with the domestic sphere; more profoundly, however, the image of the convict destabilises that of the home, suggesting Pip's fear of sliding into criminality and shame. Such class instability is fundamental to sensation fiction; it reappears in the illustrations to Part 2 (1 December 1860), which break down the distinctions between Pip's domestic world and the convict's world by showing both as fraught with angst. In the upper left corner of the page, Magwitch files his shackles against the same dark background as in Part 1, while in the lower right corner, Pip shrinks between the angular Mrs Joe and the pompous Uncle Pumblechook. In Part 5 (22 December 1860), the first image of Miss Havisham completes this destabilisation as it infuses the domestic realm (including the figure of the bride) with nightmare and terror.

Illustration and detailism

So far we have seen illustration's role in creating sensation fiction's effects of excitement and instability. A less obvious aspect of sensational illustrations lies in their contribution of the detailism that underpins the genre: unlike gothic novels, sensational fictions tantalised the reader with their realist underpinnings in contemporary everyday life. As Henry James remarked, 'those most mysterious of mysteries, are the mysteries which are at our own doors'.[12] Indeed, the illustrations to *Eleanor's Victory* offer realist details of nautical rigging as well as accurately rendered Paris street scenes;[13] those for *Lady Audley's Secret* embed the heroine in modern life as she receives telegrams (Part 3, 4 April 1863); and those for *No Name* situate Magdalen Vanstone in the mundane settings of the shop (Part 20, 26 July 1862) and Captain Wragge in the post office (Part 30, 4 October 1862). The chilling effects of turbulent smoke, wind-swept garments and unchaperoned nocturnal scenes, then, worked precisely because such *frissons* were combined with realist visual details of temporal and physical setting.

A notable aspect of this detailism appears in the sensation novel's preoccupation with documents. The genre flaunts its relation to letters, telegrams, newspapers, wills, legal papers, diaries and written proof. Indeed, many sensation novels present themselves as 'bundles of documents authored by witnesses in the case'.[14] We see this preoccupation at the level of illustration, layout and typeface, as the pages of the sensation novel reproduce the 'documents' upon which its plot relies. *The Law and the Lady* opens with a woodcut of signatures in a marriage register (Part 1, 26 September 1874); *Eleanor's Victory* features a torn suicide note, typographically rendered on the page (See Part 5, 4 April 1863); *Lady Audley's Secret* includes a death announcement in *The Times* (Part 2, 28 March 1863); and *The Woman in White* reproduces a death certificate (Part 26, 19 May 1860). Notably, a number of these documents are misleading or false: Eustace signs the marriage registry with a false name; Lady Audley publishes the false death announcement of Helen Talboys; and Sir Percival Glyde obtains a death certificate for Anne Catherick under the name of Laura, Lady Glyde. Sensation fiction's pages, then, paradoxically reproduce print documents that cast doubt on the reliability of print itself, often relying on chasms between the documented 'fact' and the improbable plot – as when Laura Fairlie appears alive over her own tombstone in Part 26 (19 May 1860).

Importantly, the sensation novel's crisis often occurs around forged, lost, missing or torn documents, many of them reproduced typographically on the page or represented in illustration. Perhaps the quintessential example of such detailism is the image of Robert Audley peeling Lady Audley's many luggage labels from her trunk (Part 11, 30 May 1863); they, rather than a marriage register or death certificate, link her many aliases to her true identity as Helen Talboys. Hood's 'Four Illustrated Sensation Novels' invokes and parodies this obsession with visual detail: it visually renders print matter such as cheques, a marriage register, a receipt, a stack of money and a 'Last Will and Testament'. It also renders other realist 'proofs' with parodic precision: a grossly exaggerated button (fig. 4.8), a bottle of poison, a corkscrew, a cash-box and parts of a disguise (moustache, glasses, hat and waistcoat). These items are isolated in individual frames, highlighting sensation fiction's obsession with concrete minutiae.

Such realist details invited the reader of sensation to become a detective of Victorian print culture. Scholars have recognised sensation fiction as a forerunner of detective fiction,[15] with its detective heroes and heroines such as Robert Audley, Sergeant Cuff, Walter Hartright, Valeria Macallan and Eleanor Vane, but they have not noted how often such detective work requires the deciphering of visual clues. In *The Moonstone*, Sergeant Cuff has to understand the process of paint drying

AND A BUTTON
FOUND IN THE
KENNEL.

4.8 [Thomas Hood], *Quintilia the Quadrigamist; or, The Heir and the Hounds*, 'Four Illustrated
Sensation Novels'. *Beeton's Christmas Annual* (1865).

on a door in order to understand the significance of a paint-smeared nightgown; in *The Woman in White*, Walter Hartright must decode a marriage
registry to recognise that the entry for Sir Percival's parents' marriage was
added belatedly; in *The Law and the Lady*, Valeria Macallan has to decipher the photograph of her husband and his first wife; and in *Eleanor's
Victory*, Eleanor has to identify the accomplice in her father's suicide by
recognising his resemblance to an illustration of a villain in a French novel.
The reader of sensation fiction must also become an expert interpreter of
Victorian visual culture, shadowing the detective's progress in deciphering
these clues. Indeed, a number of illustrations feature the process of visual
interpretation itself, as in Part 4 of *Lady Audley's Secret* (11 April 1863),
where Robert and George gaze at Lady Audley's Pre-Raphaelite portrait, or

in Part 17 of *Eleanor's Victory* (27 June 1863), where Eleanor interprets Launcelot Darrell's sketches of Bohemian Paris in order to link him to the circumstances of her father's suicide.

Placement of illustrations

The savvy reader of serial sensation novels would have realised that the detective work required of the reader extended beyond the content of illustrations to a consideration of their placement in the serial text. Most serials featured illustrations at the beginnings of instalments, which meant that they often offered visual clues to the plot of the coming episode. This was not true of volume editions, which typically tipped in illustrations beside the plot events as they occurred in the letterpress. In serial form, however, illustrations often preceded the letterpress and thus conveyed key plot developments to the reader in advance of the verbal text. For example, the chapter initial to Part 4 of *Margaret Denzil's History* (February 1864) depicts the body of a man lying on a beach under the chapter title 'Over the Cliff'. The reader thus knows that some sort of misfortune (suicide? murder? accident?) will occur and that the unknown man will be injured or perhaps killed. The astute reader of the visual plot, then, asks not simply *What will happen next?* but more focused questions such as *Who is the man on the beach? How did he fall over the cliff? And will he survive?*

The illustration to Part 2 of *Armadale* (December 1864) provides another example of this proleptic function of sensational illustration. It shows the two young Allan Armadales meeting together (fig. 4.9), whereas the previous instalment had featured the dying Allan Armadale's injunction, 'Never let the two Allan Armadales meet in this world: never, never, never!'[16] The reader of visual images, therefore, starts Part 2 knowing that a meeting will occur and asking questions such as *How will the two Armadales meet?* and *What will be the consequences of this meeting?* Such proleptic knowledge changed sensation plots from simple suspense to a complicated process of acquiring visual knowledge and then matching it to or refining it by means of the letterpress. The sensation novelists' dictum, 'Make 'em laugh; make 'em cry; make 'em wait'[17] thus becomes something more like Make 'em look, make 'em read, make 'em wonder. The pleasure of reading illustrated sensation fiction, therefore, has less to do with simple suspense and more to do with the correct deciphering of verbal and visual plots.

THE TWO ARMADALES.

4.9 Wilkie Collins, *Armadale*, *Cornhill* (December 1865).

Illustration and self-reflexivity

Indeed, sensation novels are remarkably self-reflexive about the importance of visual culture to the genre. Several feature artists or other producers of visual imagery: *The Woman in White*'s Walter Hartright is an art teacher who becomes a newspaper illustrator and *Eleanor's Victory*'s Richard Thornton paints scenes for sensation dramas while Launcelot Darrell from the same novel is a visual artist. Such self-consciousness finds expression in sensational illustrations themselves, as when Hartright finds himself at the limits of expression when he tries to describe his first meeting with Laura. In Part 3 (10 December 1859), he writes, 'How can I describe her? How can I separate her from my own sensations, and from all that has happened in the later time? How can I see her again as she looked when my eyes first rested on her – as she should look, now, to the eyes that are about to see her in these pages?'[18] Instead of using words, he turns to his watercolour portrait to evoke this powerful moment: as he records, the 'drawing that I made of Laura Fairlie, at an after-period, in the place and attitude in which I first saw her, lies on my desk while I write' (795). The illustration to Part 3 reproduces this fictional drawing, with Laura in exactly the attitude of Hartright's portrait; the caption points to Hartright's verbal description of Laura at the moment when he depicted her: 'She was standing near a rustic table –' (796). The reader, then, first sees Laura not through mimetic verbal or visual representation, but rather as mediated by Hartright's own retrospective visual reconstruction of her. This portrait of Laura, twice removed from direct mimesis, thus emphasises the complexity of the text/image relation, implying that an image is free neither of an implied viewer nor of an implied attitude to its subject.

A similarly complex relationship of text and image appears in Part 1 of Collins's *Blind Love* (6 July 1889), where the narrator avows the impossibility of representing Iris Henley in words or pictures:

> No descriptions of her will agree with each other. No existing likenesses will represent her. The one portrait that was painted of Iris is only recognisable by partial friends of the artist. In and out of London, photographic likenesses were taken of her. They have the honour of resembling the portraits of Shakespeare in this respect – compared with one another, it is not possible to discover that they present the same person.[19]

Ironically, the illustration that immediately precedes this passage represents Iris looking directly at the reader, hands behind her head, in a nonchalant but challenging pose. The caption, 'Iris Henley', effectively establishes this illustration as the very portrait that the letterpress calls into question. This ironic relation again disturbs a mimetic or direct relation between text and image, suggesting instead that '[m]eanings are generated ... in the very interaction between the textual and the visual, the points at which they coincide and conflict'.[20]

The illustrations that appeared in *Harper's Weekly*'s serialisation of *The Moonstone* similarly suggest the limits of an image's ability to represent. In this novel, the character of Rosanna Spearman challenges Victorian identity categories in multiple respects. As a lower-class woman with a significant physical disability and a criminal past, she defies conventional boundaries when she falls in love with an upper-class man, Franklin Blake. Significantly, while the verbal text describes her 'deformed shoulder',[21] the visual text never offers a realist depiction of Rosanna's disability. Instead, the chapter head for Part 7 (15 February 1868) suggests Rosanna's indecipherability and the way in which she eludes conventional representation: Rosanna appears in the middle of a small arched frame, her body across the horizon between sea and shore, her veiled figure represented by a mere series of scribbled lines. Severely simplified into a pillar-like form, her body's shape echoes the larger arch of the frame, which itself suggests the shape of a tombstone. Finally, then, Rosanna passes the limits of representation except to signify her own impending death, which occurs in the quicksand between sea and shore. Laura Fairlie, Iris Henley, Rosanna Spearman: all three women defy conventional portraiture, indicating the way in which sensation fiction pushes the limits of representation and problematises the text/image relationship.

Suggestive, complex and offering knowledge and forms of representation not available in the verbal text: sensational illustrations constituted no mere supplement but were intrinsic to sensational plots as they reached their first Victorian readers. Book historians and critics of material culture insist on the importance of the text's physical embodiment in producing meaning for the reader: as Pierre Macherey writes, 'Readers are made by what makes the book.'[22] This dictum applies forcefully to sensation fiction, whose serial form differed radically from its volume publication. In placement and number of illustrations, these serials offered a unique reading experience to their first Victorian readers and richly contributed to creating the sensational *frissons* that critics deplored and readers adored.

Modern editions of illustrated sensation novels

Ironically, many modern editions of sensation novels deny their readers such interactions of text and image, as very few reproduce illustrations at all and none reproduce the serial layouts that Victorian readers enjoyed. As Victorianist scholars develop more sophisticated understandings of text/ image relations, however, editors and publishers are increasingly producing editions that take visual matter into account. Natalie M. Houston's Broadview edition of *Lady Audley's Secret* reproduces the illustrations (though not the layout) from the *London Journal*; and Maria K. Bachman's and Don Richard Cox's Broadview edition of *The Woman in White* reproduces Frederick Walker's famous theatre poster for *The Woman in White*, as well as the illustrations (including the frontispiece) from the 1861 volume edition of the novel. Houston's edition reproduces the illustrated text of *Maurora Maudeley*, thus capturing the importance of illustration in sensation fiction's parodic forms. Moreover, digital reproductions of journals such as *Harper's Weekly* make far more accessible the original serial editions of such novels, enabling scholars and readers to recapture the Victorians' reading pleasures. The advent of digital technologies may renew the possibility for modern readers to experience text/image relationships in a way similar to that of initial Victorian readers.

If sensation fiction, then, made 'the literature of the Kitchen' into the 'favourite reading of the Drawing room', it also brought text and image together in ways intrinsic to its original form, but in ways that are lost to many modern readers. The illustrated sensation novel participated in the rich flowering of Victorian visual culture, especially as manifested in book and periodical illustration. Pen and pencil together produced sensation's thrilling atmospheric effects and excitement, its grounding in realist detail and documentary proof, its emphasis on visual reading and interpretation, and its preoccupation with social transgression and the crossing of racial, national, gender and species boundaries. Self-reflexive about their debt to visual culture, many sensation novels featured scenes of characters (especially detectives) reading or deciphering visual images, providing paradigmatic examples of how sensation readers themselves approached these texts that so richly combined verbal and visual representation. In 'The Critic As Artist' (1891), Oscar Wilde noted the tendency in Victorian literature to 'appeal more and more to the eye'.[23] Sensation fiction's complexly dual experience of verbal and visual reading thus places it centrally in the literary tradition of this consummately visual era.

NOTES

1. [Thomas Hood], 'Four Illustrated Sensation Novels', *Beeton's Christmas Annual* (1865), 77–81.
2. Forrest Reid, *Illustrators of the Eighteen Sixties: An Illustrated Survey of the Work of 58 British Artists* (New York: Dover, 1975), 1.
3. W. Fraser Rae, quoted in Mary Elizabeth Braddon, *Aurora Floyd*, ed. Richard Nemesvari and Lisa Surridge (Peterborough: Broadview, 1998), 592.

4. H. L. Mansel, quoted in *ibid*., 574.

5. ON, 259.

6. Rae, quoted in Nemesvari and Surridge (eds.), *Aurora Floyd*, 588, 591.

7. Mansel, quoted in *ibid*., 573–4.

8. Quoted in Jean-Pierre Bacot, *La presse illustrée au XIXe siècle: une histoire oubliée* (Presses Universitaires de Limoges, 2005), 80.

9. Mansel, quoted in Nemesvari and Surridge (eds.), *Aurora Floyd*, 573.

10. Nicholas Daly, 'The Woman in White: Whistler, Hiffernan, Courbet, Du Maurier', *Modernism/Modernity* 12:1 (2005), 7.

11. Wilkie Collins, *The Law and the Lady*, *The Graphic* (1874), 565. Further references to this edition will be given in the text.

12. Quoted in Lyn Pykett, *The Improper Feminine: The Women's Sensation Novel and the New Woman Writing* (London: Routledge, 1992), 6.

13. Simon Cooke, 'George du Maurier's Illustrations for M. E. Braddon's Serialization of *Eleanor's Victory* in *Once a Week*', *Victorian Periodicals Review* 35:1 (2002), 93.

14. 'Sensation, Novel of', *Concise Oxford Companion to English Literature* (Oxford University Press, 2003).

15. Ronald R. Thomas, 'Wilkie Collins and the Sensation Novel', in *The Columbia History of the British Novel*, ed. John J. Richetti (New York: Columbia University Press, 1994), 479.

16. Wilkie Collins, *Armadale*, *Cornhill* (1864), 546.

17. 'Em', *Webster's Online Dictionary* www.merriam-webster.com/dictionary/em, 21 January 2010.

18. Wilkie Collins, *The Woman in White*, *Harper's Weekly* (1859), 795. Further references to this edition will be given in the text.

19. Wilkie Collins, *Blind Love*, *Illustrated London News* (1889), 12.

20. Julia Thomas, *Pictorial Victorians: The Inscription of Values in Word and Image* (Athens: Ohio University Press, 2004), 25.

21. Wilkie Collins, *The Moonstone*, *Harper's Weekly* (1868), 21.

22. Pierre Macherey, *A Theory of Literary Production*, trans. Geoffrey Wall (London: Routledge and Kegan Paul, 1978), 70.

23. Oscar Wilde, 'The Critic As Artist', in *The Artist as Critic: Critical Writings of Oscar Wilde*, ed. Richard Ellman (University of Chicago Press, 1982), 350.

5

ANDREW MAUNDER

Sensation fiction on stage

We know more about nineteenth-century stage adaptations than we do about other popular forms of entertainment which flourished in the period. We have prints, photographs, prompt copies, posters (fig. 5.1), reviews and reminiscences, even some silent films. If stage adaptations of novels remain neglected, it is not because of a shortage of evidence but because the practice remains essentially denigrated; melodramatic and sentimental, the plays seem to represent much that is antithetical to what we admire in the novels from which they were taken.

Literary and theatrical criticism has maintained a fairly unsympathetic stance in regard to this sub-speciality, which always aimed for public approval and a fast buck. Rather unfairly it is T. A. Palmer's 1874 words which stand out when we think of the moving moments of *East Lynne* (1861), when Isabel Vane, disguised in green glasses, watches her son die ('dead, dead, dead! And he never knew me, never called me mother'[1]), obliterating Wood's writing and stealing her ideas. It is men like Palmer who are accused of enacting a form of 'assault' on the female-authored novel;[2] yet Palmer never made much of a living from the theatre, from hawking his weepy second-hand melodramas round second-rate provincial theatres.

In actuality the position of the stage adaptation on the mid-Victorian theatre was a far more complex affair than we have traditionally been led to believe, involving different cultural fields and enterprises and a variety of subject positions. When *Lady Audley's Secret* (1862) conquered the London stage in February 1863, at least two in the St James's Theatre's audience – Henry Morley and David Masson – saw Mary Elizabeth Braddon's heroine as a symptom of cultural decline: 'an appeal to that low taste for criminal horrors which is sufficiently catered for by the Old Bailey reports'.[3] Across the capital at the Effingham Theatre in Whitechapel, a different audience cheered as another Lady Audley, reconfigured in an anonymously authored script as a working-class heroine, pushed her inconvenient, upper-class husband down the well.

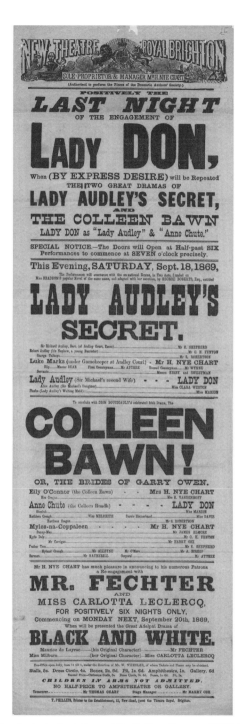

5.1 Playbill advertising *Lady Audley's Secret*, *The Colleen Bawn* and Wilkie Collins's *Black and White*. New Theatre Royal, Brighton (18 September 1869).

This chapter examines some of the artistic trends and tremors brought about by the fashion in the 1850s, 1860s and 1870s for 'refitting' novels for the stage, as well as the uneasy relationships between novelists, adaptor-dramatists and theatre critics.

Evolutionary stages

The structural and aesthetic links between Victorian novels and the stage have, of course, long been acknowledged. So, too, have the attempts by some novelists, notably Wilkie Collins and Charles Reade, but also Florence Marryat, Lucy Clifford and Hall Caine, to turn their own novels into plays or in some cases turn plays into novels – and sometimes back again. However, charting the development of this trend represents a larger challenge. Most contemporary accounts agree that, by mid-century, the appetite for stage adaptations appeared unstoppable: 'taking possession of our theatres to the exclusion of Shakespeare' and 'ousting from the stage nearly all modern compositions' – as the *Theatrical Journal* lamented in 1871.[4] In his magisterial *History of English Drama* (1955) Allardyce Nicoll located the beginning of this boom in the eighteenth century, prompted by adaptations of Samuel Richardson, Ann Radcliffe and Matthew 'Monk' Lewis, adding, nonetheless, that 'it was not until the time of Scott that the whole field of fiction was eagerly and systematically sacked'.[5] Nicoll's phraseology is, of course, significant here and the fate of stage adaptations at his hands is quickly settled: crude pieces of theatre only worth recognising in the context of the theatre industry's eye for the main chance. More recently Philip Cox in *Reading Adaptations* (2000) has found more of interest in the ways in which, between 1790 and 1840, the stage adaptation emerged as a serious competitor for theatre audiences but became stuck with a 'low' as opposed to 'high' culture label.[6] This label proved difficult to shake off. As late as 1874, the *Academy* compared the genre of the stage adaptation to the 'cheap illustrated edition'.[7] While on the one hand a reference to the idea that the adaptor's task was to make pictures – or pictorial effects – out of words, the comment is also designed to suggest 'dumbing down'. By this time the cultural landscape had altered to include such names as Colin Henry Hazlewood (1823–75), John Oxenford (1812–77) and Andrew Halliday (1830–77), reliable money-spinners who developed adaptation into a kind of sub-speciality, enabling theatres to keep afloat during quiet periods. They had to compete with what Wilkie Collins termed 'the rank and file of hack writers',[8] who made a living selling plays to working-class theatres.

Something of the extent to which stage adaptations pervaded theatrical culture in London's West End in the 1850s and 1860s can be found in the testimony of the aforementioned Henry Morley, Professor of English at University College, London, who kept a journal of his playgoing experiences. In 1863, Morley attended productions of not only *Lady Audley's Secret* but *Effie Deans* (aka *The Heart of Midlothian*) and *Aurora Floyd* (two versions). In his journal, Morley described the Adelphi Theatre's production of the latter as 'garbage', fitted only for the 'literary taste [of] the uneducated'. Charles Reade's much-misunderstood *It's Never Too Late to Mend* was likewise a 'repulsive excrescence'.[9] Occasionally Morley was willing to be seduced by the wattage of a production's star power; in 1854 he was captivated by Charlotte Cushman's turn as the gypsy, Meg Merrilies, in a new version of Scott's *Guy Mannering*. But Morley was also increasingly exasperated by what he saw as the reliance on plays taken second-hand from other sources. For Morley and other earnest theatregoers of the 1850s and 1860s it was far better to be moved by Samuel Phelps in *A Midsummer Night's Dream* (1855), Louisa Herbert in *The School for Scandal* (1866) or even Wilkie Collins's *The Lighthouse* (1855), which featured Charles Dickens as director and star, because all of these had at least some claim to originality and grandeur. Overall, Morley's attitude to stage adaptations remained ambiguous and fluctuated between appreciation of the imaginative processes involved and ridicule for the apparent superficiality of the results. For him, as for others, adaptations also served as salutary reminders of the coarsening of theatrical culture, and of drama's loss of influence as an art form.

In the 1860s, as in other decades, the notion that British theatre was in terminal decline was a common one, and because they were perceived as one of the root causes of this, stage adaptations had become the object of heated discussion. Among purists, there was a sense that, because they traded on the cultural memory of a pre-existing text, adaptations were lazy, superficial and dishonest and thus made unsatisfactory theatre.[10] Certainly adaptors could not expect much respect. 'It has been objected', noted the *Illustrated Review* in its 1877 obituary of Andrew Halliday,

> that to dramatise the creations of great writers is a very inferior branch of authorship. It has been said that those who have never read the original novel listen in helpless despair to the confused scenes unfolding themselves on the stage, while those who had read the original fail to recognise their ideal of the characters of the story in their 'counterfeit presentment' on the stage.[11]

Despite the admitted difficulty of the challenge, old prejudices died hard. Moreover, the majority of theatre managers encouraged the production of such works. Owing to the 1842 Copyright Act, they did not need permission to stage a novel. Thus in 1866 when Ellen Wood sought advice from Charles Dickens after dramatisations of *East Lynne* had started to spring up in Britain and North America, all he could tell her was that 'our English law (which has little tenderness for such an idle thing as Literature) does not, to the best of my belief, give you the power of preventing ANY stage adaptation of your book'.[12] Wilkie Collins likewise complained that 'any larcenous rascal possessed of a pot of paste and a pair of scissors can steal my novel for stage purposes – as things are'.[13] To secure rights over a stage version, a novelist had to write and register a dramatic version of their own work with the Lord Chamberlain's Office ahead of anyone else. The fact that few novelists bothered to do this meant that hardly any of them had control over what was staged, or indeed whether they wanted it staged at all. Nor could he or she expect any fee. So while some novelists – Dickens, Collins, Reade – fought against the theft of their works, they invariably lost. Sometimes they sued, but such instances were rare.

Wood, at least, seems to have accepted dramatisations of her novel with *sang-froid*, recognising that they could boost her own sales. This idea that stage adaptations could showcase a book was a popular defence used by 'literary cracksmen', as the *Theatrical Journal* termed adaptors, and as an argument had a certain amount of leverage over some novelists (Mary Braddon and Thomas Hardy being notable examples).[14] Not everyone was convinced, of course – something which comes across in an 1872 article, 'The Natural Right of Adaptation', in the *Orchestra* magazine. This Darwinian-sounding piece was an attack on veteran dramatist, J. R. Planché, who was never more comfortable than when devising stage entertainment based on someone else's material. The *Orchestra* noted that Planché tried to excuse his career as 'pirate, vampire and the like' by claiming that the typical adaptor was tempted into his morally dubious career by cunning theatre managers: 'more blameable than the adaptor, being towards him as the receiver to the thief'.[15] But why were adaptations so popular with theatres? Obviously the speed with which an efficient adaptor could knock up a play from pre-existing materials, sometimes not bothering to change the original dialogue, was part of it. And if the novel had been – or was currently being – published in instalments it would most likely have a pre-existing episodic quality to it, with perhaps a good cliff-hanger. Generally speaking, however, the processes of adaptation did not lend themselves to much written reflection, unless those involved were forced to defend themselves in the law courts or letters pages – as in the very public feud between Charles Dickens and William Thomas Montcrieff in 1837 over the unauthorised staging of *Nicholas Nickleby*. Certainly it was the case that for novelists like Wilkie Collins, who adapted their own works for the stage, there were often quite striking differences between novel and play, the result of a refusal simply to cut and paste from one medium to the other. Yet while Collins described his own stage version of

Man and Wife as an 'entirely new Dramatic Story' he was loath to write about what he actually *did*. *Man and Wife* opened at the fashionable Haymarket Theatre on 23 February 1873. Collins claimed of the novel to have aimed for 'strong drama ... making the flesh of "drawing-room audiences" creep'; in other words, he wrote in the melodramatic style.[16] What can be gleaned is that Collins seems to have regarded adaptation as part of a process of revisualising what he had originally written as fiction.

One of the surviving commentaries by an adaptor of other people's novels comes from Edward Fitzball, author of *Jonathan Bradford or, The Murder at the Roadside Inn* (1833), *Paul Clifford* (1835), *Quasimodo* (1836) and *Marmion* (1847) among many others. In his memoirs, Fitzball suggests adaptation as an ideal apprenticeship, one which 'did not require any remarkable ability, as it was only to select scenes and join them together' to form a workable melodrama.[17] Once again, it is slightly tricky to work out the process being described. Was it a case of adapting the novel to the needs of the theatre company – one thinks of Mr Crummles's valuable pump and washing tub in *Nicholas Nickleby*? Or did the theatre accommodate itself to the needs of the story? For Fitzball there was little sense of an aesthetic clash. As a task of translation from one medium to another, it did not seem much of a challenge.

This picture of hack dramatists running amok has coloured perceptions of Victorian stage adaptations, but decisions about *what* to adapt were slightly more considered. There was the lure of the tried and tested 'pre-sold' title, or what Frederick Wedmore, in a review of W. S. Gilbert's adaptation of Annie Edwardes's *Ought We to Visit Her?* (1874), called 'the embodiment of conceptions already familiar'.[18] This was also a point made by *The Times* in its review of the Surrey Theatre's production of *The Woman in White* (1860). As the paper explained:

> [O]nce a tale becomes generally popular, a desire to see it as a dramatic form immediately spreads like an epidemic ... Whether a story be fitted for stage purposes or not people do not inquire, nor even care. They only want to see the personages they have read about clothed with a visible form and turn from the book to the stage as a child turns from letter-press to pictures.[19]

One of the inferences is that there was always new business to be had from those who might not normally go to the theatre. As a reviewer of another Surrey production – *East Lynne* (1866) – noted, the steady stream of stage adaptations invariably gave audiences a special theatrical experience: edited highlights of the source novel in melodramatic mode – enhanced with 'broader and more marked effects ... judicious groupings and well-arranged masses of colour'.[20] Stripped to the bare bones with a handful of strong characters, exciting confrontations and opportunities for grandstanding (all ingredients attractive to star actors), they promised the kind of powerful dramatic experience most theatre managers could only dream about discovering in an original play. This at any rate was the pitch given by William Waldron in the Preface to Elizabeth Gaskell's *Lizzie Leigh* (1863), in which he boasts that, unlike other adaptations, his will not disappoint: 'The startling and appalling events so vividly detailed in narrative, assume in dramatic form, a terrible picture of reality of so immensely interesting and absorbing a nature that the audience are completely satisfied.'[21] In his account of the Victoria Theatre production of *Oliver Twist* (1837–9), John Hollingshead colourfully evoked the audience's response to Bill Sikes dragging Nancy round the stage by her hair ('one loud and fearful curse, yelled by the whole mass like a Handel Festival chorus'). While the piece might lack grandeur or romance, Hollingshead was in no doubt that the 'fifteen hundred perspiring playgoers' left having got the 'explosion' of passion that they had paid to see.[22] Class is an important element here, of course. Both the Victoria and Surrey theatres were situated in unfashionable Lambeth, south of the Thames, and the Victoria in particular catered to a localised, working-class audience. The adaptor took particular elements of the source text (a plot, a character, a location), and as with other plays, fitted them to meet the sympathies of the local clientele.

Of the Victorian novelists, Dickens remained the biggest draw. In 1871 the *Saturday Review* had no doubt that 'the works of Dickens form the mainstay of English theatres both at the East and the West end of London'.[23] Dickens's novels resonated with the people. Readers wanted to see Oliver, Nancy, Quilp and Joe Gargery in the flesh, and adaptations of Dickens's novels tended to follow hard on the heels of their original publications, sometimes even before they had finished serialisation. Walter Scott-inspired plays also remained popular; 'Scott spells success', noted the *Observer* in 1870.[24] So, too, did productions based on William Harrison Ainsworth's *Jack Sheppard* (1839–40) and Charlotte Brontë's *Jane Eyre* (1847) – much to the latter's alarm. In the 1850s, London also saw at least twenty different *Uncle Tom's Cabin* productions, 'all the managers [being] mad to produce [it]', Edward Fitzball recalled.[25] Harriet Beecher Stowe's other big novel, *Dred*, resulted in at least eighteen adaptations (1856–82), including an equestrian one at Astley's Amphitheatre.[26] By 1865, the *Daily Telegraph* was also able to record that 'latterly the custom [of adaptation] has been carried out to a fuller extent than usual, for the sensational element in the productions of the lady-novelists who are now in the ascendant has possessed great attractions for both actor and audience'.[27] Mary Braddon's theatrical links are well documented and were reinforced by the fifty or more dramas (re)created from her novels, including eight *Lady Audley's Secrets*, nine *Aurora Floyds*, five *Henry Dunbars* and two versions of *Eleanor's Victory*.[28] Plays taken from Anna Maria Hall's *Tales of Woman's Trials* (1835), Ouida's [Marie Louise Ramé's] *Under Two Flags* (1867) and Wood's *East Lynne* also became staples for managements and performers on a world-wide scale, the latter's sentimental and homiletic paeans to wifely loyalty and motherhood and the tragic predicament of its heroine proving the stuff of powerful 'weeping' melodrama. This is only the top of a very long list, one which also includes hundreds of plays culled from anonymous serials.

Satisfying the censor

One reason for the conflicting attitudes towards stage adaptation had to do with the types of novels being adapted. Plays taken from George Eliot's and Anthony Trollope's novels were rare. In contrast, theatres sucked up 'Newgate' novels and sensation fiction like a powerful vacuum cleaner. Critics and moralists shook their heads in horror at the prurient philistinism of the resulting plays. They were fearful, too, about the messages audiences took away from them to the extent that from the late 1830s the connection between stage adaptations and public immorality was the subject of multitudinous articles. However, it was the people giving evidence to the Parliamentary Select Committee on Theatrical Licences and Regulations of 1866 who best extrapolated these concerns. They included Charles Reade, who told the committee that 'things might be described in a book which could not be presented in a play, and which could not be even indicated without doing perhaps very considerable harm'. At the same hearings William Bodham Donne, Deputy Examiner of Plays in the Lord Chamberlain's Office, responsible for censoring plays, agreed that a story acted on stage by living, breathing people affected the senses 'much more strongly' than did the same story nestling between the covers of a book or in a magazine. Adaptation involved a move into a different cultural space and, in some cases, into a different tradition. As an 'expert' witness, Donne went on to explain the existing ban on London stage productions of *Jack Sheppard* and *Oliver Twist*. This had come about because 'the Lord Chamberlain had a great many letters from parents and masters requesting that such pieces should not be exhibited, because they had an ill effect on their sons and apprentices'.[29]

Such evidence was highly troubling, and would be a topic of conversation for years. In April 1868 the debate over the 'mischievous ideas' and 'morbid feeling'[30] which such crime-ridden dramas were deemed to encourage flared up when the Lord Chamberlain's Office refused to license a version of Dickens's novel submitted by John Oxenford. The *Orchestra* shared the institutional reservations, noting how 'Oliver Twist makes a particularly repulsive play'. It continued:

> How often have dramatists to be reminded that what of [sic] ghastly and horrible reads well enough in a book – excites just sufficient terror to fulfil its object – is often shocking on the stage. Put such scenes on the stage as we daily read of in the police reports of our newspapers and an indignant audience would pull the theatre down around our ears. The eye cannot always bear all that the imagination can master; and so it is with Oliver Twist ... We see no more good that can come of such horrors than if the worst cases in our hospital wards were suddenly lowered for public inspection into the street.[31]

Were most people really *that* impressionable, to the extent that they would be sent over the edge by what they saw on stage? Many critics believed so, and what seems neurotic now did not seem so then. Another – liberal – paper, the *Examiner*, fanned the flames of overreaction by casting the Lord Chamberlain's deputy as a kind of asylum keeper, whose proper task it was to straightjacket Oliver Twist and 'place it under restraint'. Having got off to an inauspicious start, there was some satisfaction to be had for Oxenford when his adaptation was finally put on in 1868, with a young Henry Irving making a 'hit' as Bill Sikes, modelling his character's appearance on George Cruikshank's famous illustrations. What had not gone away was the dilemma in reconciling Dickens-the-national-treasure with the originator of this cor-rupting piece. Some critics got round it by locating Oliver Twist as a product of the novelist's younger days, when he did not fully appreciate 'the incredible barbarism' of what he was writing. Others noted that adaptations invariably tore into the moral landscape of the novel from which they came. Reading Oliver Twist as Dickens wrote it involved 'embracing the green fields and pure atmosphere of morality, as well as the close and grimy haunts of vice ... it is from breathing the healthy air of these pleasant spots that the boy of tender years and the youth of passionate impulse are kept safe against the taint of infection while reading the story'.[32] But this all got polluted when people partook of the novel on stage; the novel seemed to lose the safety net of its omniscient narrator's voice. Spectators faced with the murder of Nancy experienced an onslaught on the nerves that was deemed to be hard to with-stand, and in many cases they had nothing to sustain them.

Tensions between dramatists and theatrical regulators also became appar-ent in the bad-tempered furore surrounding Charles Reade's dramatisation in October 1865 of his own novel *It's Never Too Late to Mend* (1856). Reade is a figure who embodies the complex symbiosis between the novel and the theatre; a novelist *and* a playwright, a man for whom orchestrating controversy seemed to be the breath of life. He also had enormous confidence in his abilities as a dramatist, claiming that his 'natural gift was for the drama'.[33] Accordingly, there was a great buzz surrounding this adaptation of the famous novel about penal abuses and Australian gold mining but no one was prepared for the violent intensity of the play's delivery. Act Two took the audience inside the prison, showing them the cells occupied by Tom Robinson and the fifteen-year-old boy Josephs (played by Louisa Moore), imprisoned for stealing potatoes to feed his mother. Josephs is shown strapped to an iron pillar in a punishment jacket, and faints after the gaoler, Hawes, accuses him of wanting to 'break the SYSTEM'.[34] The play script is (deliberately) vague in its stage directions, and back in the Lord Chamberlain's office W. B. Donne seems not to have picked up on any danger signals. In performance, however, Hawes's outbursts were delivered in a loud rasp together with highly physical displays of acting, 'as real as actuality could make it', as a writer for the *Reader* recorded.[35] As the scene progressed the acting became more strident. The play's producer, George Vining, later described how on stage 'the gaoler seemed to throw the boy down with ... a smack similar to a cod's tail slapped on the marble slab of a fishmonger's shop'.[36] This was – and is – strong stuff and (as in the novel), culminated in Josephs hanging himself in his cell, falling out against the door in full view of the audience.

'It's revolting', Frederic Guest Tomlins, theatre critic for the *Morning Advertiser* shouted out from the stalls, leaping to his feet while the rest of the theatre went into uproar, with 'the better part of the audience'[37] cheering the red-faced – some said tipsy – theatre critic, for interrupting the performance. Those in the gallery booed him. Many observers claimed to have been left numb with revulsion and a campaign was started against the play. Critics wrote of the 'ignoble spectacle of humanity degraded',[38] and of the play's being a throwback to a less civilised age when public torture of criminals was deemed entertainment. (The play came hard on the heels of the Royal Commission on Capital Punishment (1864–5) which had pushed the issue of how criminals should be punished to the forefront, as well as recommending that public executions be abolished.) There was also the familiar objection that these 'spiced' scenes not only encouraged the more impressionable theatregoer to sympathise with wrong-doers but helped 'create a hatred of law and its consequences'. And there was a sense – much like that which dogged sensation fiction – that a social line had been crossed or at least had been blurred thanks to the voyeurism which seemed to be the play's *modus operandi*. West-End audiences were being given the same kind of violent stage displays which their East-End counterparts enjoyed, people who would 'grossly gape on' at anything, or so it was believed.[39] Ironically, of course, the public loved the play; it took £8,000 at the box office and advertisements even carried a list of members of the royal family who had been to see it – and would presumably (if asked) vouch for its respectability. Reade himself felt persecuted *and* vindicated; he loathed the critics more than ever but was convinced that he had helped revolutionise theatre with a breakthrough brand of radical, socially committed melodrama.

Although exaggerating the potential impact of such pieces, the voices of the mid-Victorian critics who had tried to police *Oliver Twist* and attacked *It's Never Too Late To Mend* expressed genuine concern. For another example, there was the case of Augustin Daly's historical drama *Leah, the Forsaken* (1863), an adaptation of Salomon Herman von Mosenthal's *Deborah* (1849). The title role of the young Jewess forsaken by the Christian farmer she loves became a popular one, and in February 1863 Kate Bateman's interpretation was deemed to be 'blood curdling'.[40] During one performance at the Princess's Theatre, a female audience member was so affected by Bateman's histrionics that she died a few days later. The *Musical Standard* railed against these 'unwholesome exhibitions of our time' and suggested that this was proof positive of how 'attendance at the theatre . . . during bodily or mental weakness is a sad error, particularly when to cultivate the morbid tastes of the multitude is preferred by managers'.[41] Even allowing for hyperbole, such fears seemed very real.

Staging sensation

While instances of theatregoers needing to be carried out of the auditorium were not events so remote that they could be discounted (there *were* other such cases), they were hardly commonplace. What *is* true is that stage adaptation started to form its own aesthetic as new developments in playwriting, technology and performance fed into it. The tremendous impact of the adaptations of *Oliver Twist*, *Lady Audley's Secret* and *It's Never Too Late to Mend* was based not only on the adaptations' deliberate breach of *politesse* but also their so-called 'sensation scenes' (for 'sensation' read gruesome/ physically dangerous/visually impressive). These were familiar features of melodrama more generally, of course, but what seems to have intrigued theatregoers was the realisation of how excitingly a stage production could translate – and even add to – climactic scenes of a particular novel. An example comes in the Surrey Theatre's November 1852 production of *Uncle Tom's Cabin*. The posters promise 'the most startling and thrilling effect ever witnessed on stage' as Eliza flees across the ice – all this being the handiwork of the theatre's very own 'Scientific Inventor', Mr Childe.[42] Equally un-nerving was Wilkie Collins's *The Red Vial* (written in 1858 and later novelised as *Jezebel's Daughter* (1880)), the final scenes of which take place in the Frankfurt 'dead-house', where bodies are stored before burial in order to test whether life is truly extinct, and where a supposed corpse comes back to life.

The most influential developments in staging were those encouraged by actor-dramatist Dion Boucicault, who playfully claimed that '[s]ensation is what the public wants and you can't give them too much of it'.[43] His drama *The Colleen Bawn* (1860) is often cited as kick-starting a new kind of theatrical experience, although it was not the first. Like much of Boucicault's output, it was taken from a pre-existing source, Gerald Griffin's novel *The Collegians* (1829) – itself based on a real-life murder case of 1819 – in which the bound body of Ellen Hanley, a sixteen-year-old peasant girl, had been found on the banks of the River Shannon. In the resulting play, the famous 'sensation' scene is a clever fusion of speech and movement involving Myles na Coppaleen, who is observed in his cave by the lake. He sees Danny Mann, an evil boatman, push Eily O'Connor into the lake because she will not yield up her marriage certificate; Myles shoots Danny and dives into the lake (an effect created by twenty small boys shaking lengths of blue gauze) to rescue her. Such scenes became a Boucicault trademark. In *The Long Strike* (1866), taken from Gaskell's *Mary Barton* (1848), the heroine, now called Jane Learoyd, and a lawyer named Moneypenny visit a telegraph office. Boucicault's script specifies '*real apparatus*', '*gaslights*' and '*telegraph operatives working as curtain rises*'[44] and the resulting scene was one of the play's selling points, 'a marvel of fidelity to fact'.[45] As the *Examiner* observed, audiences were invariably bowled over by this scene: 'the public hears the clapping of mimic telegrams and claps with delight in answer to their clapping'.[46] In the telegraph office a message is sent, and the witness – comic Irishman, Johnny Reilly (played by Boucicault) – makes a spectacular 'header'[47] through the ship's porthole and swims to a pilot boat.

Other box-office attractions – and these could be duplicated at length – include Boucicault's *After Dark* (1868; hero bound to a rail track as a London underground train approaches); Watts Phillips's *Lost in London* (1867; an apparently faithful recreation of a coal mine); Andrew Halliday's *The Great City* (1867; Charing Cross Station and a hansom cab). Impressive, too, were Collins's and Dickens's *No Thoroughfare* (1867; villain throws himself over a precipice); T. W. Robertson's *For Love* (1867; recreation of the wreck of the troopship *Birkenhead* at the Cape of Good Hope fifteen years earlier); Andrew Halliday's *Little Em'ly*, aka *David Copperfield* (1869; the wrecking of Steerforth's yacht); and *Amy Robsart*, based on Scott's *Kenilworth* (1870). The latter was a spectacular production replete with pageants and ballets chosen to relaunch London's most prestigious 'legitimate' theatre, Drury Lane, after a refurbishment, on 24 September 1870. Residency in this

'National Temple of the Drama', as *Lloyd's Weekly Messenger* described the theatre, was irrefutable proof, if any were needed, that adaptation had finally 'arrived'.[48] As critics were quick to point out, while the play was 'not Sir Walter Scott' it was certainly 'very clever'.[49] Halliday was commended for not having vulgarised Scott, though his decision to change the novel's original ending provoked comment. In the play's final scene it is Richard Varney who, having lured the heroine on to a collapsing drawbridge in front of Mervyn's Tower as part of his plan to murder her, plummets to his death, while Amy is left hanging over the precipice as the curtain drops (a stuntman stood in for the actor playing Varney). By most accounts this scene received the greatest applause of the night. But Halliday was also accused of having 'violate[d] the tragic issue of the novel' in the interests of conventional melodramatic justice.[50] It would have been better, claimed the *Morning Post*, if Halliday had had the courage of his convictions and let Amy die – an experiment which would have had the effect of 'producing a *real* sensation'.[51] The *Saturday Review* likewise felt cheated:

> Some of us resemble the old lady who liked to enjoy her murders when she read the newspaper, and if we go to see a sensational drama we expect as much sensation as can be got out of the story which is dramatized ... We pay our money in the expectation of seeing Amy Robsart murdered, and we feel that we are taken in when she has the audacity to continue to exist at the fall of the curtain.[52]

In some respects, the furore provoked by these scenes was rather similar to the the publicity which in 2010 surrounded Danny Boyle's film *127 Hours*. This is the film with a notorious scene in which a climber trapped in a crevasse is forced to amputate his forearm – a depiction which has caused more than one person to watch through their fingers. Victorian stage adaptations often relied on this kind of 'punch' scene (to use a term employed by film-makers of the early 1900s). W. S. Gilbert noted: 'Every play which contains a house on fire, a sinking steamer, a railway accident, and a dance in a casino, will (if it is liberally placed upon the stage) succeed in spite of itself. In point of fact, nothing could wreck such a piece but carefully written dialogue and strict attention to probability'.[53] Later examples include *The Ruling Passion* (1882; the heroine and an escaped lunatic begin a balloon ascent from the Crystal Palace), and Charles Reade's *Drink* (1879), an adaptation of an adaptation of Emile Zola's *L'Assommoir* (1877) replete with a gruesome death scene showing the effects of delirium tremens. Reade's play seemed to bear out an earlier prediction made by the *Pall Mall Gazette* that it would not be long before 'dissecting rooms and hospitals' would be put on stage: 'Operations will be performed with faithful attention to realism; the shrieks of the patients; and the white faces of the attendants will all be presented, and should the audience protest against these assaults on their patience the answer will be, "It is true, such scenes are daily acted."[54] By the 1870s some stage technicians like Frederick Lloyd had started to become theatrical celebrities in their own right, and some, like John Johnson, who designed the sets for the 1868 *Oliver Twist*, even started to take their own curtain calls when a set or special effect elicited an audience's approval – which was frequently.[55] In an 1864 letter to John Forster, Dickens reported how *The Streets of London*, an otherwise underwhelming play with a prosaic script, was, thanks to its fire scene, 'drawing all the town'. Dickens thought it 'depressing' and 'degrading' that 'not only do the audiences – of all classes – go, but they are unquestionably delighted'.[56] Such comments suggest not only the need for successive productions to outdo previous ones, but an increase in the tension between the spoken text and the visual one. An actor's ability to move an audience via dialogue seemed to be getting less important than his ability to do acrobatics, while being able to fall over, or scream piercingly on cue – as Julia Neilson did repeatedly in *Amy Robsart* – was the first requirement for an actress. One wag reckoned that technological advances would soon enable Neilson and her ilk to be replaced by specially designed steam whistles. As for those adapting novels, it was claimed that they were more interested in finding employment for the stage carpenter and scene painter than bringing out a text's 'inner life'.[57]

Not everyone disapproved, however. The ability to be shaken or stirred by such scenes was for Clement Scott not a bad thing, but testament to man's essential humanity. In *Thirty Years at the Play* (1890), Scott quotes approvingly John Ruskin's remarks from 'Of Kings' Treasuries' (1865), to the effect that 'sensation *is* good for us':

> If we were sponges, perhaps sensation might not be easily got for us; if we were earth worms, liable at every instant to be cut in two by the spade, perhaps too much sensation might not be good for us. But being human creatures *it is* good for us; nay, we are only human in so far as we are sensitive . . .
>
> You will find it a fruitful subject of thought; but briefly, the *essence* of all vulgarity lies in want of sensation . . . a deathful callousness which, in extremity, becomes capable of every sort of bestial habit and crime, without fear, without pleasure, without horror and without pity. It is in the blunt hand and the dead heart, in the diseased habit, in the hardened conscience that men become vulgar . . .[58]

Whether watching from the stalls as an adult or remembering the plays he had seen as a boy from the gallery in the 1860s, it *was* possible for Scott to imagine that theatre was offering a deeper physical–emotional experience than detractors claimed. He could not quite explain what it was but clues can be found in Jeffrey Cox's recent analysis of the dynamics of Victorian melodrama. Cox argues that the sensational devices did not just involve 'some set of cheap, stagey tricks' but were part of an artistic plan to ensure that audiences 'felt the action on stage in a visceral way'. According to Cox, great sensational moments are flash-points 'where the audience's attention, often wandering, is firmly arrested and fixed on the action ... passions may be aroused ... affective responses engaged'. What happens is that audiences leave 'having had a "real" experience, having really "felt" something while ... in the theatre, but the experience is closer to that of an amusement park ride ... than to that of traditional drama'.[59] It is certainly the case that commentaries, diaries and reminiscences of the period suggest that these kinds of reactions were common. Both Queen Victoria and Matthew Arnold were profoundly moved after their (separate) visits to Charles Kean's production of the 'creepy'[60] *Corsican Brothers* from the 1844 novel by Alexandre Dumas, *Père*. Arnold confessed to being a hundred times more shaken up by this play than *King Lear*.[61] In 1890, Clement Scott could still recall John Palgrave Simpson's version of *The Master of Ravenswood* (1865) and the 'shiver' induced by 'the weird effect of the last scene, and the rising tide that swallowed up Edgar'.[62] However, none of this tops the most famous account of a different – more agonised(?) – physical reaction to the whole adaptation business. This is the one given by John Forster of Dickens lying on the floor of his box at the Surrey Theatre unable to watch what had been done to *Oliver Twist*.[63]

However difficult it is to recapture the excitement of Victorian theatre, it is apparent that stage adaptations raise important questions about the angles from which Victorian audiences viewed and re-viewed characters like Josephs, or Oliver Twist, or Amy Robsart. Across the cultural landscape of the 1860s and 1870s, a pattern started to repeat itself: stripped-down versions of popular novels, refitted with considerable technical ingenuity. Yet while the processes involved deserve further investigation, the business of adaptation raises additional questions. There is the disappearance from nineteenth-century literary history of a particular body of work which says much about the ways in which different social classes were fed the works of different authors. The early-Victorian period saw adaptations of popular novels produced at what seemed like industrial speed. It was a fashion whereby adaptors pilfered novels to suit 'star' performers but also produced subversive adaptations for different kinds of audiences, which repositioned characters and re-emphasised certain plot lines. Critics of sensation novels, and of Victorian popular culture more generally, have paid only limited attention to the working-class appeal of characters such as Lady Audley, Isabel Vane and Lizzie Leigh – but it is a topic which deserves to be an important part of discussions of the ways in which fiction was disseminated. And, for all its ambivalent press, the process was undoubtedly a powerful one. Stage adaptations did not damage novels but transformed them, affecting the audience's interpretations of them – an experience which even we can appreciate. After all, who, nowadays, does not think of *Oliver Twist* without also calling to mind *Oliver!*?

NOTES

1. T. A. Palmer, *East Lynne: A Domestic Drama in a Prologue and Four Acts* (London: Samuel French, nd.), 38.
2. Kerry Powell, *Women and Victorian Theatre* (Cambridge University Press, 1997), 101.
3. Unsigned review, '"Lady Audley" on the Stage', *London Review* (7 March 1863), 244–5.
4. Unsigned, 'Playwrights of the Period', *Theatrical Journal* 32 (1871), 297–8 (297).
5. Allardyce Nicoll, *A History of English Drama 1600–1900*. Volume IV: *Early Nineteenth Century Drama 1800–1850* (Cambridge University Press, 1955), 92.
6. Philip Cox, *Reading Adaptations: Novels and Verse Narratives on the Stage, 1790–1840* (Manchester University Press, 2000), 167.
7. Unsigned review, 'The Stage', *Academy* (5 September 1874), 278–9 (278).
8. Wilkie Collins, 'Dramatic Grub Street', *Household Words* 17 (1858), 265–70 (269).
9. Henry Morley, *Diary of a London Playgoer* (Leicester University Press, 1974), 243, 313.
10. See John Ellis, 'The Literary Adaptation: An Introduction', *Screen* 23:1 (1982), 3.
11. Unsigned, 'Andrew Halliday', *Illustrated Review* 1 (1877), 81–3 (82).
12. Charles Dickens to Ellen Wood, 19 January 1866, in *The Letters of Charles Dickens 1865–1867*, ed. Graham Storey (Oxford: Clarendon, 1999), 143.
13. Wilkie Collins to William Moy Thomas, 6 February 1888, in BGLL, vol. IV, 297.
14. 'Willis Redshanks', 'British Drama', *Theatrical Journal* (12 August 1857), 251–2 (252).
15. Unsigned article, 'The Natural Right of Adaptation', *Orchestra* 468 (1872), 379–80 (379).
16. Wilkie Collins to John Hollingshead, 1 July 1869, BGLL, vol. II, 136.
17. Edward Fitzball, *Thirty-Five Years of a Dramatic Author's Life*, 2 vols. (London: T. C. Newby, 1859), vol. II, 261.
18. Frederick Wedmore, 'Royalty Theatre – "Ought We to Visit Her"', *Academy* (24 January 1874), 103.
19. Unsigned review, 'Surrey Theatre', *The Times* (8 November 1860), 6.
20. Unsigned review, 'Dramatised Versions of Novels: *East Lynne* at the Surrey', *Sunday Times* (11 February 1866), 8.
21. William Waldron, 'Preface', *Lizzie Leigh; or the Murder near the Old Mill* (London: Thomas Hailes Lacy, 1863), 2.
22. John Hollingshead, *My Lifetime*, 2 vols. (London: Sampson, Low, Marston, 1895), vol. I, 188–90.

23. Unsigned review, 'Great Expectations', *Saturday Review* (17 June 1871), 770–1 (770).
24. Unsigned review, 'Drury Lane Theatre', *Observer* 9 (1870), 6.
25. Fitzball, *Thirty-Five Years of a Dramatic Author's Life*, vol. II, 234.
26. Judie Newman, 'The Afterlife of *Dred* on the British Stage', in *Transatlantic Stowe*, ed. Denise Kohn, Sarah Meer and Emily Todd (University of Iowa Press, 2006), 208–24 (209–10).
27. Unsigned review, 'Surrey Theatre', *Daily Telegraph* (7 February 1865), 8.
28. Jenifer Carnell, 'Introduction', William Suter, *Lady Audley's Secret* (Hastings: Sensation Press, 2008), 7–12.
29. Quoted in James F. Stottlar, 'A Victorian Stage Censor: The Theory and Practice of William Bodham Donne', *Victorian Studies* 13:3 (1970), 253–83 (257; 258).
30. Viscount Sydney, Lord Chamberlain to William Donne, 20 August 1862. Quoted in Dominic Shellard and Steve Nicholson with Miriam Handley, *The Lord Chamberlain Regrets. A History of British Theatre Censorship* (London: British Library, 2004), 42.
31. Unsigned review, 'The Theatres', *Orchestra* 10 (1868), 52–3.
32. See 'The Drama: The Queen's Theatre', *Examiner* (18 April 1868), 249.
33. Quoted in Malcolm Elwin, *Charles Reade* (London: Jonathan Cape, 1931), 111.
34. Charles Reade, *It's Never Too Late to Mend* (1865), British Library Add. Mss. 53044, 35.
35. Unsigned review, 'The Theatres', *Reader* 6 (1865), 438.
36. Wayne Burns, *Charles Reade* (New York: Bookman Associates, 1961), 235.
37. Unsigned review, 'The Theatres', *Saturday Review* 20 (1865), 785.
38. 'L.', ''Tis Never Too Late to Mend', *Pall Mall Gazette* (6 October 1865), 5.
39. Unsigned review, 'The Theatres', *Reader* 6 (1865), 438.
40. Edward L. Blanchard, *The Life and Reminiscences of E. L. Blanchard*, ed. Clement Scott and Cecil Howard, 22 vols. (London: Hutchinson, 1891), vol. I, 283.
41. Unsigned, 'Table Talk', *Musical Standard* 2:38 (1864), 224.
42. British Library Playbills, Surrey Theatre 'November' 1852, 311–13.
43. Quoted in Richard Fawkes, *Dion Boucicault* (London: Quartet, 1979), 118.
44. Dion Boucicault, *The Long Strike* (New York: Samuel French, 1870), 31.
45. Unsigned review, 'The Long Strike', *Examiner and London Review* (4 December 1869), 776.
46. Unsigned review, 'The Theatrical Examiner: Lyceum', *Examiner* (6 October 1866), 632.
47. Unsigned review, 'Fine Arts: The London Theatres', *London Review* (22 September 1866), 325.
48. Unsigned review, 'Opening of Drury Lane Last Night', *Lloyd's Weekly Messenger* (25 September 1870), 1.
49. Unsigned review, 'Drury Lane Theatre', *Observer* 9 (1870), 6.
50. Unsigned review, 'The Theatres', *Orchestra* 366 (1870), 4.
51. Unsigned review, 'Amy Robsart', *Morning Post* (25 September 1870), 6.
52. Unsigned review, 'Sensation Dramas Old and New', *Saturday Review* 30 (1870), 427–8 (427).
53. Quoted in J. O. Bailey, 'Introduction', *British Plays of the Nineteenth Century* (New York: Odyssey, 1966), 6.
54. 'L.', ''Tis Never Too Late to Mend', 5.

55. See unsigned, 'Public Amusements', *Lloyd's Weekly Messenger* (14 April 1868), 6.
56. Charles Dickens to John Forster, quoted in Fawkes, *Dion Boucicault*, 149–50.
57. Unsigned, 'Andrew Halliday', *The Theatre* (17 April 1877), 140–1 (141).
58. Clement Scott, *Thirty Years at the Play* (London: The Railway & General Automatic Library, 1890), 60–2.
59. Jeffrey Cox, 'The Death of Tragedy; or, the Birth of Melodrama', in *The Performing Century*, ed. Tracy C. Davis and Peter Holland (London: Palgrave, 2007), 161–81 (169, 170–1).
60. Queen Victoria, *Journal* (30 April 1852), cited in Richard Schoch, *Shakespeare's Victorian Stage* (Cambridge University Press, 1998), 134.
61. Quoted in Jane Stedman, *W. S. Gilbert's Theatrical Criticism* (London: Society for Theatre Research, 2000), 4.
62. Scott, *Thirty Years at the Play*, 71.
63. John Forster, *The Life of Dickens, Volume One 1812–1842* (London: Chapman and Hall, 1872), 152. Quoted in Cox, *Reading Adaptations*, 121.

6

RICHARD NEMESVARI

Queering the sensation novel

For Victorian readers and critics, three novels were uniformly granted the honour (or assigned the blame) of establishing sensation fiction as a culturally significant literary form: Wilkie Collins's *The Woman in White* (1859–60), Ellen Wood's *East Lynne* (1861) and Mary Elizabeth Braddon's *Lady Audley's Secret* (1862). Although at first glance the structural differences that characterise these works might seem to separate more than join them, they do share thematic and plot elements that justify their being grouped together. Most obviously, each is centred on a mystery that drives the story, and whose solution is meant to resolve all other aspects of the narrative. Thus Kathleen Tillotson, in an early formative statement, asserts 'the purest type of sensation novel is the novel-with-a-secret'.[1] Yet Jonathan Loesberg, in another important essay, points to an equally significant aspect of how these texts function when he notes '[q]uestions of identity not only are central to the plots of the three genre-establishing novels of Collins, Braddon, and Wood but also play a role in the other works of the genre'. Thus the nefarious theft of Laura Fairlie's identity in *The Woman in White*, the transformation-through-railway-accident of Lady Isabel Vane into the French governess Madame Vine in *East Lynne* and the protean ability of Lucy Graham to pass through various self-willed identity transmutations to become Lucy, Lady Audley in *Lady Audley's Secret*, all demonstrate the centrality of this trope. Loesberg's argument, however, is more specific in its insistence that 'the difference between this use of the question of identity in sensation fiction and that of other works of fiction is that the sensation novel sees the problem in its legal and class aspects rather than in its psychological aspect'.[2] This is certainly defensible, and the fact that the main-character transformations listed above all involve some type of rise or fall in class status fully supports Loesberg's position.

There is, nonetheless, another Victorian cultural concern that has the potential to unite the dominant sensationalist elements of secrecy and identity even more tightly. Each of these foundational novels explores as a significant subtext the issue of *sexual* identity by providing characters whose deviation from an acceptably gendered heteronormativity introduces the sensational possibility of queer alterities, but without ever explicitly acknowledging what is being suggested. In other words, Collins, Wood and Braddon bring into play the mysterious fluidity of sexuality while at the same time ensuring that the potentialities on display dare not speak their name. By focusing on acts of transgression both overt and covert such texts were ideally positioned to explore the problematics of gender performance even as their plots attempted, through their restoration of the status quo, to reassure their audience that cultural norms were secure.

The distinctive ambivalence that results has crucial implications for the ideological representation of queerness in sensationalism, since if gender multiplicity is invoked only to be reprobated then the form is not so much queer as anti-queer. There can be little doubt that insistently gender-problematised figures such as Count Fosco in *The Woman in White*, or Cornelia Carlyle in *East Lynne*, are presented as negative, but they are also two of the most striking characters in their texts and provide a great deal of necessary narrative energy. The reader thus finds herself/himself engaged with them in a way that, if it does not necessarily overcome the primary text's judgemental criticism, nonetheless prevents a total rejection, and thus opens the way to a reflexive identification and possible understanding. Indeed, what is so striking about many of these characters is the sheer satisfaction they seem to take in the supposedly unacceptable identities created for them by authors who, at least nominally, censure their various orientations. The disjunction between professed narrative/textual disapproval, and the pleasure queer characters take in their constructed perversity, makes the machinations of plot required to suppress and punish them appear excessive and unconvincing, resulting not in the undercutting of the non-normative, but in a questioning of the normative instead.

The textual tensions that result, and their resolutions, can hardly avoid having political implications. Sensation fiction, by exposing the fabrication of core identity at its most fundamental level, leads to a questioning of other core assumptions that ramify out from the individual, including the problematic constructions of Victorian domesticity, desire, criminality, Englishness, madness and, finally, class. Queer characters both cause trouble *in* their narratives, by introducing conflict into the plot, and are troubling *to* their narratives, because they embody disruptive possibilities that are only barely containable. For the three authors under discussion this disturbance finds its most explicit expression through Collins's creation of Marian Halcombe and Count Fosco, through Wood's creation of Cornelia Carlyle and through Braddon's creation of Phœbe Marks as well as, most centrally, Lady Audley herself. Whether these figures are eventually reintegrated into normative culture, or are expelled or even killed in order to neutralise their nonconformity, is less significant than that they have dramatically impinged on the text and the reader's consciousness, and thus forced that reader into a confrontation with social complacencies that turn out to be radically unstable.

The initial encounter of Walter Hartright, the hero of *The Woman in White*, with Marian Halcombe demonstrates the disconcerting power queerness has to disrupt categorical thinking. Walter, perceiving her first silhouetted in a window, is 'struck by the rare beauty of her form, and by the unaffected grace of her attitude', so that when Marian turns and walks towards him 'the easy elegance of every movement of her limbs and body ... set [him] in a flutter of expectation to see her face clearly'.[3] The subsequent discovery that 'the lady's complexion was almost swarthy, and the dark down on her upper lip almost a moustache', that '[s]he had a large, firm, masculine mouth and jaw' and that 'her expression – bright, frank, and intelligent – appeared ... to be altogether wanting in those feminine attractions of gentleness and pliability, without which the beauty of the handsomest woman alive is beauty incomplete' (74) is extremely disturbing. Walter's response is 'to be almost repelled by the masculine form and masculine look of the features in which the perfectly shaped figure ended ... to feel a sensation oddly akin to the helpless discomfort familiar to us all in sleep, when we recognise yet cannot reconcile the anomalies and contradictions of a dream' (74–5).

This uncanny 'sensation', communicated to the reader as so many of Walter's sensations are throughout the plot, aligns the audience's perceptions with his, yet not in the way that might at first seem indicated. His declaration that 'never was the old conventional maxim, that Nature cannot err, more flatly contradicted' (74) is an attempt to constitute Marian as an unnatural error by invoking an aphorism that she apparently nullifies. But as he increasingly learns to appreciate and admire her, it is his 'conventional' reaction that is exposed as inadequate. It thus becomes clear that in fact Nature is *not* errant, but that rote and constrictive assumptions about gender identity certainly are, revealing the limitations of Walter and the culture that has shaped him.

It is significant, therefore, that Marian's gender inversion finds its most explicit expression in her attempts to protect her half-sister, Laura Fairlie. Since the only available way for Walter to deal with his growing and inappropriate love for Laura is to abandon his position as drawing master at Limmeridge House, Marian is left alone to defend Laura from her increasingly sinister fiancé and eventual husband, Sir Percival Glyde, and his seemingly affable but considerably more dangerous friend, Count Fosco. Indeed, it is Marian who directs Walter to curtail his wayward attachment, urging him to ' "Crush it! . . . Don't shrink under it like a woman. Tear it out; trample it under foot like a man!" ' (110). This appeal to gendered behaviour, however, is ironic, in that Marian is later called upon to enact it as well. The closer that Laura's marriage approaches, the more distraught she becomes, eventually declaring '[b]efore another month is over our heads, she will be *his* Laura instead of mine! *His* Laura! I am as little able to realise the idea which those two words convey – my mind feels almost as dulled and stunned by it, as if writing of her marriage were like writing of her death' (211, emphasis in original). The implications of Marian's attachment to Laura find an even more explicit expression in a passage that shortly follows, in which she twice describes herself as a possible 'rival' to Sir Percival before warning Laura that his 'jealousy' is already putting the continuing closeness of their relationship in danger (212).

The erotic response underlying Marian's possessiveness towards Laura is apparent as she reacts to the thought of the sexual initiation the wedding entails. An implied lesbian attachment between the half-sisters, at least on Marian's part, shows the text invoking putatively improper desire as a way of generating a sensational subtext while at the same time signalling her 'unwillingness to lend her full cooperation to male appropriations'.[4] Further, since Marian's unease concerning the wedding proves justified, her 'unnatural' feelings are pragmatically validated even if their foundations are culturally suspect; in this case her otherness generates a forceful premonition of the disempowerment of women through matrimony.

Thus Marian's energetic defence of Laura after her marriage to Glyde takes the form of a series of 'masculine' assertions of agency. Her direct refusal to act as a witness when he attempts to coerce Laura into blindly signing away her inheritance leads him to insult her, at which point she declares 'if I had been a man, I would have knocked him down on the threshold of his own door' (268), an unladylike declaration that the reader fully endorses. Subsequently she creeps from her bedroom on to the roof of the veranda in order to eavesdrop on Glyde and Fosco's plotting, effects Laura's escape from the asylum in which that plotting had imprisoned her, reunites Walter with Laura and while he struggles to restore Laura's stolen identity, contributes to this small group of outcasts by providing 'for [their] household wants by the toil of her own hands' (422). Some critics view this last element as the beginning of a textual process reintegrating Marian into the domestic sphere, marginalising and potentially erasing the challenge her gender subversion has posed. Such a reading is, however, an overstatement. Although Walter's return into the plot certainly re-establishes his voice, perspective and character as dominant, Marian's character remains unchanged. Collins obviously wishes to make Walter a more conventional hero as the story proceeds, and he does this by pushing all other characters into the background. He also, however, gives Marian the last word in the novel. Her concluding, triumphant identification of Walter and Laura's baby boy as '*the Heir of Limmeridge*' (617, emphasis in original) seals their victory over its villains, while Walter's own concluding lines insist that 'Marian was the good angel of our lives – let Marian end our Story' (617). Far from simply reducing Marian to the caricatured Angel in the House, this expands the dominant Victorian discourse by explicitly endorsing an improper mode of female expression and suggesting its acceptability. She remains 'this sublime creature ... this magnificent Marian' (351), to the end, although the character who thus apostrophises her, Count Fosco, and who shares her queerness, will meet a very different fate.

It is unsurprising that Fosco expresses a deep admiration for Marian, since he is presented as possessing the same kind of gender inversion as hers. The reader is informed that 'his movements are astonishingly light and easy. He is as noiseless in a room as any of us women; and, more than that ... he is as nervously sensitive as the weakest of us' (242). Also, he 'has all the fondness of an old maid for his cockatoo' and 'devours pastry' as Marian has 'never yet seen it devoured by any human beings but girls at boarding-schools' (243, 246).

One thing that Marian finds particularly amazing is Fosco's relationship with his wife, Laura's aunt the former Eleanor Fairlie, who before her marriage 'was always talking pretentious nonsense, and always worrying the unfortunate men with every small exaction which a vain and foolish woman can impose' (239). As Madame Fosco, however, 'she sits for hours together without saying a word' and has been transformed 'into a civil, silent unobtrusive woman, who is never in the way' (239), proof that 'the foreign husband ... has tamed this once wayward English woman till her own relations hardly know her again' (240). The ominous use of the word 'tamed' here, however, finds further emphasis in Marian's later, fraught observation that in this matrimonial relationship 'the rod of iron with which he rules her never appears in company – it is a private rod, and is always kept upstairs' (244), so that Fosco's coercively phallic assertiveness is announced about as overtly as is possible in a novel of the period. This being the case, his patriarchal influence is not restricted to women, as Marian notes:

> He can manage me, as he manages his wife and Laura ... as he manages Sir Percival himself, every hour in the day ... He puts the rudest remarks Sir Percival can make on his effeminate tastes and amusements, quietly away from him ... smiling at [Sir Percival] with the calmest superiority; patting him on the shoulder; and bearing with him benignantly, as a good-humoured father bears with a wayward son. (245)

The Count's effortless blending of effeminate tastes with masculine dominance demonstrates a queer self-assertiveness that, in its absolute confidence, simply refuses to accept any need to be other than he is.

Further, the enjoyment Fosco so obviously experiences through his self-performance draws the reader in, creating an energetic attractiveness in the novel's main villain that seriously complicates its ostensible values. After Marian becomes ill by being soaked and chilled through her adventure on the veranda, providing Fosco the opportunity to purloin and read her diary, he adds his comments to that text and declares

> [t]he presentation of my own character is masterly in the extreme. I certify, with my whole heart, to the fidelity of the portrait. I feel how vivid an impression I must have produced to have been painted in such strong, such rich, such massive colours as these ... Under happier circumstances how worthy I should have been of Miss Halcombe – how worthy Miss Halcombe would have been of ME. (351–2)

There is no room here for what Michael D. Snediker designates the 'queer-pessimistic constellation', the '[m]elancholy, self-shattering, shame'[5] that supposedly must mark non-normative alterities. Even Walter is not immune to the power of Focso's personality. Having blackmailed the Count into providing a written confession of the plot against Laura, and watching his enemy prepare to create his own *tour de force* narrative, the upright Englishman cannot help but make the following observation:

> The enormous audacity with which he seized on the situation in which I had placed him, and made it the pedestal on which his vanity mounted for the one cherished purpose of self-display, mastered my astonishment by main force. Sincerely as I loathed the man, the prodigious strength of his character, even in its most trivial aspects, impressed me in spite of myself. (586)

Indeed, despite Walter's successful efforts to restore Laura's identity and drive Fosco out of England, it is possible to argue, as does George Levine, that 'the brilliant Fosco ... in fact virtually wins'.[6] He is allowed to keep the ten thousand pounds that has been his goal all along and, by forcing Walter to become a blackmailer in order to re-establish Laura's proper status, confirms what he has suggested throughout the story – that the English are no more virtuous than foreigners such as himself; they are just better at self-justification.

The introduction into the novel of an Italian secret society that eventually avenges Fosco's betrayal of it by murdering him adds yet another extra-judicial level to a narrative that seems increasingly uncertain about the efficacy of established social systems to defend its values, so that while the

Count is made to pay for his crime, it is 'through a contrivance of plot that has nothing to do with the crime itself'.[7] It is as if Fosco's 'extraordinary mixture of prompt decision, far-sighted cunning, and mountebank bravado' (584) is too much for even the author who created him, so that Collins is himself forced into desperate narrative remedies to ensure his required punishment.

In a novel such as *The Woman in White*, which raises the sensational possibility that all levels of identity are inherently fragile, and then attempts to assuage the anxiety thus produced by restoring status quo normalcy through its closure, characters such as Marian Halcombe and Count Fosco are both thematically appropriate and yet threateningly excessive. Marian may not be fully satisfied with the circumscribed agency available to her womanly masculinity, but she never apologises for what she is, while Fosco is absolutely satisfied with the manly effeminacy that allows him to manipulate everyone around him. As main characters in the story their queerness cannot help but render its happy ending problematic, because they emphasise the tenuous assumptions about gender identity upon which that ending relies. In contrast, the role played by Cornelia Carlyle in *East Lynne* appears much less prominent, but the disruption she embodies, and causes, is equally revelatory.

If Collins's novel could be described as an anatomy of identity, then Ellen Wood's might be designated an anatomy of domesticity. The book presents a series of failed households, while the collapse of the most central one, the one created by Archibald Carlyle's marriage to Lady Isabel Vane, generates the main melodramatic action. And a major contributor to that collapse is Archibald's half-sister, Cornelia. More interesting, however, is that although her role is clearly presented as negative, she does not bear the brunt of the blame for the disaster that occurs. Instead, as a secondary character whose queer sensibility is expressed through a rejection of the conventional female domestic influence found in a husband/wife dyad, and through a masculine focus on economic power, she foregrounds the ways in which standard patriarchal gender roles are so imperceptive, and thus so vulnerable, that they cannot cope with her aggressive self-assertion. The result is an affective identification with Isabel as the fallen woman, a response reinforced by the sympathy created through her later, sensationalised suffering. Cornelia Carlyle thus illustrates Alex Woloch's observation that '[m]inor characters exist *as* a category, then, only because of their strange centrality to so many texts, perhaps to narrative signification itself',[8] in that her striking alterity to the marriage plots surrounding her calls attention to the narrative signification of the novel's cultural critique.

That Cornelia is Archibald's half-sister creates an echo of Marian and Laura's relationship in *The Woman in White*, and there is a hint of transgressive desire in Wood's text as well. The reader is told that 'Cornelia ... was grown up when her father married again', that when the second Mrs Carlyle dies in giving birth to Archibald, 'his half-sister reared him, loved him, and ruled him', and that she had 'never relaxed her rule; with an iron hand she liked to rule him now, in great things as in small, just as she had ruled in the days of his babyhood'.[9] This suggestion of unwomanly dominance through surrogate maternity is problematic, but the narrator then takes this questionable attachment one step further:

> Miss Carlyle, or, as she was called in the town, Miss Corny, had never married; it was certain she never would; people thought that her intense love of her younger brother kept her single, for it was not likely that the daughter of Mr Carlyle had wanted for offers. Other maidens confess to soft and tender impressions; to hope of being some time or other, solicited to abandon their father's name, and become somebody's better half. Not so Miss Carlyle: all who approached her with the love-lorn tale, she sent quickly to the right-about. (79)

Although 'Miss Corny' does not bear Marian's manly appearance, her intense attachment to her brother allows for a similar masculine identification, both through a repudiation of 'soft and tender impressions', and through her choice to remain his half-sibling rather than become the 'better half' of a man under whose authority she would have to bend.

Predictably, then, when Archibald announces his sudden and unexpected marriage to Isabel the result is a paroxysm of anger, along with another echo of *The Woman in White*:

> 'As sure as we are living here, I would have tried for a commission of lunacy against him, had I known this ... Better have him confined as a harmless lunatic for a couple of years, than suffer him to go free and obtain his fling in this mad manner. I never thought he would marry: I have warned him against it ever since he was in leading-strings.' (181)

The excessiveness of Cornelia's reaction, with its sensational evocation of internment in a private asylum, cannot fully be explained even by Archibald's slipping of the 'leading-strings' that Cornelia had so clearly intended to keep attached for ever. The queer household that she had meant to establish is exposed fully when she passes on word of the marriage to Barbara Hare, a character who had herself entertained hopes of receiving a proposal from Archibald. Cornelia's pleasure in the younger woman's barely contained anguish leads to a startling moment of insight when Barbara asks, '"Are you sure you are not jealous?"', to which the older woman replies, '"Perhaps I am ... Perhaps, had you brought up a lad as I have brought up Archibald, and loved nothing else in all the world, far or near, you would be jealous, when you found him discarding you with contemptuous indifference, and taking a young wife to his bosom, to be more to him than you had been"' (182). The jealously incestuous desire hinted at here, like the jealously lesbian desire hinted at in Collins's text, suggests the kind of perversity sensation fiction often evokes. Far from admitting defeat at having apparently lost the coveted role of mother/wife to her half-brother, however, Cornelia instead sets out with evident relish to sabotage the marriage she cannot abide, and she is able to do so because her own ambiguous gender assignment allows her to exploit broader gender constructs for her advantage.

Earlier in the novel the reader has been told that the other 'ruling passion' of Miss Corny's life, aside from the passion for her brother, was 'love of saving money' (78). Cornelia's cunning strategy, therefore, is to insist on moving into East Lynne with her half-brother and his new wife, in order supposedly to help Isabel learn the economics of running a middle-class household, a task which, as the daughter of an earl, she has had no experience of. Archibald, being used to giving his half-sister her way, raises no objection to this, and the result is that Cornelia completely usurps Isabel's place:

> Isabel would have been altogether happy but for Miss Carlyle: that lady ... inflicted her presence upon East Lynne, and was the bane of the household. She deferred outwardly to Lady Isabel as mistress; but the real mistress was herself, Isabel little more than an automaton. Her impulses were checked, her wishes frustrated, her actions tacitly condemned by the imperiously willed Miss Carlyle ... Mr Carlyle suspected it not. At home only morning and evening, and then more absorbed with the cares of his business, which increased upon him, he saw not that anything was wrong. (216)

In other words, Cornelia has managed to abrogate to herself the roles of both the husband *and* wife of the house, a gender fusion which well suits her character, as she controls the specifics of household management along with the money that finances it, even after Isabel has fulfilled her most important normative role and provided that household with children. The most disastrous expression of this queer situation then arises with Isabel's proposed recuperative trip to Boulogne after her last pregnancy. When she asks why her children cannot accompany her, her sister-in-law is adamant: '"Why should they not?" retorted Miss Corny. "Why, on account of the expense, to be sure. I can tell you what it is, Lady Isabel, what with one expense and another, your husband will soon be on the road to ruin"' (249). That this claim is utterly false is bad enough, but the more serious problem is that Archibald allows Cornelia to have her way at the 'expense' of his wife's manifest wishes. This, in turn, leaves her more open to the blandishments of

Francis Levison, the novel's cad and serial seducer, whose appearance at the French resort town reawakens an infatuation that eventually leads to Isabel's abandonment of the home that has never really been hers, and her descent into fallen woman status.

The key to all of this, however, lies in the previous statement that 'Mr Carlyle suspected it not'. Too busy with his work to notice that his wife is both desperately unhappy and, indeed, drifting towards infidelity, it is Archibald who is the unstated culprit in the novel. As John Tosh puts it, 'the [Victorian] separation of the spheres was centrally a matter of mental compartmentalization ... Whether the husband worked at home or used it merely as a refuge, he had little to do with domestic labour or domestic management',[10] and this rigid bifurcation pushes an already teetering household to its destruction. Ironically, it is Cornelia's ability to combine masculine and feminine attributes that gives her power, while her half-brother's hyper-masculine unwillingness (or inability) to understand the female space he ostensibly inhabits as 'home' leaves him blind to the danger that will bring it down. Further, like Fosco, Cornelia's queer behaviour is both chastened and yet victorious. Although with Isabel's adulterous elopement her sister-in-law's persecution is revealed, resulting in Archibald's searing castigation '"May God forgive you, Cornelia!"' (331), she has nonetheless won the battle to expel this unsuitably upper-class rival for her half-brother's affection – but only because of that half-brother's own socially conditioned limitations. Both Collins and Wood, therefore, employ queer characters to explore the weaknesses of their culture's primary gender discourses, so that we should hardly be surprised when Mary Elizabeth Braddon does something very similar when following in her precursors' steps.

Lady Audley's Secret combines explicit class transgression with implicit sexual transgression to create a doubled commentary on female disempowerment. And, given what Helena Michie describes as 'the novel's insistent thematization of doubling',[11] it is completely appropriate that that commentary finds expression through the paired figures of Lucy, Lady Audley and her maid, Phœbe Marks. The connection of these two characters is established immediately by their names, 'Lucy' deriving from the Latin word for 'light' and 'Phœbe' tracing back to the Greek words 'bright' and 'radiant', an ironic set of associations given their shared predilection for working in the shadows. The linkage, and the irony, is then made more direct by the novel's narrator:

> The likeness which the lady's-maid bore to Lucy Audley was perhaps, a point of sympathy between the two women. It was not to be called a striking likeness; a stranger might have seen them both together, and yet have failed to remark it. But there were certain dim and shadowy lights in which, meeting Phœbe Marks

gliding softly through the dark oak passages of the Court, or under the shrouded avenues in the garden, you might have easily mistaken her for my lady.[12]

Phœbe is most like her mistress when moving through 'dim and shadowy lights', or through 'dark ... passages', or through 'shrouded avenues', so that this paragraph, which reinforces the text's consistent evocation of Audley Court as a gothic setting, helps reveal Phœbe's function as a *doppelgänger* to Lucy. Lady Audley herself recognises the similarity, declaring early on that ' "you *are* like me [Phœbe], and your features are very nice" ' (95), invoking the idea that same-sex desire can be constructed as a kind of narcissism, since it centres on a version of the self rather than on the embodiment of an other, so that elements of what Elizabeth Lee Steere suggests could be a 'covertly implied ... lesbian relationship'[13] are hinted at in the two women's relationship.

Their problematic intimacy arises because Lucy 'hated reading, or study of any kind, and loved society; rather than be alone she would admit Phœbe Marks into her confidence, and loll on one of the sofas in her luxurious dressing-room, discussing a new costume for some coming dinner party, or sit chattering to the girl, with her jewel box beside her, upon the satin cushions' (90). This 'luxurious' indolence leads to an informality that Alicia Audley, Lucy's stepdaughter, sees as more than distasteful. Upon finding 'the maid and mistress laughing aloud over one of the day's adventures', Alicia, 'who was never familiar with her servants, withdrew in disgust' (95). This fortuitous withdrawal then leads to a scene in which Lucy, after 'smooth[ing] her maid's neutral-tinted hair with her plump, white, and bejewelled hand', asks Phœbe to do her a favour, which in turn leads, after the maid agrees, to her mistress retiring to bed, 'curl[ing] herself up cosily under the eider-down quilt', and suddenly declaring ' "Kiss me, Phœbe" ... as the girl arranged the curtains' (96).

Lucy's ability to break boundaries by moving from employment as the governess at Audley Court to being its lady continues through an illegitimate familiarity with a female servant that implies even greater illicit activity. The necessary secretiveness of such a liaison feeds into Victorian anxieties about servants as the potential enemy-within, an idea the novel's narrator seems to endorse with the observation '[a]mongst all privileged spies, a lady's-maid has the highest privilege ... She has a hundred methods for the finding out of her mistress's secrets' (346). On one level, Lucy's compromise of Phœbe through a shared sexual secret is a way of ensuring the protection of all her other secrets, since the maid now has as much to lose by exposure as the mistress. However, it is just this idea of shared secrets that ends up broadening the implications of Braddon's doubled female characters, most directly in the context through which Phœbe becomes increasingly complicit with Lucy.

The first secret Phœbe discovers pits her against her mistress, since the revelation in a hidden drawer of 'a baby's little worsted shoe rolled up in a piece of paper, and a tiny lock of pale and silky yellow hair, evidently taken from a baby's head' (70) provides all the evidence needed to blackmail Lucy. Although these 'Hidden Relics' (64), as this chapter is called, do not reveal the ultimate secret of Lady Audley's bigamy, they expose the existence of a concealed child, and that is more than enough. However, Phœbe's decision to use her knowledge to force Lucy to purchase a public house for her loutish cousin Luke, and thus facilitate her marriage to him, has unexpected repercussions. When Lucy 'remonstrate[s] with her maid upon her folly in wishing to marry the uncouth groom' by asking ' "You surely are not in love with the awkward, ugly creature, are you Phœbe?" ' (140), Phœbe's response is instructive:

> 'I don't think I can love him. We have been together from children, and I promised, when I was little better than fifteen, that I'd be his wife. I daren't break that promise now ... I've often watched and watched him, as he has sat slicing away at a hedge-stake with his great clasp-knife ... When he was a boy he was always violent and revengeful. I saw him once take up that very knife in a quarrel with his mother. I tell you, my lady, I must marry him.'   (140–1)

The coercive nature of male power is made blatant here, with Luke's threateningly phallic knife representing the vulnerability of women who, whether fulfilling the role of fiancé, wife or mother, are always potentially victims. Lucy, after she is abandoned by her first husband, George Talboys, attempts to find what agency she can through her bigamous marriage with Sir Michael Audley, but she is no less trapped and dependent than Phœbe, even if the economic desperation driving her is more subtle than the fear of being stabbed. When Lucy suggests that she will prevent the marriage Phœbe is moved to extremities: ' "My lady – my good, kind mistress!" she cried vehemently, "don't try to thwart me in this – don't ask me to thwart him. I tell you I must marry him. You don't know what he is. It will be my ruin, and the ruin of others, if I break my word. I must marry him!" ' (141). Lucy's sense that there ' "must be some secret at the bottom of all this" ' (141) is about to be proven true, but the crucial revelation is that, far from positioning herself as the blackmailer of her 'good, kind mistress', Phœbe has come to identify with her, a collusion created through the queer attachment that has grown between them through shared female intimacy.

Thus when Luke insolently insists on being given one hundred pounds to establish himself as the proprietor of a public house, instead of the fifty pounds Lucy originally offers, the reader is provided with the kind of melodramatic scene that made sensation fiction so popular:

> Lady Audley rose from her seat, looked the man steadfastly in the face till his determined gaze sank under hers; then walking straight up to her maid, she said ... 'Phœbe Marks, you have told *this man!*'
>
> The girl fell on her knees at my lady's feet.
>
> 'Oh, forgive me, forgive me!' she cried. 'He forced it from me, or I would never, never have told!'   (142, emphasis in original)

The betrayal is clear, both through Lucy's shocked disbelief that Phœbe could have revealed her secret to a '*man*', and through Phœbe's histrionic reaction to the exposure of this gender treachery. Yet even here her deeper loyalty is demonstrated. She is no longer marrying Luke simply out of fear for herself, but also in order to protect Lady Audley from the ruin that will overtake her should Luke expose the secret he has forced out of his reluctant wife-to-be. Although in Braddon's text we are dealing with two female criminals, there is still some sympathy available as these women end up at risk from a male figure that has earlier been described as a 'broad-shouldered, stupid-looking clodhopper' (65). The context seems very different, but it is not inappropriate to invoke *The Woman in White* here, and Marian's evaluation of the impact of heteronormativity:

> No man under heaven deserves these sacrifices from us women. Men! They are the enemies of our innocence and our peace – they drag us away from our parents' love and our sisters' friendship – they take us body and soul to themselves, and fasten our helpless lives to theirs as they chain up a dog to his kennel. And what does the best of them give us in return? ... I'm mad when I think of it!   (208)

Both novels use queer female relationships to problematise marriage, the institution that most directly embodies Victorian gender interaction. But because Lucy, through her bigamy, radically enacts the dissatisfaction *Lady Audley's Secret* subtextually invokes, her expression of Marian's rhetorical declaration of madness will be much more direct.

The famous (or infamous) conclusion of Braddon's novel, in which Robert Audley's relentless detection finally exposes all of his aunt-by-marriage's secrets, leads to this declaration by Lucy: '"God knows I have struggled hard enough against you, and fought the battle patiently enough; but you have conquered, Mr. Robert Audley. It is a great triumph, is it not? a wonderful victory! You have used your cool, calculating, frigid, luminous intellect to a noble purpose. You have conquered – a MADWOMAN!"' (254). Lucy's supposed hereditary insanity acts as a metaphor for all her subversive/criminal activity throughout the plot, but it also provides Robert with the opportunity to use the same kind of extra-judicial means to deal with her that Walter used to deal with Fosco. As numerous critics have pointed out, Robert's self-interested desire to avoid any scandal involving his family and Lucy leads him to 'simply [arrange] for her to be pronounced "mad" and imprisoned accordingly in a *maison de santé* abroad. The "secret" let out at the end of the novel is not, therefore, that Lady Audley is a madwoman but rather that, *whether she is or not*, she must be treated as such.'[14] Interestingly, by this point Phœbe has essentially dropped out of the story, and when Robert subsequently interviews Luke Marks to fill in the remaining gaps of his investigation, that erstwhile caring husband declares '"Bother Phœbe … whose a talkin' of Phœbe? what's Phœbe that anybody should go to put theirselves out about her?"' (422). More secrets than one disappear when Lucy is 'Buried Alive' (387) in a Belgium sanatorium, and the text's concluding disregard of its evocation of same-sex attraction, while fastidiously tying up every other loose end of its tangled narrative, suggests that some transgressions need to be buried more deeply than others. Lucy's despairing cry '"You have brought me to my grave, Mr. Audley … you have used your power basely and cruelly, and have brought me to a living grave"' (396) manages, against all apparent odds, to leave the reader commiserating with the novel's dangerously unconventional anti-heroine, and with her fruitless struggle to evade the constraints of her culture. Early in the novel a minor character declares to Sir Michael '"it's a queer world"' (159), and although that Victorian use of the word is not the same as the predominant usage in this essay, Braddon's main character has queered her readers' conventional responses in multiple ways.

The non-normative gender performance of certain characters in *The Woman in White*, *East Lynne* and *Lady Audley's Secret*, along with the 'perverse' sexualities this type of performance implies, provided their audiences with the thrilling *frisson* such transgression provokes (and which the newly identified genre of sensation fiction demanded). They achieve more than that, however, in the textual economy of their narratives. By challenging standard cultural exchanges of value, and disrupting status quo discourses of propriety, instantiations of queerness provide the authors of these novels with a mode of social analysis that clearly struck a nerve with Victorian reviewers. And, of course, striking the nerves is exactly the effect sensationalism aims for. Negative responses to sensation novels often emphasised what the critic viewed as an unnatural and unhealthy focus on aberrant attitudes and behaviour, an accusation that inevitably contains its own unexamined assumptions. Literary fictions expose cultural fictions, and these three texts invoke queer energies that resonate long after the excessively overdetermined, and, therefore, questionable, restoration of order that closes their plots has been imposed. Gender is troubled in order for that trouble to be allayed, but the disturbances generated by Collins, Wood and Braddon remain the foundation of their sensational success.

NOTES

1. Kathleen Tillotson, 'The Lighter Reading of the 1860s', Introduction, Wilkie Collins, *The Woman in White* (Boston: Houghton, Mifflin, 1969), xv.
2. Jonathan Loesberg, 'The Ideology of Narrative Form in Sensation Fiction', *Representations* 13 (1986), 117.
3. Wilkie Collins, *The Woman in White*, ed. Maria K. Bachman and Don Richard Cox (Peterborough, ON: Broadview, 2006), 73–4. Further references to this edition will be given in the text.
4. D. A. Miller, '*Cage aux Folles*: Sensation and Gender in Wilkie Collins's *The Woman in White*', *Representations* 14 (1986), 128.
5. Michael D. Snediker, *Queer Optimism: Lyric Personhood and Other Felicitous Persuasions* (Minneapolis: University of Minnesota Press, 2009), 4.
6. George Levine, *How to Read the Victorian Novel* (Malden, MA: Blackwell), 117.
7. *Ibid.*, 116.
8. Alex Woloch, *The One vs. the Many: Minor Characters and the Space of the Protagonist in the Novel* (Princeton University Press, 2003), 37, emphasis in original.
9. Ellen Wood, *East Lynne*, ed. Andrew Maunder (Peterborough, ON: Broadview, 2000), 78. Further references to this edition will be given in the text.
10. John Tosh, 'Domesticity and Manliness in the Victorian Middle Class: The Family of Edward White Benson', in *Manful Assertions: Masculinities in Britain since 1800*, ed. Michael Roper and John Tosh (London: Routledge, 1991), 49.
11. Helena Michie, *Sororophobia: Differences among Women in Literature and Culture* (Oxford University Press, 1992), 65.
12. Mary Elizabeth Braddon, *Lady Audley's Secret*, ed. Natalie M. Houston (Peterborough, ON: Broadview, 2003), 138. Further references to this edition will be given in the text.
13. Elizabeth Lee Steere, ' "I Thought You Was An Evil Spirit": The Hidden Villain of *Lady Audley's Secret*', *Women's Writing* 15:3 (2008), 307.
14. Miller, '*Cage aux Folles*', 121.

7

JANICE M. ALLAN

The contemporary response to sensation fiction

In an 1852 review of what is arguably the most obvious example of sensationalism *avant la lettre*, a critic for *Bentley's Miscellany* claims that 'To write effectively of *Basil* we ought to have another vocabulary at command.'[1] Regardless of whether Wilkie Collins's novel represents a genuinely innovative form of writing, or is merely a hybrid of existing modes and genres, this comment signals how the literary productions that came to be labelled 'sensational' were *experienced* by their contemporary critics as something new or unprecedented: a phenomenon that required reviewers to adjust their critical vocabulary and discursive practices. Produced and consumed within a culture obsessed with establishing and defending clear taxonomic classifications, the indeterminate and polymorphic nature of 'the sensational' was perceived as a problem to be investigated, a riddle to be solved, and literary critics embarked on a self-conscious attempt to determine what it might signify, both in and of itself, and for mid-Victorian culture and society more generally. The resulting literary debate, waged in the pages of the periodical press, was unprecedented in terms of both its vehemence and intensity.

The critical response to this new phenomenon was not, by any stretch of the imagination, universally hostile; indeed, the most aggressive attacks on sensation fiction tended to be confined to the elite quarterlies (the *Edinburgh Quarterly*, *Quarterly Review*, *Westminster Review* and *North British Review*) and the reception offered in many of the shilling monthlies, literary weeklies and daily newspapers was both more measured and more welcoming. At the same time, the genre had a number of cogent and persuasive defenders who, after too many examples of staid domestic fiction, welcomed the thrills it offered. Nevertheless, it is still true that a significant proportion of the reviews are characterised by an exaggerated rhetoric, occasionally verging on the hysterical, that had rarely been seen in previous literary discussions. Constructing the genre as 'a pestilence so foul as to poison the very life-blood of our nation',[2] these reviews betray an almost paranoid fear of the dangers, both moral and social, posed by the nation's light reading. Consider a single significant example from 1866:

> There is no accounting for tastes, blubber for the Esquimaux, half-hatched eggs for the Chinese, and Sensation novels for the English. Everything must now be sensational . . . Just as in the Middle Ages people were afflicted with the Dancing Mania and Lycanthropy, sometimes barking like dogs, and sometimes mewing like cats, so now we have a Sensational Mania. Just, too, as those diseases always occurred in seasons of dearth and poverty, and attacked only the poor, so does the Sensational Mania in Literature burst out only in times of mental poverty, and afflict only the most poverty-stricken minds. From an epidemic, however, it has lately changed into an endemic. Its virus is spreading in all directions, from the penny journal to the shilling magazine, and from the shilling magazine to the thirty shillings volume.[3]

Littered with allusions to disease, contamination and degeneration – the discursive fields that came to dominant the debate – reviews such as this construct the sensation novel not simply as a threat to literary standards, but to the bedrock of values that ground the English middle-class subject. While more level-headed critics were quick to point out that this type of heightened rhetoric brought the reviewer into dangerous proximity with the genre being attacked – in the words of one, 'this cry of horror strikes us as being itself rather sensational'[4] – there is no doubt that the anxiety displayed in many reviews was real rather than feigned. In addition to tracing the contours and terrain of the critical debate surrounding the sensation novel, this chapter will attempt to account for its emotive intensity, an intensity markedly at odds with both the supposed ephemerality of the genre and the professional authority of its critics.

Defining the concept of sensation

At the heart of this discussion is the elusive concept of sensation itself: a 'popular and very expressive term, and yet one much more easy to adopt than to define'.[5] It first appears within theatrical discourses of the late 1850s and early 1860s, where it was applied to 'sensation dramas' such as *The Colleen Bawn* (1860) by the Irish playwright, Dion Boucicault. Within a few years, the word became ubiquitous and was applied, with little discrimination, to a wide range of cultural productions. *Dublin University Magazine*, for example, employed the term to refer not only to the latest works of fiction but also to 'Blondin on the high-rope, or Leotard flying from his perilous trapeze, or Olmar, a human spider, walking on a lofty ceiling, with head downwards, or Boucicault taking his famous "header" '[6]. Other critics lamented the 'curse' of 'sensational journalism', where 'everything must yield to "sensation" and "excitement"',[7] as well as the new tendency towards 'sensational art' that is 'intended to work on our feelings'.[8]

Occluding the formal differences between these very different modes of representation, it becomes clear the term 'sensational' was employed, not to refer to some common formal property intrinsic to each of its various manifestations but, rather, to their perceived effect on the audience. Unlike 'legitimate' art that attempts to elevate or ennoble through, for example, instruction or appeals to the sympathetic faculties, the sensational was condemned because it aimed only to shock and excite: to produce a literal sensation upon the body. In this sense, it matters little whether one is reading the latest sensation novel or watching the spectacle of Jules Leotard somersaulting between trapezes. In the words of Henry Mansel, one of the most hostile and influential critics of sensationalism, 'excitement, and excitement alone, seems to be the great end at which they aim – an end which must be accomplished at any cost'.[9] Believing that 'the taste of a generation, and the art of a generation, are mutually informed, and are bastard or legitimate, false or correct, flagitious or respectable, alike and together',[10] the public demand for sensation was read by many critics as a worrying sign of cultural degeneration. For others, such as the prolific novelist and reviewer, Margaret Oliphant, sensationalism was a sign of the times, a reflection of the 'changed world in which we are now standing'.[11] Paradoxically, the term thus came to designate that which was distinctly modern, even up-to-the-minute, as well as that which was decidedly retrograde, a throwback to an earlier, more primitive state of civilisation. As we shall see, concerns relating to sensationalism's affective potential and its implications for cultural standards loomed large in the critical discussion of its most troubling manifestation: the sensation novel.

Constructing a new genre

It has often been claimed that the appearance of Collins's *The Woman in White* (serialised in Charles Dickens's weekly magazine, *All the Year Round*, between 26 November 1859 and 25 August 1860) initiated a new literary genre: the sensation novel. It is, however, worth noting that while several critics, including that of *The Times*, were willing to concede that the novel's mode of narration – where different characters each contribute a portion of the narrative – was innovative, it was still described as 'a novel of the rare *old* sort'.[12] In fact, for the majority of critics, Collins's latest novel, while being the most perfectly executed of his works to date, remained 'pretty nearly of the same stamp with his earlier creations'.[13] In purely formal terms it is, therefore, difficult to defend the novel's status as originary.

Moreover, as Graham Law suggests elsewhere in this volume, the term 'sensation novel' was already in use in the American press in 1858 while, in the United Kingdom, it appears in *Blackwood's Edinburgh Magazine* as early as January 1860, when *The Woman in White* was still a full seven months away from completion. Associating their appearance with the advent of the railway, the author of 'Rambles at Random in the Southern States' queries how 'James Watt would have regarded the flood of light literature with which the world is now deluged' and, more specifically, the 'piles of "sensation novels" at 25 cents each, by eminent American authors'.[14] While the use of inverted commas suggests that the term may have been unfamiliar to British readers, the fact that 'piles' of these novels are available for American travellers to 'devour' implies a well-established demand in their native country. Thus it appears that the sensation novel, as a recognised and named literary category, predates Collins's novel by some margin and, moreover, that *The Literary Budget* was right to claim, as it did in 1861, that 'we owe the epithet "sensation" to the candid or reckless vulgarity of the Americans'.[15]

It is significant that the term did not assume a prominent place in the British critical vocabulary until 1862, when the public impression created by *The Woman in White* had been intensified by the appearance of Ellen Wood's *East Lynne* (serialised in W. H. Ainsworth's *New Monthly Magazine* between January 1860 and September 1861) and not one, but two, novels by Mary Elizabeth Braddon (*Lady Audley's Secret* ran from January to December 1862 in the *Sixpenny Magazine* while *Aurora Floyd* was serialised in *Temple Bar* between January 1862 and January 1863). The phenomenal popularity of each these works, together with the fact that they appeared in such close succession, allowed them to be constructed – despite being formally and thematically diverse – as a collective phenomenon that marked a new direction in literary production. In this sense, the term 'sensation' refers as much to their reception in the literary marketplace as any particular characteristic within the novels themselves. As *Fraser's Magazine* explains to its readers, 'a novel comes out which "makes a sensation," and "has a run"; that is to say, it goes through a number of editions – large and small – and serves as a fertile topic of conversation for the whole-novel reading population of Great Britain and Ireland for some weeks at a time'.[16]

This comment provides a salient reminder of how closely the advent of the sensation novel was, for its contemporary critics, bound up with the changing material conditions of literary production and consumption. Only a few decades earlier, it would have proved impossible for a novel to 'make a sensation' in the manner described in *Fraser's*. Yet, by the early 1860s, all the necessary conditions were in place. Growing literacy rates, combined with a gradual reduction in working hours, had produced an ever-growing mass readership. At the same time, advances in printing technologies, modes of distribution (including the railway and the advent of the lending library), as well as the removal of what were known as the 'taxes on knowledge' (stamp duty was repealed in 1855 and the duty on paper in 1861) led to an explosion in print culture. Particularly relevant to a discussion of sensation fiction was the rise of the serial. In the minds of many contemporary critics, the worst faults of sensation fiction – particularly its emphasis on physical affect and shocking, fast-paced plots – were directly attributable to this fragmented mode of publication. At the same time, the symbiotic relationship between the serial and sensation – a relationship governed by market forces rather than any 'higher' artistic considerations – signalled, for many critics, the growing commodification of literature. This commodification, moreover, was taken as *prima facie* evidence of a decline in literary standards. According, for example, to the *London Quarterly Review*:

> Our magazines are largely to blame for the multiplication of this species of literary trash. It seems now to be thought essential to the success of any periodical that it should have two or three serial tales regularly going on in its pages, and that it should secure the services of some writers whose names have secured a certain notoriety, and who often continue in this way to palm very inferior wares upon the market. Under such circumstances, indeed, the authors neither do justice to themselves nor to their readers. They are compelled to produce a certain portion at regular intervals, and it is almost necessary that every portion should produce some sensation. Hence the spasmodic, feverish, exciting style in which the tales are written, often regardless alike of the dramatic unities and of all literary finish.[17]

I would suggest that the critical perception that sensationalism represented something new, or unprecedented, stemmed as much from its association with these new market conditions as any particular characteristic of Collins's or Braddon's writing. As suggested by a reviewer for *The Times*: 'There has never been anything like it before. To the literary historian it is an unparalleled phenomenon, and people know not what to make of it.'[18]

The question of how to interpret this phenomenon preoccupied the critical establishment and, as is now widely recognised, the furore surrounding sensation fiction cannot be disassociated from a generalised anxiety about what these new market conditions signalled for the nation's cultural standards and boundaries. In 1861, for example, an advertisement for the newly launched *Sixpenny Magazine* (the future home of *Lady Audley's Secret*) claimed that 'the removal of Duty on Paper creates a new era in Literature; it compels cheapness; and it enables the combination of quality with quantity'.[19] Yet for many critics, this 'new era in Literature' was marked by nothing so much as the complete severing of quality from quantity. Seemingly cut adrift from the dictates of taste and discrimination, literature entered a free-market economy, governed only by the law of supply and demand. Within this climate, the act of reading – 'so long a virtue, a grace, an education, and, in its effects, an accomplishment'[20] – is refigured, by the critics, as an appetite, even an addiction, that the new mass readership cannot, or will not, control. According to Thomas Arnold (brother of the more famous defender of cultural standards, Matthew Arnold), these readers would not be deterred by 'bad taste, bad English, and literary crudity, from reading what is suited to the barbarous condition of their intelligence. So the law of supply and demand works; and, to meet the notions of such readers, a plentiful crop of like-minded writers arises; and an unprecedented circulation of worthless books is the inevitable result.'[21]

Such comments betray what Susan David Bernstein has termed 'an anxiety of assimilation'. As she suggests, this anxiety 'signifies the threat of altering social boundaries. With sensation fiction, "worthless" mass culture masquerades as valuable elite culture, while the tastes of upper-class readers replicate the uncultivated, exaggerated appetites of the underclass.'[22] These fears are writ large in W. Fraser Rae's often-quoted accusation that Braddon 'may boast, without fear of contradiction, of having temporarily succeeded in making the literature of the Kitchen the favourite reading of the Drawing room'.[23] They are, however, more interestingly teased out in the 1862 article, 'The Last Sensation Novel'. According to its anonymous author:

> So long as this detective-officer style of literature was confined to one shilling volumes and railway platforms, no great harm was done ... When we buy one of these shilling volumes we know exactly what to expect. At first the position of this school was not a high one. But it has of late risen in the literary scale. As Becky Sharp won her way into society by dint of powers of attraction unworthy of the stately queens of fashion, so the policemen line of writing was found to possess an interest often sadly wanting to more decorous publications ... The result is that instead of a dozen criminals, discoveries, and executions from 'Waters', in the space of one volume, and for the price of one shilling, we have the detection of only one criminal – without any execution at all – extending over three volumes, and charged at the exorbitant rate of thirty-one shillings and sixpence.[24]

Like the titular Lady Audley, sensation fiction is threatening because it is able to transgress the boundaries of class and culture by disguising its dubious origins and masquerading as something better and more worthy than it is.

It is this very mutability that makes the sensation novel such a useful if ambiguous term within the critical vocabulary of the period. As a polyvalent term that could be manipulated to reflect the attitudes and presumptions of individual critics, the designation 'sensation novel' was, from the start, applied both loosely and inconsistently. For example, while some critics identified Collins as the leader of the school, others exempted him from it altogether, arguing that his writing represented something higher and better than mere sensation. Similarly, Ellen Wood remained, throughout her long and prolific career, precariously perched on the border between sensationalism and domestic realism. The critical positioning of writers such as Charles Reade, Rhoda Broughton and Ouida (the pseudonym adopted by Maria Louise Ramé) was similarly ambiguous.

Turning to the typical features ascribed to the genre – most obviously, its incident-laden plots, emphasis on crime, secrecy, class transgression and aggressive, passionate heroines – we run into similar difficulties. As a number of critics were quick to point out, these features were neither new nor unique to the works deemed sensational. Indeed, this recognition opened the door for the genre's defenders to construct what Solveig Robinson identifies as 'a kind of "counter canon" of sensation fiction' which aligns it with recognised great works of the past.[25] In one such defence, 'The Sensational Williams', the author claims that:

> It is very easy to cry 'Sensational!' but the word proves nothing … The Œdipus of Sophocles is in the highest degree sensational; so are half the plays of Shakespeare, at a moderate computation; so is the Satan of Paradise Lost; so is Raphael's Massacre of the Innocents; so is the Laocoon; so, one may say, are the Oratorios of Handel, since they dealt with tremendous elements of suffering and wonderment, of aspiration and triumph. Whenever humanity wrestles with the gods of passion and pain, there, of necessity, is that departure from our diurnal platitudes which the cant of existing criticism denounces by this single word.[26]

Nor is the affective potential of these narratives – 'begun, continued, and prolonged for the sole purpose of creating and heightening a feverish excitement'[27] – any better able to anchor a definition of the genre. As even its staunchest opponents were forced to acknowledge, the ability to produce affect cannot be limited to any one single type or period of cultural production. In the words of one such critic, 'Sensation writing is an appeal to the nerves rather than the heart; but all exciting fiction works upon the nerves, and Shakspeare can make "every particular hair to stand on end" with anybody.'[28] Thus, it is hardly surprising that, as late as 1870, the critic Alfred Austin was still demanding, 'what is a sensation novel?': a question 'which has been put over and over again by extremely reasonable objectors, and to which, as far as we know, there has never yet been given an adequate and satisfactory reply'.[29]

Given the various ambiguities and inconsistencies with which the label was adopted and applied, it seems increasingly clear that, far from referring to a distinct and coherent body of texts, or a particular style of writing, it is little more than a discursive construction invented by the reviewers. Indeed, as early as 1874, the novelist, poet and critic, Mary Isabella Irwin Brotherton, suggested that while 'Coleridge, I think, called turnips the first Cause of boiled mutton ... critics appear to me to be the First Cause of sensation novels'.[30] But if the label 'sensation fiction' cannot shed much light on the products so named, it can tell us a good deal about those who were involved in naming it. As Nicola Diane Thompson suggests, a careful analysis of such critical classifications helps to 'reveal the reviewer's own aesthetic and ideological preconceptions and provides insight into how both the individual critic and contemporary literary conventions process a new work'.[31] It seems to me that this assertion is particularly apposite to the sensation genre as the critical response it generated cannot be disassociated from a complex interstice of anxieties relating not only, as we have already seen, to cultural standards, but also to class and gender boundaries, and to the professional standing of the critic 'him'self. Turning to two of the most common objections to the genre – its affiliation with 'low' and popular forms and its affective impact on female readers – we can begin to trace these 'aesthetic and ideological preconceptions' at work.

The literature of the kitchen

As suggested above, sensation fiction was perceived as a threat, not simply because it was associated with a variety of 'lower' forms, such as melodrama or the penny dreadfuls consumed by an 'unknown public' that Collins numbered at over three million, but because it was able to disguise such dubious origins and masquerade as more worthy reading material for the middle classes.[32] According to *The Broadway*, it was Collins who first discovered that 'tales of crime and horror, which had hitherto thrilled the hearts of scullery-maids, might, if more artistically sated, be rendered acceptable in the drawing-room'.[33] But for many other critics, the mutability of the genre was associated not with Collins, but with the so-called queen of sensation: Mary Elizabeth Braddon. In part, this was because Braddon, more than any of the other sensation novelists, openly defied the critical injunction to respect the boundaries between different literary markets. Not only did she simultaneously supply novels to cheap periodicals aimed at the working classes and to the middle-class circulating libraries but, at times, the same fare was offered at both tables. According, for example, to the *Examiner*'s review of her 1864 novel *Henry Dunbar* (originally serialised as *The Outcast* in the pages of *The*

London Journal): 'This is a highly-seasoned dish of tainted meat that has been already contrived and served up for a kitchen dinner by the great *chef* of the kitchen maids, and is now brought upstairs for the delectation of coarse appetites in the politer world.' Distinguishing his own superior taste from such uncultured 'appetites', the critic concludes that while Braddon's novels 'are at the head, perhaps, of Kitchen Literature ... In every other respect we recognise the same appeals from a coarse taste to a taste that cannot in many kitchens of the land be coarser.'[34] This determination to 'recognise' and expose sensation fiction as a low and 'coarse' form is a prominent feature, not only within the reviews of Braddon, but of the genre as a whole. Like Robert Audley peeling away the layers of Lucy Audley's deception, the critics attempt, in Mansel's words, to reveal the sensation novel as it appears to their 'superior' judgement: 'pure and undisguised, exhibited in its naked simplicity, stripped of the rich dress which conceals while it adorns the figure of the more ambitious varieties of the species'.[35]

In their attempts to relegate the genre back to the kitchen, critics lost no opportunity to remind their readers of its menial origins. While Mansel claims that a 'commercial atmosphere floats around works of this class, redolent of the manufactory and the shop',[36] other critics strip the sensation novelists of their individuality as artists, reducing them to 'a number of deserving work-men and workwomen [who turn their products] with strict punctuality, despatch, and attention to business'.[37] Adopting a different strategy to effect the same end, the reviewers also used the genre's interest in topical crime, divorce and scandal to align it with the daily newspapers. This comparison emphasised not only the sensation novel's status as cheap, mass-produced reading material, but also its ephemerality: 'the excitement of it once over, it is fit for nothing but the waste-paper basket or the back of the grate. It is an egg-shell, a yesterday's newspaper, a sucked orange, a heap of withered leaves in autumn-time, a last year's almanack, savourless salt.'[38] Even when not ostensibly addressing the issue of the genre's origins, the language of the critics is imbued with class metaphors and allusions. In a review of Matilda Houstoun's *Such Things Are* (1866), for example, the author's grammar is compared to 'the Cockney [who] enrich[es] as many words by the illegitimate addition, as he impoverishes by the illegitimate abstraction, of the "h." Her idioms and phrases sometimes have a smack of the servants' hall.'[39] However such attacks are couched, their purpose is always the same: 'to make as distinct a separation as the printer's skills can indicate between the lower and the higher ground in fiction' and, by so doing, to reinstate clear class and cultural boundaries.[40]

Jonathan Loesberg has traced the critical anxiety generated by the genre (as well as its narrative structures) to concerns about the stability of class identity in the build-up to the Second Reform Act. Bradley Deane, however, argues that this context 'does not sufficiently explain the particularity of the moment of sensationalism as a literary development'.[41] Instead, he asserts that it must be read, not simply as a reaction to the changes in the literary market-place outlined above but, in addition, as a response to the threat such changes posed to the authority of the critics themselves. For as Deane suggests, 'the greatest threat to writers whose job is distinguishing the "best" of cultural productions … is a form of production that seems universally embraced'. To counteract this threat, certain critics became 'outspoken opponents of the literary market itself. To justify their new claims to be guardians of culture, they endorsed the notion that culture required guarding, that without their stewardship the public would inevitably err … As a genre, sensationalism … was destined from its inception to be the threat against which critics defined their cultural aspirations.'[42] For an example of this oppositional logic at work, we need only turn to Arnold's 'Recent Novel Writing', where he claims that

> as the Bankruptcy Court purifies commerce from rotten speculations, and parliamentary committees, however imperfect as tribunals, do knock on the head many worthless railway schemes, it is much to be wished that criticism, instead of suffering itself to be deluged by the flood or silenced by the din that issues incessantly from all our literary workshops, should assert its right and function more stiffly than ever.[43]

Given that Arnold and his peers are trying, precisely, to disassociate (and protect) literature from the corrupting influence of market forces, his choice of metaphors is slightly ironic. At the same time, however, such metaphors testify to a heightened anxiety about the insecurity of capital, cultural or otherwise, within a commodity-led market. Situating the response to sensation fiction within this context, we can begin to understand the exaggerated and emotive rhetoric employed in many reviews. What the critics did not appear to recognise is that this rhetoric was in danger of undermining the disinterested, professional authority it was designed to protect.

Gendering the response to sensation fiction

If the sensation novel debate was shaped by a range of anxieties arising from changes within the literary marketplace, it also bears the imprint of the increasingly complex constructions of middle-class femininity. Indeed, as a genre primarily produced and consumed by women and, moreover, dominated by unruly yet attractive heroines, it is hardly surprising that 'a distinctly gendered aesthetics of reception' is in evidence in many of the reviews.[44] At the heart of this gendered response are two related assumptions about the woman writer and reader. According to the first, the office of the woman writer should be an extension of her domestic role within the home: to promulgate appropriate moral values and support the socialisation of young women into properly feminised (and classed) subjects. Turning from the point of production to that of consumption, the second assumption constructs the female reader as both less critical and more porous (and hence more open to influence) than her male counterpart. It, therefore, stands to reason that if 'novels may be, and are, the medium through which moral poison is frequently administered',[45] women are in far greater need of protection than men. Indeed, the critic's role as the regulator of literary standards was, in part, justified by this construction of women as vulnerable readers.

We can detect these assumptions at work in many of the gender-specific attacks on the genre where aesthetic and ideological considerations routinely collapse into one another. It is significant, for example, that while realism is the critical yardstick against which sensationalism is routinely judged and found lacking, this yardstick is often most forcefully employed in discussions of female transgression and deviance. Thus W. Fraser Rae, responding to Aurora Floyd's violent attack on 'the Softy' in chapter 12 of Braddon's novel, claims that 'no lady possessing the education and occupying the position of Aurora Floyd could have acted as she is represented to have done'. Operating under the assumption that a 'novel is a picture of life, and as such ought to be faithful',[46] Aurora's 'unrealistic' actions are seen to contribute to the novel's overall *artistic* failure. At the same time, however, there is both a moral and social dimension to Rae's judgement as his assertions bolster public faith in normative middle-class femininity by denying the very existence of the deviance embodied in Braddon's character.

According to many critics, these unrestrained and passionate heroines constituted the most distinctive and disturbing aspect of sensation fiction; women who, in the words of Oliphant, 'give and receive burning kisses and frantic embraces, and live in a voluptuous dream'.[47] Given that the female reader was believed to have 'a dangerous habit of identifying the situations of a novel with the circumstances of her own life, and of speaking and acting as she thinks a young lady in a novel would speak or act',[48] the hostility expressed towards the genre is hardly surprising. Through their affective potential, moreover, sensation novels were seen to 'stimulate the very feelings which they should have sought to repress'[49] and, by encouraging unregulated and excessive desires (both material and sexual), would effectively unfit the reader for the responsibilities of middle-class life. As suggested by *The Spectator*, such novels encourage her to 'long for inaccessible heroes, people of boundless wealth and heroic horsemanship, perfect natures and an irresistible smile … till they hate the thought of life with that struggling doctor, or rising lawyer, or pre-occupied man of commerce'.[50]

For other critics, the only thing more shocking than the passionate heroines, plots and language of sensation fiction was the fact that it was produced by women. As Francis Paget claims, in one of the most inflamed and hyperbolic of attacks, 'No *man* would have dared to write and publish such books': 'No! they are women, who, by their writings, have been doing the work of the enemy of souls, glossing over vice, making profligacy attractive, [and] detailing with licentious minuteness the workings of unbridled passions.'[51] Paget's judgement is typical of a tendency to judge women writers according to their adherence to – or deviation from – the domestic role described above. Unlike the 'proper' woman writer who offers her readers an appropriate education and role models, the female sensationalists proffer an inappropriate version of each. As Henry James wrote of Braddon, 'She knows much that ladies are not accustomed to know, but that they are apparently very glad to learn.'[52] The possession of such improper knowledge called into question the author's femininity, even her respectability, and many of the attacks on female sensationalists were unabashedly personal. Oliphant, for example, queried whether Braddon was 'aware how young women of good blood and good training feel'.[53] While Braddon's irregular personal life left her vulnerable to such charges, her position as editor of *Belgravia Magazine* gave her the power to retaliate and she promptly commissioned G. A. Sala to write 'The Cant of Modern Criticism', one of the most cogent defences, not simply of Braddon, but of the genre as a whole. Indeed it was, as Beth Palmer suggests, 'by dramatizing and sensationalizing the debate on sensation taking place in the periodical press, [that] Braddon made herself its key player and made her magazine a significant site'.[54]

A product of its time

As we have seen from the discussion above, the critical response to the sensation genre was – no less than the novels themselves – the product of a particular historical moment. Inextricably bound up with changes in the literary marketplace, as well as shifting definitions of class and gender identity, the genre provided a convenient locus for the discussion of a range of extra-literary concerns and anxieties. It was thus, for its critics, so much more (if also so much less) than a literary category and, in this, it was helped rather than hindered by its polymorphic indeterminacy. Yet as time passed and such concerns fell by the wayside, the term lost its critical charge. By the mid 1880s, it came to name a decidedly old-fashioned type of writing – 'harmlessly exciting stories of plot and accident' – as a nostalgic signifier of a simpler, bygone era.[55] Yet, if the sensation novel was invented by its reviewers, it has, even as anticipated, outlived them. In the words of A. C. Swinburne: 'though Dickens was not a Shakespeare, and though Collins was not a Dickens, it is permissible to anticipate that their names and their works will be familiar to generations unacquainted with the existence and unaware of the eclipse of their most shining, most scornful, and most superior critics'.[56]

NOTES

1. Unsigned, '"Esmond" and "Basil"', *Bentley's Miscellany* 32 (November 1852), 576–86 (584).
2. Vincent E. H. Murray, 'Ouida's Novels', *The Contemporary Review* 22 (1878), 921–35 (935).
3. John Richard de Capel Wise, '*Belles Lettres*', *Westminster Review* 30:1 (1866), 268–80 (269–70).
4. Unsigned, 'Cecil Castlemaine's Gage', *Saturday Review* 24 (1867), 414–15 (414).
5. Unsigned, 'Our Female Sensation Novelists', *Christian Remembrancer* 46 (1863), 208–36 (210).
6. Unsigned, 'Modern Novel and Romance', *Dublin University Magazine* 61 (1863), 436–42 (438).
7. Unsigned, 'Sensational Journalism', *London Review* (4 May 1861), 502–3 (502).
8. Unsigned, 'Sensational Art', *Saturday Review* (22 August 1863), 252–4 (252).
9. Mansel, 482.
10. Unsigned, '"Sensation" Literature', *The Literary Budget* 1 (1861), 15–16 (16).
11. OSN, 564.
12. E. S. Dallas, '*The Woman in White*', *The Times* (30 October 1860), 6, emphasis added.
13. Unsigned, 'The Woman in White', *The Saturday Review* 10 (25 August 1860), 249–50 (249).
14. Laurence Oliphant, 'Rambles at Random in the Southern States', *Blackwood's Edinburgh Magazine* 87 (1860), 103–16 (103).
15. Unsigned, '"Sensation" Literature', 15.
16. Unsigned, 'The Popular Novels of the Year', *Fraser's Magazine* 63 (1863), 253–69 (253).
17. Unsigned, 'Recent Novels: Their Moral and Religious Teaching', *London Quarterly Review* 27 (1866), 100–24 (102).
18. Unsigned, 'Novels', *The Times* (30 December 1864), 8.
19. Unsigned, Advertisement for *The Sixpenny Magazine*, *The Publisher's Circular* 24 (1861), 288.
20. Alfred Austin, 'The Vice of Reading', *Temple Bar* 42 (1874), 251–7 (251).
21. T. A. [Thomas Arnold], 'Recent Novel Writing', *Macmillan's Magazine* 13 (January 1866), 202–9 (204).
22. Susan David Bernstein, 'Dirty Reading: Sensation Fiction, Women, and Primitivism', *Criticism* 36:2 (Spring 1994), 213–41 (217).
23. Rae, 204.
24. Unsigned, 'The Last Sensation Novel', *London Review* 5 (1862), 481–2 (481).

25. Solveig C. Robinson, 'Editing Belgravia: M. E. Braddon's Defense of "Light Literature"', *Victorian Periodicals Review* 28:2 (Summer 1995), 109–22 (113).

26. Unsigned, 'The Sensational Williams', *All the Year Round* 11 (1864), 14–17 (14).

27. Unsigned, '"Sensation" Literature', 15.

28. Unsigned, 'Our Female Sensation Novelists', 210.

29. Alfred Austin, 'Our Novels. The Sensational School', *Temple Bar* 29 (1870), 410–24 (410).

30. Mrs Brotherton, *Old Acquaintances*, 1874, quoted in Unsigned, '*Belles Lettres*', *Westminster Review* 46 (1874), 283–98 (288).

31. Nicola Diane Thompson, *Reviewing Sex: Gender and the Reception of Victorian Novels* (Basingstoke: Macmillan, 1996), 10.

32. Wilkie Collins, 'The Unknown Public', *Household Words* 18 (1858), 217–22 (217).

33. Unsigned, 'Women's Novels', *The Broadway* 1 (1868), 504–9 (505).

34. Unsigned, 'Kitchen Literature', *Examiner* (25 June 1864), 404–6 (404).

35. Mansel, 506.

36. *Ibid.*, 483.

37. Unsigned, 'New Novels', *The Graphic* (9 May 1891), 531.

38. Unsigned, '"Sensation" Literature', 15.

39. Arnold, 'Recent Novel Writing', 203.

40. ON, 275.

41. See Jonathan Loesberg, 'The Ideology of Narrative Form in Sensation Fiction', *Representations* 13 (Winter 1996), 115–38; Bradley Deane, *The Making of the Victorian Novelist: Anxieties of Authorship in the Mass Market* (New York and London: Routledge, 2003), 149.

42. *Ibid.*, 72, 68.

43. Arnold, 'Recent Novel Writing', 202.

44. Thompson, *Reviewing Sex*, 10.

45. Unsigned, 'Novel-Reading', *The Saturday Review* 15 (1867), 196–7 (196).

46. Rae, 190, 203.

47. ON, 259.

48. Unsigned, 'Novels, Past and Present', *The Saturday Review* 21 (1866), 438–40 (440).

49. Unsigned, 'Recent Novels', 102.

50. Unsigned, 'The Effect of Novel-Reading on Girls', *The Spectator*, rpt. in *Littell's Living Age* 83 (1864), 569–72 (570).

51. Francis Paget, 'Afterword' to *Lucretia. Heroine of the Nineteenth Century* (1868), quoted in Andrew Maunder, ed., *Varieties of Women's Sensation Fiction, 1855–1890*, 6 vols. (London: Pickering and Chatto, 2004), vol. I, 210–18 (215).

52. Henry James, 'Miss Braddon', *The Nation* 1 (1865), 593–4 (594).

53. ON, 260.

54. Beth Palmer, *Women's Authorship and Editorship in Victorian Culture: Sensational Strategies* (Oxford University Press, 2011), 16.

55. Unsigned, 'Novels of the Week', *Athenaeum* 3226 (1889), 251–2 (252).

56. Algernon Charles Swinburne, 'Wilkie Collins', *Fortnightly Review* 46 (November 1889), 589–99 (589–90).

8

MARIACONCETTA COSTANTINI

Sensation, class and the rising professionals

A new 'class of literature'

In an 1863 review published anonymously, the theologian Henry Longueville Mansel manifested his concern about the literary vogue for sensationalism, which he felt both fed and whetted the mid-Victorian appetite for excitement. An object of moral opprobrium, which threatened to corrupt 'the habits and tastes of its generation', the sensational 'class of literature' was also disparaged, in Mansel's view, by its association with a world of trade 'redolent of the manufactory and the shop'.[1] While expressing his moral reservations, Mansel suggested that the new form reeked of the coarse materialism of a commercialised society dominated by profit-oriented producers and a tasteless mass of purchasers.

Other detractors of the sensation novel strengthened their moral censure with social and aesthetic arguments. A recurrent accusation against the new genre was that it debased high standards of living and literariness through contamination with lower standards. This view is effectively expressed by W. Fraser Rae in an unsigned review of the novels of Mary Elizabeth Braddon. With sarcastic wit, Rae credits Braddon with creating a cheap kind of literature that lowers the tastes of her respectable audience: 'She may boast, without fear of contradiction, of having temporarily succeeded in making the literature of the Kitchen the favourite reading of the Drawing room.'[2] The figurative link with domestic space connotes the new popular form as a threat to social stability. A generic hybrid appealing to servants and masters alike, the sensation novel is alarmingly conceived as an agent of chaos that blurs the socialised borders dividing labour from leisure, bad taste from good.

The disquiet evinced by mid-century reviewers is proof of the growing attention paid to class issues at the time. As a literary phenomenon that flourished in the 1860s, the sensation novel provided a variety of fictional responses to these issues, while its specific modes of production and circulation raised doubts about its affiliations to old and new social groups. A first element that demands consideration is the socio-political context in which the genre rose. The late 1850s and 1860s were years of intense debate over parliamentary reform. Supporters and opponents of the reform, in discussing the extension of the franchise, gave voice to underlying fears of disintegration, since they worried about the loss of identity resulting from the collapse of class barriers. Sensation fiction encodes these fears in its obsessive handling of plots of lost identity. As Jonathan Loesberg contends, however, the genre conveys no anodyne social views: its 'contradictoriness, dissociations, and willed nonseriousness . . . indicate an ambivalence about the ways the various ideological structures were emplotting class conflict'.[3]

The ambivalence Loesberg ascribes to sensation novels is a sign of the complexity of the mid-century language of class. After replacing old-fashioned ideas of rank and order, the notion of class posed new problems of definition, since it evolved in accordance with the changing roles of differently oriented groups. The middle class, in particular, had developed into a multi-layered social entity. Its internal subdivisions, ranging from gentrified plutocracy to lower-class employees, made it a class of contending opinions and fluctuating markers of status – a class whose ideological signs were given a 'multi-accentual'[4] quality by the intersection of various group interests. It suffices to consider the differences in objectives, sources of income and lifestyles between captains of industry and professionals, traders and clerks, to have an idea of the diversity of their social roles and views. The multi-accentuality of the Victorian middle class is evident in sensational representations of its identity. Less willing than other writers to explore the misery of industrial labourers, and generally distrustful of the aristocracy, sensation novelists were enthralled by the heterogeneity of their own class, which they described in ambivalent terms. However different their political orientation might appear, these novelists seldom proposed unambiguous models of middle-class conduct and ideology. In depicting upward mobility, for example, they condemned the breaching of ethical precepts but generally attached an idea of progress to the rise of worthy individuals. Half-ironic and half-serious was their challenge to bourgeois values. Although they wove criminal plots that exposed the performative nature of respectability, they revealed ideals of worthiness and trust pertaining to middle-class morality.

This ambiguous approach to the class with which they identified was due to the novelists' divided loyalties. As freelance writers belonging to a group of rising professionals, they had an experience of mobility that compelled them to negotiate their social identity anew. The fact that they used literature as a source of income, moreover, complicated their relations with the world of art. Torn between opposing drives, they gave fictional shape to their anxieties by characterising writers and artists who, as will be shown, embodied their creators' search for a professional model that should reconcile economic exigencies with artistic aspirations.

A further element of ambiguity was their treatment of violence and sexual deviancy. Reviewers like Mansel condemned the commercial exploitation of these themes as a sign of the authors' affiliation to profit-seeking groups. But there was another spectre evoked by the sensational staging of scandals: class debasement. The genre had low origins in working-class melodrama and penny fiction and, because of its explicit use of deceit and crime, appealed to readers from different classes. As Deborah Wynne explains, the broadening fascination with lawbreaking in the 1860s was a result of the growing sense of social insecurity, which was given fictional shape by reworking popular reportage and literature into exciting stories destined for a cross-class audience.[5] Generally serialised in middle-class family magazines and republished in 'respectable' triple-decker volumes, sensation novels nonetheless retained distinct elements of working-class literature. Rae's complaint about the lowering of bourgeois tastes is a worried response to the incorporation of low-brow elements into successful stories for middle-class consumption. Although they toned down the crudity of their sources and often closed their narratives with positive images of domesticity, sensation novelists were accused of endangering the stability of a social order founded on clearly defined boundaries between bourgeois and lower-class values.

Cross-class transgression informed the relations between these novelists and their audience. An emblematic case is the professional history of Mary Elizabeth Braddon, the writer against whom Rae launched his scathing attack. After starting her career as a penny-weekly author, Braddon composed highly successful sensation novels for middle-brow magazines and triple-volume editions. Her formative work for proletarian journals exerted a significant influence over her career even though she later attempted to elevate sensationalism to art. Braddon's experience in the working-class literary market was doubtlessly unusual. Most practitioners of the sensation genre shunned the world of penny dreadfuls and deliberately aimed at the audience of middle-brow magazines. Still, the separation between the two categories of journals and fiction was not so drastic. In addition to using low-brow ingredients, sensation novelists shared part of their audience with penny-novel authors, since growing numbers of readers targeted by penny journals were attracted to less cheap miscellanies.

The changing identity of the periodical readership did not escape Wilkie Collins's notice. In an article titled 'The Unknown Public' (1858), he manifested his curiosity about the 'unknown public' of weeklies that, by his reckoning, outnumbered the largely middle-class 'known public'. Collins uses a comic tone to describe the plebeian world of penny-novel readers, whom he identifies with working-class semi-literates. Nevertheless, he betrays a genuine attraction to this gigantic mass of consumers. What he announces in the concluding paragraph is the imminent future for the rise of the 'unknown public' who, once 'taught the difference between a good book and a bad', might give 'the widest reputations' to 'the best writers of their time'.[6]

Collins's exploration of an unfamiliar audience is further testimony to the interest sensationalists felt in the changing alliances between classes. Distinctively middle class in their aspirations to wealth and recognition, these writers served an expanding literary market that brought them into contact with lower social strata. The experiences they had in an urbanised, increasingly anonymous world became fictionalised in their stories of domestic crime, which disclose the fragility of a middle-class identity in need of redefinition.

The Woman in White (1859–60), the novel that inaugurates the decade of sensationalism, bears traces of the genre's problematic representation of a fast-changing society. What Collins tells in this novel is a complex story of lost identity imbricated with class and legal anxieties. Faced by the danger of losing his standing, the baronet Percival Glyde asks the help of a cunning aristocrat, Count Fosco, to achieve a double criminal objective: to gain control of his wife's property, and to silence a woman who is supposed to know the secret of his illegitimacy. The striking resemblance between the two women enables the plotters to stage a perturbing exchange of identities, which is given official sanction by a law that too often sided with the powerful. While the upper-class Laura Fairlie is incarcerated in an asylum under the name of Anne Catherick, her lower-class double is buried in a grave inscribed with the lady's name.

Another transgression of class boundaries is the rise of Laura's drawing master and lover, Walter Hartright, who marries his former pupil and fights against the two plotters to restore her identity. Through his agency, Laura finally regains her name and status, but the original balance of her world is lost for ever. This idea is conveyed by the death of the two upper-class plotters, whose role is symbolically taken by Hartright, as Laura's husband and father of her son. While confirming the desirability of the world of rank and property, Collins depicts the historical process of gentrification of some middle-class individuals who, through marriage or wealth, were substituting 'degenerate' upper-class members. As is often the case in Collins's fiction, however, the characterisation of the rising man is not devoid of ambiguities. Hartright's transition from patronage to professional illustration, his parallel careers as amateur sleuth and attorney, and his final integration into the gentry,[7] configure his path to self-development as a winding one. The difficult choices he is forced to make during his ascent give clues to the author's thoughts on a thorny problem confronting Victorian social climbers: the problem of marking out the ethical and behavioural spheres of their agency within a class system they were contributing to upset.

Artistic vocation and materialistic drives

'So glad to possess you at Limmeridge, Mr Hartright.'[8] These words of welcome uttered by Mr Frederick Fairlie to his newly employed drawing teacher are revelatory. An advocate of feudal class relations, the invalid squire patronisingly adds Hartright to his many 'possessions' which, together with the enslaved valet Louis, comprise a valuable collection of art objects. Humiliating in its implications, the master–servant relation established by Fairlie is the first obstacle the protagonist must overcome. After leaving Limmeridge for sentimental reasons, Hartright serves as draughtsman for an expedition to Central America and, on his return to England, makes a career as illustrator for periodicals. The new occupations he accepts mark his emancipation from the fetters of upper-class employment and patronage, and his entry into a competitive job market. The struggle for survival he has learned abroad is successfully applied to the new life he leads in London as illustrator and amateur detective. Constrained to act for himself by poverty, he makes progress towards a permanent engagement in his job while his investigation into the secrets of Laura's enemies paves the way to his marriage into the landed gentry. The achievement of both goals is granted by his newly adopted conduct. 'There was no choice but to oppose cunning by cunning' (467), he confesses to the reader, when he resolves to defeat his upper-class antagonists through spying and blackmail. His ambiguity is increased by the role of amateur attorney he comes to play by editing the novel's narratives into a pseudo-legal text that is meant to validate his agency.

Hartright's promotion from reified employee to leisure-class gentleman sheds light on Collins's view of social mobility. As John Kucich demonstrates, the author's sympathies lay with a group of 'cultural intellectuals', 'a mobile segment of middle-class society ... allied with the arts' and yearning for social recognition.[9] In representing this cultural fringe, which included drawing masters, writers and amateur art practitioners, Collins brought into focus their unstable class identity. Anti-bourgeois in feelings but hungering for insiderhood, idealistic but attracted to wealth, the members of this sub-class were coming to terms with the prospect of making a professional use of their gifts to earn money and status. The main drawbacks of such a prospect were the sacrifice of high-art aspirations and the moral deterioration resulting from the adoption of profit-seeking motives.

These contradictions are embodied by the protagonist in *The Woman in White*. A devotee of the fine arts, Hartright takes up low-brow illustration to earn a living and resorts to deceit when necessary. The relation he establishes with Fosco is equally laden with ambiguities. Although he is a criminal and a traitor, the Italian count provides an imitable model of cunning for the rising teacher. With regard to manners, however, Hartright draws little inspiration from the grandiloquent Fosco, who is a master of courtesy and an upholder of the old code of honour. In the end, the author sides with the drawing teacher, who is shown to be victorious over the aristocrat. But he avoids solving the ambivalence of Hartright's newly acquired identity. Principled and pragmatic, cultured and unrefined, the protagonist reveals the complexity of the historical process through which middle-class groups were trying to redefine their standards at the mid-century. Not surprisingly, Hartright's demeanour is evocative of the behavioural paradigm elaborated by Samuel Smiles in *Self Help* (1859). Smiles aimed to harmonise old notions of gentlemanliness with middle-class ideals of work, uprightness and self-reliance. In the same year, Collins explored this possibility by creating a fictional intellectual who negotiates his way between contending models and principles.

Hartright is the prototype for other cultural intellectuals featured in Collins's novels. Their characterisation enabled the author to focus on his own role as a literary professional yearning for success within a highly stratified society. An intriguing figure, in this sense, is Ozias Midwinter, the racial hybrid who plays a central role in *Armadale* (1864–6). His rise from vagrancy to the caste of literati, which he enters in the double role of journalist and prospective novelist, epitomises the opportunities offered to talented individuals by the expanding literary market. Midwinter is initially hyper-connoted in terms of marginality, as a mixed-race heir turned vagabond who accepts menial jobs and is prone to hysterics. In the course of the narration, however, he slowly evolves into a self-assured professional who is legitimately rewarded with social prestige. To make his growth more remarkable, Collins juxtaposes the dark outcast with a fair double, Allan Armadale, who rises to squirehood through inheritance. Although he is honest and generous, Armadale is shown to be too indolent and uncultured to embody his new role successfully. His social ascent is thus meant to reveal ironically the stagnancy of the leisured classes who seldom earned their privileges. By contrast, Midwinter's mobility and success are ascribed to his work ethic and his adherence to the culture of self-help. By associating his two protagonists with 'the embattled site of the gentleman', Collins shows the extent to which an old-fashioned concept was being appropriated by different groups and turned into a signifier of multifarious class ideologies.[10] At the novel's conclusion, it is Midwinter's model that proves more successful. While the lazy Allan embodies a declining leisure-class ideal, Midwinter benefits from the democratisation of gentlemanliness. Sensitive and hard-working, toiling to make a career without being tainted with the vulgarity of the cash nexus, he achieves an honourable middle-class identity.

By adding gentility to the writer's hallmarks, Collins confirmed his desire to redefine the social and moral position of his professional sub-class. An analogous preoccupation is displayed by Braddon, who, in *The Doctor's Wife* (1864), draws the intriguing portrait of Sigismund Smith, a novelist who makes his second appearance in *The Lady's Mile* (1866). A hack writer working for the 'unknown public' of penny dreadfuls, Smith is said to enjoy 'an immense popularity amongst the classes who like their literature as they like their tobacco – very strong'.[11] Well paid for his job, which is preferred to a legal career, he dismantles most prejudices attached to his professional group, since he is a hard-working young man immune from the violent passions that shake his fictional creatures. In imitation of Braddon, who tried to evade the strictures of sensationalism in *The Doctor's Wife*, Smith cherishes the hope of writing for a middle-brow readership. This hope starts to takes shape in the novel's conclusion, in which he is attracted by a young woman who could be a 'charming subject for three volumes of the quiet and domestic school' (404). In a tongue-in-cheek remark on his new interest, Braddon links Smith's admiration of quiet domesticity to another middle-class virtue: the ability to save money. Defined as 'a gentleman' who has amassed 'a very comfortable little independence from the cultivation of sensational literature in penny numbers' (404), Braddon's alter ego is culturally assimilated within the bourgeois audience for whom he aims to work. His independence, diligence and ambition are middle-class qualities that grant his social rise while preserving him from the debasing effects of his penny-novel experiences. This potential for elevation explains why Smith is the only thriving young man at the conclusion. More industrious than the upper-class Roland Landsdell, who is too idle to pursue an objective, he has more imagination than George Gilbert, the good surgeon devoted to his mission but unwilling to change his drab life. The tragic deaths of both the squire and the doctor are signs of their respective failure to adapt to an evolving society. Quite different is Smith's ability to shape his own destiny. An amusing but painstaking emblem of Braddon herself, he manages to harmonise the ambiguities of his cross-class relations and to offer a more agreeable model of professional conduct.

Outsiders looking in: surplus women and detectives

The efforts sensation novelists made to determine their role in mid-Victorian society were due to the contending meanings of literary labour. More strongly than other writers, they perceived their dependence on market laws of supply and demand, and suffered from the class blight cast on them by being money earners. Defensive, ironic and sometimes provocative in their strategies of self-representation, they laid stress on their heteronomous position as professionals aiming at artistic independence but also resolved to sell the products of their labour to a cross-class readership. This difficult position increased their interest in other rising groups that were trying to adjust their occupational models to the class and moral requirements of their society. Two groups, in particular, embodied an idea of low-ranking occupation that was felt as threatening by their contemporaries: working middle-class women and detectives. Respectively associated with ideals of nurture and lawfulness, working women and sleuths were embroiled in a capitalist system that tainted the symbolic integrity of their work. The ambiguity of their standing attracted the attention of sensation novelists who represented the multiple tensions clustering around them.

Women's occupation was a controversial issue at mid-century. The domestic model of female propriety on which middle-class ideology hinged clashed with the prospect of paid labour outside the home. The ideal wife was financially dependent on her husband; she was expected to display his wealth, supervise the household management and incarnate a ladylike ideal that combined upper-class refinement with bourgeois morality. The incongruities of this role were exposed by sensation novelists, who unveiled the mercenary motives of marriages, related bourgeois domesticity with crime and dramatised the collision between morality and social performance. The eponymous protagonists of Braddon's best-known novels, *Lady Audley's Secret* (1862) and *Aurora Floyd* (1862–3), bear evidence of this process of narrative deconstruction. If the upwardly mobile Lucy Audley learns to conceal her greed and crimes under a ladylike demeanour, the wealthy Aurora Floyd ignores her household duties and establishes dangerous cross-class liaisons. Despite their differences of status and morality, both protagonists are vehicles for Braddon's double-edged view of the bourgeois ideal of femininity, an ideal founded on desirable qualities but too rife with contradictions to be attained unquestionably.

What made the domestic model more elusive was the emergence of new figures demanding recognition in their occupations. In 1851, a census revealed the existence of a surplus of middle-class unmarried women who needed to make a living through paid employment. These women were excluded from traditional professions, such as those in law and medicine, which they began to pursue only later in the century. What they were offered, at mid-century, was a limited range of occupational choices: they could either opt for paid household work (as governesses or housekeepers) or try one of the new jobs in nursing, professional writing and acting. In either case, they had to fight against the prejudices of a society that considered middle-class women's paid labour as unfeminine and redolent of working-class vulgarity. Sensation novelists represented these emergent figures as a liminal group aspiring to bourgeois insiderhood but menacingly at odds with gender prescriptions. The precariousness of their position is well rendered by the recurrent characterisation of duplicitous governesses and housekeepers. The scheming Mrs Powell who spies on her mistress in *Aurora Floyd*, the refined governess with a secret who becomes Lady Audley, and the divorced lady who re-enters her home disguised as an employee in Ellen Wood's *East Lynne* (1861) are fictional variants of an ambiguous model of femininity which expressed a number of coeval anxieties.[12] Most novels close with the removal of their threat from the household. But the disquiet these characters convey is not obliterated, since their domestic invasion signals the instability of traditional divisions between mistress and servant, leisure and labour.

The transgressive story of Magdalen Vanstone, the heroine of Collins's *No Name* (1862–3), gives interesting clues to the hardships of female occupation. A wealthy young lady deprived of her property and status by a legal technicality, Magdalen is forced to abandon her life of leisure and enter the job market. After starting a disreputable career as an actress, she decides to make use of her theatrical skills to get her wealth back. Through deceitful impersonation, she traps her cousin Noel Vanstone into a mercenary marriage, and later continues to pursue her goal in the role of parlour-maid. Although she renounces her claim in the end, Magdalen discloses the illusoriness of class confines, since she symbolically appropriates the social status of the people she impersonates (namely her governess, a respectable young woman, her maid). The last part she performs before her final redemption adds a further element of transgression to her conduct. While trying to convince her maid Louisa to exchange their roles, she describes the difference between mistress and servant in terms of performance: 'Shall I tell you what a lady is? A lady is a woman who wears a silk gown, and has a sense of her own importance. I shall put the gown on your back, and the sense in your head.'[13] The perturbing implications of this statement are reinforced by her actual wavering between leisure and labour, affluence and poverty. As a declassed working lady experiencing extreme class mobility, Magdalen reveals the problems faced by Victorian surplus women, who were suspended between the yearned-for sphere of the privileged and the scary underworld of the labour classes.

The aggressiveness attributed to surplus women was indicative of their location on the fringes of a class that feared their anomalous status. With similar distrust, the Victorian bourgeoisie responded to the rise of a figure associated with the forces of law and order: the detective. The institution of the new Detective Police in 1842 and the changes occurring in policing techniques had given more visibility to the role of investigators, who came to be perceived as painstaking agents of a disciplinary system enforcing social control. The growing power they were assigned was a source of both relief and disquiet for the middle class. On the one hand, they were expected to grant order and protect respectable citizens. On the other, they were perceived as menacing intruders by the bourgeois people they met during their investigations.[14] Usually of low-class origins, detectives lacked the good taste and manners of the well-to-do, who resented their plebeian inquisitiveness. As officers of the law, moreover, they challenged social hierarchies, since they were empowered to control and censure the lives of their social superiors. On a professional level, finally, the uncertainty of their status was determined by their 'uneasy transition' from private employees to public servants which occurred in the first half of the century. Although the role of private hiring diminished after 1828, the change in professional status they experienced was gradual and laden with ambiguities: 'For many years … individuals applying for police assistance continued to have a major – often determining – voice in the choice of the officer and his rate of pay.'[15]

All these concerns come to light in the portraits of professional and amateur detectives drawn by sensation novelists. The narrative experiments they conducted gave birth to a new genre that later overpowered its source models, as Margaret Oliphant foresaw in an article that appeared in *Blackwood's Edinburgh Magazine* ('Sensation Novels', 1862). Before the detective genre gained its autonomy, however, sensationalists used its ingredients to express the tensions generated by contemporary reforms. The mixed feelings that the upper classes had for investigators are discernible in the characterisation of Detective Joseph Grimstone and Sergeant Richard Cuff, who respectively appear in Braddon's *Aurora Floyd* and Collins's *The Moonstone* (1868). Both working for Scotland Yard, and both charged with the delicate task of investigating a crime committed in a wealthy family, these detectives fight against the suspicions of the household masters and servants, who view their inquiries as violent intrusions. The two novels end with the partial success of the detectives, who make good guesses but fail to come to a full solution of the cases. Meticulous and rational though they are in their job, Grimstone and Cuff enter into social relations that prevent them from achieving an unambiguous status. If Cuff's association with the house-steward and the gardener is suggestive of cross-class identity, the fact that both detectives accept money from the investigated families – in the form of rewards or fees – casts a shadow on their professional duties.

The profit motive acquires full relevance in the sensational depiction of the host of Victorian private eyes, who spied on people's secrets to make a living. Their liability to break a wide range of laws is epitomised by the disreputable conduct of James Bashwood, 'the Confidential Spy of modern times',[16] satirised in *Armadale*. Greedy, stony-hearted and prone to act dishonestly, Bashwood bears witness to Collins's reflection on the traps of this modern occupation which could endanger society if unregulated. Although he provides an extreme example of corruption, this minor character confirms the suspicion with which sensation novelists looked upon detectives, who were often represented as liminal figures seeking for moral and social identification.

Old professions, new challenges

In addition to police investigators and private eyes, the sensation genre offers an array of amateur detectives belonging to different classes. Their investigations are spurred by the wish to make up for the flaws of the Victorian legal system, even though they are often shown to adopt a lawbreaking, self-interested conduct. The inquiry conducted by the protagonist of *The Woman in White* reveals this incongruity, since he combines unlawful espionage methods with legal knowledge. On a symbolic level, the convergence of Hartright's amateur roles of detective and attorney raises questions of deontology concerning the legal profession. To what extent were mid-Victorian lawyers entitled to circumvent rules in their practice? And which conflicts of interest did they face? These questions reflected complex mid-century debates about the legal professions, law and morality which attracted attention in the sensational decade and would become more pressing at the *fin de siècle*.

The old professions underwent significant changes during the nineteenth century. A main catalyst for transformation was the rise of a middle class demanding services and occupational chances previously reserved for the privileged classes. The legal and medical professions were particularly affected by the reshaping of socio-economic structures. Traditionally recruited among the landed classes and bound to a high-status clientele, barristers and physicians suffered from the competition of lower-branch groups of practitioners, which included attorneys, solicitors, surgeons and apothecaries. The emergence of these groups brought about important reforms in their systems of recruitment, training and practice. But it also raised controversies over the ethos of lower-status professionals who lacked cultivation, served a cross-class clientele and bartered their duties for money.

The interest sensation novelists had in lawyers and doctors is hardly surprising. In the same way as their literary counterparts, rising professionals in law and medicine bid for social recognition and were likewise charged with misusing their vocation for commercial purposes. These parallels account for the genre's depiction of surgeons and solicitors who face professional discrimination, but finally prove to be superior to their elite rivals. In other cases, however, the characterisation of both high- and low-status professionals is rife with contradictions or bleakly suggestive of depravity. What the genre responded to in these cases were specific apprehensions about the power of legal and medical experts within a society that was growingly influenced by a capitalist economy. The more competitive professionals became, the more complex their ideology appeared, since they met challenges that confounded their ethical points of reference. Because of their traditional relations with the gentry, the status professionals had appropriated some elements of the gentlemanly ideal, such as the notion of service and the disdain for competition. Quite different were the values shared by the members of the lower branches, who had introduced entrepreneurial notions of profit and self-help into their professional conduct. Their rise posed the problem of elaborating a model that could incorporate the bourgeois gospel of work and merit without yielding to the imperatives of commercialism. This model, which was still in the making in the heyday of sensationalism, came to define the specificity of middle-class professionalism later in the century when its practitioners acquired consciousness of their belonging to an internally stratified 'fourth class'.[17] Their autonomy from the tripartite structure of owners of land, owners of capital and owners of labour was negotiated between contending values, which were gradually adapted to the changing exigencies of professional training and practice.

By writing at an early stage of this process, sensation novelists captured crucial elements of the clash between elite and emergent professionals. Their pictures of the world of the law, for example, show the attorneys' efforts to develop an occupational model that satisfied their economic needs while being socially agreeable. Collins offers multiple variants of this model. Now ironic, now serious, his fictional attorneys range from the greedy but skilful Mr Boxsious, the lawyer-detective of an early tale reprinted as 'The Lawyer's Story of a Stolen Letter' (1856), to the industrious and trustworthy Pedgifts, Senior and Junior, featured in *Armadale*. More critical is, instead, the sensational depiction of high-status lawyers and prospective barristers, who conceal moral and professional weaknesses behind a façade of respectability. The characterisation of Robert Audley in *Lady Audley's Secret* is emblematic. A leisure-class young man qualified as a barrister but too lazy to work, Robert starts a legal career at the novel's close after training as amateur detective. His final growth as professional is, however, obscured by his equivocal demeanour. Led into the inquiry by a morbid attraction for his aunt, he incarnates different conflicts of interests when he decides on her future. Apart from being a relative and heir of Lady Audley's husband, he symbolically conflates the discordant roles of prosecutor and judge of the woman, whom he commits to an asylum with the complicity of a thinly scrupled physician, Dr Mosgrave.

Mosgrave's comments on the lady's potential (but still undeveloped) insanity suggest that Braddon's reservations about high-status lawyers were also applicable to their medical counterparts. Physicians and eminent surgeons were often depicted as snobbish and self-righteous by sensation novelists, who tended to favour the professional zeal of rising doctors. The contrast between the two medical sub-groups is sarcastically rendered by Charles Reade in *Hard Cash* (1868), where the honest Dr Sampson is opposed to distinguished medical rascals. In this highly sensational novel, Sampson not only proves to be morally superior to the venal specialists that incarcerate the sane Alfred Hardie into an asylum; he also exhibits great competence in diagnosing illnesses, since he derives his knowledge from bedside practice rather than classical erudition. In the same year as Reade, Collins drew the sympathetic portrait of Ezra Jennings in *The Moonstone*. A mixed-race doctor's assistant suffering from slander and affected by a terminal disease, Jennings nonetheless offers an outstanding professional model. His care in treating the ill Dr Candy and the experiment he conducts to clear Franklin Blake's name of infamy prove him to be a committed medical man who combines expertise with moral courage, ingenuity with an unwavering service ethic.

Later in his career, Collins dealt with specific issues of medical deontology and scientific experimentation. In the 1860s, however, his attention was focused on the inner dynamic of a profession that was redefining its class alliances and ethical standards. Collins had a keen interest in lower-branch medical men. In his fiction, he laid stress on their expertise and industry but also explored their relations with a free-market economy that risked compromising their integrity. This danger is well rendered by his mocking pictures of quack doctors and patent medicine sellers who capitalise on gullible patients. Their deceitful practices are epitomised by Dr Downward (alias Dr Le Doux), the medical swindler portrayed in *Armadale*. A former abortionist who fashions for himself the role of worthy proprietor of a Hampstead sanatorium, Downward hides his crimes under a mask of respectability that favours his social ascent, as ironically suggested by the higher principled solicitor Pedgift: 'in an age favourable to the growth of all roguery . . . I look upon the doctor as one of our rising men' (673).

By representing the conflict between entrepreneurial and service ideals, sensation novelists gave visibility to the uncertain position of rising groups of the old professions with whom they partly identified. The challenges they faced were many, but the counter-model they offered to the idle classes was promisingly connoted. 'How many a grief has been bred of idleness and leisure!' exclaims Braddon in *Aurora Floyd*, before commenting on the busy life led by all professionals: 'we have no time to pine or die'.[18] The heterogeneous group of journalists, lawyers, nurses, curates and medical attendants with whom Braddon aligns herself in this passage embodied a positive ideal of middle-class industry – an ideal which, if purged from the corruptive influence of the cash nexus, provided a social alternative to the useless, degenerate lifestyle of the do-nothing classes.

NOTES

1. Mansel, 482–3.
2. Rae, 204.
3. Jonathan Loesberg, 'The Ideology of Narrative Form in Sensation Fiction', *Representations* 13 (1986), 115–38 (133).
4. Patricia Ingham, *The Language of Gender and Class: Transformation in the Victorian Novel* (London and New York: Routledge, 1996), 3.
5. Deborah Wynne, *The Sensation Novel and the Victorian Family Magazine* (Basingstoke and New York: Palgrave, 2001), 8–14.
6. Wilkie Collins, 'The Unknown Public', *Household Words* 18 (1858), 217–22 (222).
7. See Ronald R. Thomas, 'Wilkie Collins and the Sensation Novel', in *The Columbia History of the British Novel*, ed. John Richetti (New York: Columbia University Press, 1994), 479–507.
8. Wilkie Collins, *The Woman in White*, ed. Julian Symons (London: Penguin, 1985), 66. A further reference to this edition will be given in the text.
9. John Kucich, *The Power of Lies: Transgression in Victorian Fiction* (Ithaca, NY and London: Cornell University Press, 1994), 109.
10. Raffaella Antinucci, '"Not another like him in the world": Wilkie Collins and the Gentleman Within', in *Armadale: Wilkie Collins and the Dark Threads of Life*, ed. Mariaconcetta Costantini (Rome: Aracne, 2009), 133–54.
11. Mary Elizabeth Braddon, *The Doctor's Wife*, ed. Lyn Pykett (Oxford University Press, 1998), 11. Further reference to this edition will be given in the text.
12. Bronwyn Rivers, *Women at Work in the Victorian Novel: The Question of Middle Class Women's Employment* (Lampeter: The Edwin Mellen Press, 2005), 86–107.
13. Wilkie Collins, *No Name*, ed. Mark Ford (London: Penguin, 1994), 503.
14. Patrick Brantlinger, 'Class and Race in Sensation Fiction', in *A Companion to Sensation Fiction*, ed. Pamela K. Gilbert (Oxford: Blackwell, 2011), 430–41.
15. Anthea Trodd, *Domestic Crime in the Victorian Novel* (Basingstoke: Macmillan, 1989), 18–19.
16. Wilkie Collins, *Armadale*, ed. John Sutherland (London: Penguin, 1995), 516. A further reference to this edition will be given in the text.
17. Harold Perkin, *The Rise of Professional Society: England since 1880* (London and New York: Routledge, 1989), 116.
18. Mary Elizabeth Braddon, *Aurora Floyd*, ed. P. D. Edwards (Oxford University Press, 1996), 77–8.

9

SAVERIO TOMAIUOLO

Sensation fiction, empire and the Indian mutiny

Of all the great events of this century, as they are reflected in fiction, the
Indian Mutiny has taken the firmest hold on popular imagination.[1]

Sensationalising mutiny/mutinying sensation

In a letter to Angela Burdett-Coutts dated 4 October 1857, Charles Dickens
suggested the measures he would take to end the insurrection commonly
known as the Indian mutiny, begun on 10 May: 'I wish I were the
Commander in Chief in India. The first thing I would do to strike that
Oriental race with amazement ... should be to proclaim to them in their
language ... that I should do my utmost to exterminate the Race upon whom
the stain of late cruelties rested.'[2] Dickens's words have an uncanny resemblance to Kurtz's 'beautiful piece of writing' in Conrad's *Heart of Darkness*
(1899), which gave Marlow 'the notion of an exotic Immensity ruled by an
august Benevolence'.[3] Kurtz's concluding remark ('Exterminate all the
brutes!') recalls Dickens's aim to 'to exterminate the Race upon whom the
stain of late cruelties rested'. The repeated use of the term 'race' – instead of,
say, 'people' or 'Indians' – is also indicative of the cultural and ideological
background of Dickens's letter, since the studies in the field of 'racial science'
(which mixed anthropological research and phrenological measurements)
functioned at the time as a fundamentally imperialistic practice to justify
British economic, political and cultural domination through an antithesis
between the Saxons and the so-called 'dark races' of mankind, as Robert
Knox defined them in *The Races of Men* (1850).[4] Dickens's aggressive verbal
reaction gives voice to a widespread counter-attack against the rebellion of
the sepoys of the Bengal Presidency army, which originated in Meerut and
then spread through central India. Along with the storming of Seringapatam
(1799), the violent suppression of the Jamaican ex-slaves by Governor Eyre
(1865) and General Charles Gordon's martyrdom in the Sudan (1884), the
Indian Mutiny (1857–8) was reputed as one of the most tragic events in
Victorian colonial and imperial history, as well as a cultural trauma that
affected the public opinion and the literary world in unprecedented ways.

Represented in melodramatic terms in contemporary newspapers and in more than seventy novels, it featured a sequence of recognisable gothic and sensational tropes such as 'exotic' settings, male violence, rape and brutality. According to some historians, one of the reasons for the outbreak was that Indian soldiers were increasingly upset by the attempts to convert Hindus and Muslims to Christianity. For others, the sepoys were also afraid of losing their power as landed gentry and opposed to land-revenue payments following the annexation of Oudh. Another cause, which was the more easily 'justifiable' in popular accounts (but also the least reliable), was based on the controversy over the new Pattern 1853 Enfield Rifle, whose paper cartridges, which had to be bitten to be opened, were said to have been greased with pork and beef fat, two animals considered by Hindus and Muslims as unclean. As Benjamin Disraeli declared before the House of Commons on 27 July 1857, 'the decline and fall of empires are not affairs of greased cartridges', and the Indian war was in truth 'the result of two generations of social disruption and official insensitivity'.[5] The insurrection ended in 1858, when a peace treaty was signed on 8 June, three months after the recapture of Lucknow.

The sepoy rebellion was an important watershed in Victorian culture and in British colonial politics, leading to the dissolution of the East India Company and to a general reform of the colonial army. For the first time, an 'Oriental race' (as Dickens put it) dared to fight against its rulers and, even worse, dared to commit 'cruelties' against the two emblems of Victorian domesticity, women and children. The enormous media coverage given to the revolt was generally focused on a rigid juxtaposition between British innocent victims (and heroic soldiers) and violent Indian sepoys. Reports centred in particular on the massacres that took place during the sieges of Delhi and Cawnpore (the English term for Kanpur), its Bibigarh well becoming the emblem of Indian brutality, and a symbol of colonial martyrdom. The story goes as follows: on 15 July 1857, Nana Sahib, who commanded the siege of the town of Cawnpore, ordered the sepoys to kill all those who were confined in Bibigarh (the home of the local magistrate's clerk). Because of their refusal to carry out his orders, Nana Sahib employed two Muslim butchers, two Hindu peasants and one of his personal bodyguards to slaughter the 120 sieged people (mainly women and children) with knives and hatchets. At the end of the massacre, the house walls were covered with blood, and the floor littered with fragments of human limbs. According to contemporary accounts, the dead, and even those who were wounded, were thrown into a nearby well.

The journalistic dispatches from India, usually based upon hearsay, as well as the political debates reported by newspapers and periodicals such as *The Times*, the *Westminster Review*, *Blackwood's Edinburgh Magazine* and the *Quarterly Review*, influenced public opinion by turning the mutiny into a 'sensational' narration of colonial atrocities. Among the many examples, it is useful to refer to a typical piece of Victorian journalism from an anonymous article published in *The Times* on 25 August 1857. It describes in detail the sepoys' brutal actions in the streets of Delhi: 'They took 48 females, most of them girls of [*sic*] from 10 to 14 … violated them and kept them for the base purposes of the heads of the insurrection for a whole week … Then they commenced the work of torturing them to death, cutting off their breasts, fingers, and noses, and leaving them to die.'[6] By focusing on the use of violence against British women and children, in a way, these accounts prepared the public for (and implicitly justified) the brutal retaliations of the so-called British 'Armies of Retribution', which consisted, among other things, in exploding rebellious sepoys from cannons' mouths. Charles Ball, R. Montgomery Martin and Colin Campbell's books are probably the most famous 'historical narrations' of the Indian war, featuring violence upon children as well as torture and rape of defenceless English women. As the nature of these 'narrations' suggests, the mutiny was not simply a historical event of great relevance that generated a plethora of usually unreliable tales (rapes by Indian people on British women, for instance, were never proven). It was, above all, a sensational story centred on questions of colonial power and on the defence of Victorian institutions, such as the family and the nation, against any form of violent otherness, in which the image of rape turned into a recurring trope connecting gender issues to colonial concerns. The 'fictional' quality of the sepoy rebellion entails a reflection on the journalistic and historical (or rather parahistorical) documents, with an eye also to the rhetorical strategies employed by the various writers in their reconstructions of the events taking place in 1857. The use of traditional gothic and sensational tropes, the presence of (prevalently) male villains of foreign origin, the depiction of physical pain and the reiteration of terms such as 'horror' prove that historical facts were given a narrative structure to justify a return to familial and colonial order in the publicly acceptable form of military reaction.

These 'historical narrations' anticipated in many ways the textual strategies and themes of sensation novels by Wilkie Collins and Mary Elizabeth Braddon, who, in turn, referred in direct or indirect ways to colonial issues and, most notably, to the Indian uprising. For Christopher Herbert, the traumatic impact on Victorian and post-Victorian consciousness of the 1857 rebellion 'can only be meaningfully studied by considering it not as a geopolitical event but as a literary and in effect a fictive one – as a story recounted over and over, in one stylistic inflection and literary register after another'.[7] The mutiny became a source of narrative inspiration for a great number of short stories and novels which explicitly or implicitly alluded to it. The first narration devoted to it was, significantly, Charles Dickens's and

Wilkie Collins's collaborative piece 'The Perils of Certain English Prisoners' (published in 1857, in the Christmas issue of *Household Words*), which discusses the mutiny question in an indirect way, by dealing with what happened in South America nearly one century before. The action takes place in a British mining colony during the reign of George II. Collins's article entitled 'A Sermon for Sepoys' (included in *Household Words* on 27 February 1858), written in the form of an Eastern parable, had a more religious or philosophical tone than Dickens's and Collins's text. Here Collins goes back to the example of Shah Jehan (1592–1616), whose fame is mainly related to the building of the Taj Mahal, to demonstrate that the past history of India offers models of pacification that should be imitated as a lesson to tame (as he says) the 'human tigers'.[8] In the list of mutiny-inspired fictions it is also necessary to include novels such as *The Wife and the Ward; or a Life's Error* (1859) by Edward Money, Sir George Trevelyan's half-historical and half-narrative treatment of the Bibigarh siege and massacre in *Cawnpore* (1865), in which the author comes to the point of admitting British racist attitudes against Indians, H. P. Malet's *Lost Links in the Indian Mutiny* (1867), James Grant's *First and Last Love* (1868), *Seeta* (1872) by Phillip Meadows Taylor, *The Afghan Knife* (1879) by Robert A. Sterndale, George Chesney's *The Dilemma* (1876), Jack Muddock's *The Great White Hand or the Tiger of Cawnpore* (1896) and Flora Annie Steele's *On the Face of the Waters* (1896), a more balanced narration of events. These texts are all examples of the ways in which the memory of the Indian insurrection outlived and often reinvented history. But there are also fictional texts which refer to the Indian insurrection and, more generally, to colonial and imperial issues in indirect or metaphorical ways, and whose message is not always politically and culturally orthodox, as the examples of Wilkie Collins's *Armadale* (1866) and *The Moonstone* (1868), or Mary Elizabeth Braddon's *Lady Audley's Secret* (1862) and *Aurora Floyd* (1863) demonstrate.

Although Collins's *The Moonstone* is set in the years 1848–9, during the second Anglo-Sikh War in India (its historical frame being represented by the events that surrounded the storming of Seringapatam), the inclusion of mysterious Indian characters represented a 'topical' allusion to the mutiny that readers could easily recognise. Nevertheless, the stealing of the 'cursed' Indian jewel becomes in Collins's novel an occasion to depict the unevenness of British colonial politics. In having the 'pure' upper-class Englishman John Herncastle as the true villain of the tale, Collins turns the Indians into victims of imperial violence. In line with his interest in cultural, sexual and racial outsiders, Collins gives prominence to the role played by the racial hybrid Ezra Jennings (whose father is English but who has been educated and reared in the colonies), who helps solve the mystery of the stolen diamond. However,

Collins's handling of the colonial question in *The Moonstone* is not exempt from ambiguities. The narration is in fact framed by the point of view of one of the novel's primary narrators, Gabriel, whose love for Daniel Defoe's *Robinson Crusoe* – one of the cornerstones of the colonial frame of mind – sets the novel in a contradictory ideological position.

Collins's multi-plot sensation *Armadale*, published when the echoes of the mutiny were still resonating, features the 'dark' Ozias Midwinter expiating the colonial crimes committed by his father Allan Wrentmore Armadale, who prospered in Barbados as a slave-owner during the 1820s. In a reformulation of Darwinian ideas on the inheritance of criminal attitudes, Collins destabilises and complicates the traditional paradigms of good and evil, empire and colony, by having Ozias as the cultural and racial outsider who lays claim to an English origin. Ozias's 'tawny, haggard cheeks; his bright brown eyes', as well as his 'rough black beard', make him a 'startling object to contemplate' for Mr Brock: 'The rector's *healthy Anglo-Saxon flesh* crept responsively at every casual movement of the usher's supple brown fingers, and every passing distortion of the usher's haggard yellow face.'[9] Finally, Mary Elizabeth Braddon's sensational blockbusters and 'pair of bigamy novels' (as she called them),[10] *Lady Audley's Secret* and *Aurora Floyd*, were both published at the dawn of the mutiny. Set during or soon after the uprising, these texts deploy the traditional rhetoric and iconography of the Indian insurrection in very different ways, and can be discussed in detail as case studies of the complex textual dialogue between colonial issues and sensation fictions.

Struggling with the tiger: *Lady Audley's Secret* and *Aurora Floyd*

At the beginning of the mutiny, when Braddon was entering the literary world and was still acting in provincial theatres under the stage-name of 'Mary Seyton', she had in fact already dealt with the Indian war. In poems such as 'Delhi' (*Beverley Recorder*, 26 September 1857), 'Captain Skene' (*Beverley Recorder*, 17 October 1857), 'The Old Year' (*Beverley Recorder*, 2 January 1858) and 'Havelock' (*Brighton Herald*, 2 January 1858), her views on the insurrection were in line with the need for retribution which was typical of that historical phase.[11] Moreover, *Lady Audley's Secret* and *Aurora Floyd* are not the only novels in which Braddon, in her long literary career, treated colonial and imperial issues. *Sons of Fire* (1895), for instance, is a late sensation fiction partially set in Africa during an expedition that involves its main characters (Africa is also mentioned in the detective novel *Rough Justice* (1898) as a place of racial degeneration). In one of her last novels, entitled *Dead Love Has Chains* (1907), the seventeen-year-old Irene is sent home from India in disgrace, being pregnant and unmarried. Like *Phantom Fortune*

(1883) before it, which centred on the crimes committed by the Governor of the Madras Presidency, Lord Maulevrier, India represents the site of moral corruption whose main agent is, however, of a British origin.

Set around 1857, *Lady Audley's Secret* is a narration of the 'traumas' experienced by the two antithetical characters of the text: by George Talboys, first after his reading of the news of his wife's death and then after his discovery of her adultery and bigamy; and by Helen Talboys, after she realises that her husband has abandoned her (and her baby) to seek his fortune abroad and, finally, after she is locked in an asylum. Through its complex characterisation of Lady Audley as a 'beautiful fiend',[12] whose story only partially motivates her unlawful and criminal actions, Braddon's novel puts into question the stereotypically antithetical roles of hero and villain, stainless husband and 'mutinous' wife. In *Lady Audley's Secret*, Braddon explicitly refers to gothic tropes and updates them on many occasions in order to prove that 'the mysteries which are at our own doors' (as Henry James said) are 'infinitely the more terrible' than those of Udolpho.[13] At the same time, she introduces new declinations of the gothic through her dislocation of the Indian rebellion in the domestic setting of Audley Court. Here the figure of the sepoy mutineer corresponds to the character of Lady Audley. Indeed, the most important events of the novel are set around the 'infamous' year of 1857: Lucy Graham (formerly Helen Talboys) marries Sir Michael Audley at midsummer, and her first husband George Talboys reads the false news of Helen Talboys's death in a number of *The Times* dated 30 August (the date of Helen's death on her tombstone is 24 August). Finally, Lady Audley is sent to the Belgian asylum of Villebrumeuse, where she will die, on 28 March 1859. Moreover, *Lady Audley's Secret* alludes to and filters historical events set in distant India in a metaphorical way, in order to discuss gender issues that are firmly located at home in Victorian Britain. For instance, in the course of a dialogue between Robert Audley and the ex-dragoon George Talboys one year after Helen Talboys's (supposed) death, Talboys compares his bitter sense of loss to the psychically shattered condition of British soldiers in India, suggesting an implicit connection between his individual tragedy and the national 'trauma' caused by the mutiny:

> 'when some of our fellows were wounded in India, they came home bringing bullets inside them. They did not talk of them, and they were stout and hearty, and looked as well, perhaps, as you and I; but every change in the weather ... brought back the old agony of their wounds as sharp as ever they had felt it on the battle field. I've had my wound, Bob; I carry the bullet still, and I still carry it to my coffin.' (87)

India becomes a nightmarish place in the reference to the Bibigarh well of Cawnpore, displaced in Braddon's novel in the apparently peaceful country setting of Audley Court. Instead of old medieval castles, the novel relocates the conventions associated with the gothic tradition into a Victorian context haunted by colonial ghosts. This approach to domestic policy seems to be miles away from John Ruskin's depiction of the ideal Victorian house in 'Of Queen's Gardens' (1865) as 'the place of Peace; the shelter, not only from all injury, but from all terror, doubt, and division'.[14] In the following quotation, for instance, the old well in Audley Court is described by Braddon not in bucolic terms but rather in apocalyptic tones that recall the 'historical narrations' of the Cawnpore well:

> A fierce and crimson sunset. The mullioned windows and the twinkling lattices are all ablaze with the red glory ... *even into those recesses of briar and brushwood, amidst which the old well is hidden*, the crimson brightness penetrates in fitful flashes, till the dank weeds *and the rusty iron wheel and broken woodwork seem as if they were freckled with blood.*
> (64, my italics)

This scene is a weird anticipation of Lady Audley's unsuccessful attempt to kill her first husband by pushing him into the old well, and replicates the image of the throwing of the British victims' bodies into the Cawnpore well. Braddon's decision to use the well as a criminal locus is an attempt to connect what was happening in India and in Britain in 1857, as well as a warning about the dangers deriving from violent assertions of independence coming from inside the margins of empire. Nevertheless, *Lady Audley's Secret* confirms and complicates these assumptions. Like Bram Stoker's *Dracula* (1897), it represents another example of what Stephen Arata defines as 'reverse colonization', according to which, in the invasive sexual, cultural and racial other, 'British culture sees its own imperial practice mirrored back in monstrous forms.'[15] Written soon after the Divorce and Matrimonial Causes Act was passed by Parliament (1858) as one of the first attempts to give Victorian women more legal rights, *Lady Audley's Secret* has been considered by feminist scholars like Elaine Showalter as one of the leading novels in the depiction of women's emancipation. However, in the light of the allusions to the Cawnpore well, the implications of *Lady Audley's Secret* seem, on the contrary, to call into question Braddon's 'status as a feminist writer'.[16] The impression is that, somehow, Braddon dramatised a problematic need of governance (both of assertive women and rebellious Indians) which came to the foreground at the dawn of the infamous year of the mutiny. At the same time, despite the presence of a dangerously 'mutinous' wife, the message between the lines of *Lady Audley's Secret* implies counter-interpretations of this text, because Lady Audley remains both a villain and a victim of

Talboys's decision to leave her to starve to death with her baby, and later (after his discovery of her change of identity and bigamous marriage) of his verbal menaces and physical violence. Indeed, the threat to denounce her crimes, along with the marks and 'bruises' (398) Talboys leaves upon the lady's wrist in their quarrel next to the well, will be the last spark leading to Lady Audley's reaction, which is not motivated by intermittent madness – as Braddon tried unconvincingly to explain, in an attempt to prevent negative criticism (which came all the same) – but by her desperation as a legally, politically, sexually and culturally powerless Victorian woman.

Although the Indian mutiny seemed, at least according to many accounts and reports, a rebellion guided by male leaders, some other commentators underlined the role played by the Rani of Jhansi (1828–58), queen of the Maratha-ruled princely state of Jhansi in North India, commonly known in Victorian Britain as 'the Jezebel of India'. After the outburst of the Indian rebellion of 1857, Rani Lakshmi Bai decided to strengthen the defence of Jhansi and assembled a volunteer army of rebels, which included women. When the British attacked Jhansi in March 1858, the Rani, with her faithful warriors, decided to fight back for about two weeks, dying during the battle for Gwalior. According to reports, she wore warrior's clothes and (being an expert horse rider) rode into battle to save Gwalior Fort, about 120 miles west of Lucknow. This woman became, for conflicting reasons, one of the emblems of the Indian war to the point that, in the opinion of Sir Hugh Rose (the British officer responsible for her defeat), the mutiny 'was produced by one man, and that man was a woman'.[17] This perception of India, and of the Indian insurrection, figured as an aggressively assertive woman, represents another facet of Western conceptions of the Orient. Indeed, Indian women were stereotyped both as passive creatures who were victims of 'uncivilised' rituals and traditions such as the *sati*, and as female fiends, witches and bazaar whores. Whereas on the one hand Philip Meadows Taylor's successful *Confessions of a Thug* (1839) paved the way for future representations of Indian superstitions and brutality through its male character Ameer Ali, it suffices to refer to the writings of Edward William Lane, who translated *The Thousand and One Nights* into English from 1838 to 1841, to have an idea of the way Oriental women were depicted in the British press. In *Manners and Customs of the Modern Egyptians* (1836), for instance, Lane represents Oriental women's unrestrained sexuality and trust in barbaric traditions through the use of morbid details, depicting a gothic scene that is on the verge of necrophilia: 'Some women step over the body of a decapitated man several times, without speaking, to become pregnant; and some, with the same desire, dip in the blood a piece of cotton wool, of which they afterwards make use in a manner I must decline mentioning.'[18] Sir Richard Francis Burton, another expert in Oriental and Indian culture who translated *The Book of the Thousand Nights and A Night* (10 vols., 1885–8), and wrote *Sciende, or the Unhappy Valley* (1851), *Sindh, or the Races that Inhabit the Valley of the Hindus* (1851) and *Personal Narrative of a Pilgrimage to Al-Madinah and Meccah* (1855–6), reported that Indian men were prone to laziness and treachery, while Indian women were considered as 'naturally' dangerous.

These pictures of unchecked female sexuality did not simply have a documentary aim but also a more subtle cultural resonance, since they reinforced the patriarchal attempt at controlling and managing improper manifestations of femininity *inside* the geographic and cultural boundaries of Victorian Britain. The contextual references to Eastern culture, along with the example of the warrior queen of Jhansi, are important elements to introduce Braddon's second 'bigamy novel', *Aurora Floyd*, where the allusions to the Indian insurrection, and to the 'Orient' in general, are more pervasive than those included in its famous predecessor. The impression is that, as time passed, Braddon filtered and gave fictional form to her notions of the Orient using more articulate narrative strategies. In *Aurora Floyd* India is a historical, geographical and cultural entity which is constantly evoked and embodied in female shape by the eponymous character. Raised by her father Archibald Floyd, a rich Scottish banker, Aurora Floyd is a passionate young woman whose mother, an actress of unknown origin, died when she was still a child. The novel opens at the peak of the mutiny in late August 1857, with Aurora's return from a Protestant finishing school in France, where she secretly married her father's groom James Conyers. Because of her dark hair and eyes (contrasted to Lady Audley's blonde ringlets) and assertiveness, she attracts her two suitors, namely a proud Captain of her Majesty's 11 Hussars, Talbot Bulstrode (who finally decides to marry the tame and tender-hearted Lucy Floyd, Aurora's cousin), and John Mellish, who succeeds in winning Aurora's heart. Like the Rani of Jhansi, Aurora is a 'fast lady' fond of horses and horse riding, enjoying herself in a hobby often considered by Victorians as a sign of moral lassitude in women.

Along with her name, which suggests an Eastern nature (Aurora was the Roman goddess of dawn) and a potentially corrupting and corruptible nature (the girl's name was chosen by her vain and capricious mother Eliza Prodder), the novel repeatedly associates Aurora with famous Oriental women. In the following excerpt, for instance, Aurora's seductive Eastern beauty – compared in the novel to that of a 'rising sun' – overcomes Lucy Floyd's homely and domestic charms. In this respect, Aurora's traits are not too different from those of an 'Eastern empress' such as the Rani of Jhansi: 'The thick plaits of her black hair made a great diadem upon her low forehead, and crowned her *like an Eastern empress*, an empress with a doubtful nose, it is true, but an empress who reigned by right divine of *her eyes and hair*.'[19] On other occasions, Aurora is compared to immoral and powerful Oriental queens such as Semiramide and Cleopatra by her suitors Mellish and Bulstrode, who wish to 'domesticate' her as if she were a rebellious (female) colonial subject. Nevertheless, their perception of Aurora's nature does not usually correspond to her behaviour. In this way, Braddon suggests a significant dichotomy between male gaze and female reality. Aurora is in fact neither a murderer nor a sexually promiscuous woman but, basically, a very impulsive and spoilt young girl.

The characterisation of Aurora as a (potentially) corrupting Oriental woman is reinforced in the novel in particular by Captain Bulstrode. His experience as an Indian officer often becomes the filter through which he reads and interprets Aurora's nature. In particular, he repeatedly compares Aurora to an intoxicating and alcoholic Indian beverage (called *bang* or *bhang*, a preparation from the leaves and flowers of cannabis that should be smoked), and expresses his fears of being poisoned by her beauty. A typical representative of the colonial officer, Bulstrode finally decides to marry the more yielding Lucy Floyd, epitomising the Victorian feelings of attraction to and repulsion for the Orient, perceived as a source of pleasure and corruption, of sensuality and death:

> A divinity! Imperiously beautiful in white and scarlet, painfully dazzling to look upon, intoxicatingly brilliant to behold. Captain Bulstrode had served in India, and had once tasted a horrible spirit called *bang*, which made the men who drank it half mad; and he could not help fancying that the beauty of this woman was like the strength of that alcoholic preparation; barbarous, intoxicating, dangerous and maddening. (77–8)

In the most sensationally theatrical scene of the novel, set near a stable yard, Aurora Floyd whips Steeve 'The Softy' Hargraves (a servant who was also the murderer of Conyers) after he had kicked her dog Bow-wow. While it is evident that Softy's physical violence towards Bow-wow represents a surrogate expression for his desire to exert violence on Aurora, her whipping epitomises a form of feminine revenge. In a reversal of gothic codes, it is the male villain who is now beaten by a woman. In the meantime Mellish, who is casually witnessing the scene, looks at this 'beautiful fury' with a voyeuristic mixture of horror and attraction:

> Aurora sprang upon him *like a beautiful tigress*, and catching the collar of his fustian jacket in her slight hands, rooted him to the spot upon which he stood. The grasp of those slender hands, convulsed by passion, was not to be easily shaken off ... She disengaged her right hand from his collar, and rained a shower of blows upon his clumsy shoulders with her slender whip ... John Mellish, entering the stable yard by chance at this very moment, *turned white with horror at beholding the beautiful fury*. (193–4, emphasis added)

The comparison of Aurora with a tiger is another indirect reference to her 'Orientalisation'. Indeed, tigers represented for Victorians the quintessential Indian animal and a symbol of India, and were perceived as another expression of what was violent, but also fascinating, in that faraway country. As far as the figurative representation of the Indian mutiny is concerned, many drawings and cartoons of the time convey the clash between British civilisation and Indian brutality by using a recognisable iconography. For instance, *Punch* censored its usually ironical attitudes and decided, on the contrary, to defend British vengeance against native Indian troops in a series of prints by Sir John Tenniel. In *Justice* (published on 12 September 1857), the personified figure of Britannia is about to hit with a sword mutinous Indians (fig. 9.1). The tone of the image is belligerent and the expression of Britannia, figured as a Minerva-like woman warrior, is extremely resolute and firm. Nevertheless, it is in particular in *The British Lion's Vengeance on the Bengal Tiger* (22 August 1857) that the Indian war is described in animal terms. In this cartoon, a lion that embodies England lunges against a tiger (India) that is trying to kill an undefended mother and her baby (fig. 9.2). As these prints demonstrate, the feeling of retribution and the use of violence in order to 'exterminate' the rebellious sepoys occur between and beneath the lines of the British press in figuratively emblematic translations. The fact that in the course of Braddon's novel Aurora is associated with (or compared with) tigers proves the novelist's complex negotiation with the Indian rebellion and with the use of colonial imagery to portray her heroine. Whereas Aurora's uncle Samuel Prodder wishes only 'to see this beautiful tigress in her calmer moods, if she ever had any calmer moods' (459), Bulstrode and Mellish describe Aurora's 'animal' nature in more subtle forms. In the attempt to inspect Steeve Hargraves's waistcoat (to find proofs of his involvement in Conyers's murder), Bulstrode evokes his battles in India and his struggles with tigers as proofs of his masculinity and of his ability to 'tame' Aurora's tiger-like instincts: 'I've been accustomed to deal with refractory Sepoys in India and I've had a struggle with a tiger before now' (544). Talbot identifies with the imperialist who perceives tiger hunting as a literal and symbolical manifestation of the Victorian desire to exert power and to rule over its colonies. According to this view, hunting required all the most 'virile' attributes of the imperial male such as courage, endurance, individualism, sportsmanship and even knowledge of natural history.

On the surface, the ending of *Aurora Floyd* appears a conciliatory one, featuring a domesticated heroine turned from 'tigress' into 'tame' Victorian wife and mother by John Mellish. Nevertheless, a distracted glance at the epilogue does not take into account or give justice to Braddon's recourse to irony, which perhaps resurfaces from the interstices of her seemingly

Fig. 9.1 Sir John Tenniel, *Justice*, *Punch* (12 September 1857).

Fig. 9.2 Sir John Tenniel, *The British Lion's Vengeance on the Bengal Tiger*, *Punch* (22 August 1857).

institutional claims: 'So we leave Aurora, a little changed, a shade less defiantly bright, perhaps, but unspeakably beautiful and tender, bending over the cradle of her first-born' (549). The epilogue conveys a sense of creeping nostalgia for the fact that Aurora is now 'a little changed' and 'a shade less defiantly bright', as though Braddon wanted to suggest that the loss of independence (and of legal identity) in Victorian wives remained a sad price to pay.

The parable of Aurora Floyd recalls not only the ambivalent approaches to Victorian femininity of other sensationalists like Wilkie Collins and Ellen Wood, but also Braddon's personal story. For a writer like her, who will choose to live with her publisher John Maxwell when his wife was still alive (and incarcerated in an Irish asylum) and who will become the mother and stepmother of eleven children (some hers and some from Maxwell's previous marriage), the question of individual freedom was counterbalanced by a firm belief in traditional Victorian familial roles. Braddon's negotiation with colonial questions and with gender issues is another attempt to find a middle ground and an 'in-between space' to articulate 'hybrid' strategies of social renewal. To quote from Homi Bhabha, who writes in a different historical and cultural context from Braddon's but whose ideas find some support in *Lady Audley's Secret* and *Aurora Floyd*, 'these "in-between" spaces provide the terrain for elaborating strategies of selfhood – singular or communal – that initiate new signs of identity, and innovative sites of collaboration, and contestation, in the act of defining the idea of society itself'.[20] In reshaping her notion of Victorian society and of the role of women in a complex alternation of tradition and innovation, Braddon (like Wilkie Collins and other sensationalists) was not depicting her 'struggle with the tiger' in faraway exotic countries but in peaceful British country houses, where the fiercest battles for the survival of the fittest were still taking place.

NOTES

1. Hilda Gregg, 'The Indian Mutiny in Fiction', *Blackwood's Edinburgh Magazine* 7 (1897), 218.
2. Charles Dickens, *The Letters of Charles Dickens*, ed. Madeline House, Graham Storey and Kathleen Tillotson, 12 vols. (Oxford: Clarendon Press, 1995), vol. VIII, 459. Expressions like 'mutiny', 'rebellion', 'uprising' and 'insurrection' will be used interchangeably. Nevertheless, it must be acknowledged that each term alludes to a specific political agenda and cultural attitude. (It is significant that Victorian historians tended to prefer 'mutiny' or 'rebellion', whereas Indian scholars now use 'insurrection' or 'First War of Independence'.)
3. Joseph Conrad, *Heart of Darkness and Other Tales*, ed. Cedric Watts (Oxford University Press, 1998), 208.

4. Robert Knox, *The Races of Men: A Fragment* (Philadelphia: Lea and Blanchard, 1850), 153.

5. *Hansard's Parliamentary Debates. Third Series 147. 20 July 1857–28 August 1857* (London: Thomas Curson Hansard *et al.*, 1857), 475.

6. Quoted in Jenny Sharpe, *Allegories of Empire: The Figure of Woman in the Colonial Text* (Minneapolis and London: University of Minnesota Press, 1993), 66.

7. Christopher Herbert, *War of No Pity: Indian Mutiny and Victorian Trauma* (Princeton and Oxford: Princeton University Press, 2008), 3.

8. Wilkie Collins, 'A Sermon for Sepoys', *Household Words* 414 (1858), 244–7 (244).

9. Wilkie Collins, *Armadale*, ed. Catherine Peters (Oxford University Press, 1999), 73, emphasis added.

10. Robert Lee Wolff, *Sensational Victorian: The Life and Fiction of Mary Elizabeth Braddon* (New York: Garland Publishing, 1979), 203.

11. See Jennifer Carnell, *The Literary Lives of Mary Elizabeth Braddon* (Hastings: The Sensation Press, 2000), 401–6. Braddon's novel *The Story of Barbara* (1880) is dedicated to Major W. S. R. Hodson, one of the most controversial figures of the Indian Mutiny.

12. Mary Elizabeth Braddon, *Lady Audley's Secret*, ed. Natalie M. Houston (Peterborough, ON: Broadview Press, 2003), 107. Further references to this edition will be given in the text.

13. Henry James, 'Miss Braddon', *The Nation* (3 November 1865), 593–5 (595).

14. John Ruskin, *Selected Writings*, ed. Dinah Birch (Oxford University Press, 2004), 158.

15. Stephen Arata, 'The Occidental Tourist: *Dracula* and the Anxiety of Reverse Colonization', *Victorian Studies* 33 (1990), 621–45 (623).

16. Lillian Nayder, 'Rebellious Sepoys and Bigamous Wives: The Indian Mutiny and Marriage Law Reform in *Lady Audley's Secret*', in *Beyond Sensation, Mary Elizabeth Braddon in Context*, ed. Marlene Tromp, Pamela K. Gilbert and Aeron Haynie (New York: State University of New York Press, 2000), 31–42 (32). See also Lillian Nayder, 'The Empire and Sensation', in *A Companion to Sensation Fiction*, ed. Pamela K. Gilbert (Oxford: Blackwell, 2011), 442–54.

17. Sir Hugh Rose, *The Times* (16 October 1885), quoted in Sharpe, *Allegories of Empire*, 75.

18. Edward William Lane, *Manners and Customs of the Modern Egyptians* (London: Charles Night, 1836), 257.

19. Mary Elizabeth Braddon, *Aurora Floyd*, ed. Richard Nemesvari and Lisa Surridge (Peterborough, ON: Broadview Press, 1998), 87, emphasis added. Further references to this edition will be given in the text.

20. Homi K. Bhabha, *The Location of Culture* (London and New York: Routledge, 2004), 2.

10

TARA MACDONALD

Sensation fiction, gender and identity

The heroine of Wilkie Collins's *The Law and the Lady* (1875), Valeria Macallan, is in many ways a typical sensation heroine. She is resilient, independent and determined to get what she wants. What she wants, however, is not to marry rich, hide her bigamous past or inherit a fortune that is rightfully hers, but to prove her husband's innocence. I begin this chapter with an example that emphasises women's complex representation in sensation fiction, and the way that male characters were often secondary to the action of the story, reduced to observing 'high-strung women, full of passion, purpose, and movement'.[1] Valeria is married only a short time before she discovers that her husband was once on trial for the murder of his first wife and that he received the ambiguous verdict 'Not Proven'. Valeria's excessive, selfless devotion to her husband seems to make her the epitome of the good Victorian wife; however, her fidelity is paired with an independent streak, as she determines to prove her husband's innocence despite his protests. When he insists, 'A good wife should know better than to pry into affairs of her husband's', she inwardly retorts, '[h]e was treating me like a child'.[2] Valeria ignores her husband's wishes and stubbornly gathers evidence; in one instance, she goes so far as to permit a hotel chambermaid to improve her appearance so that she can draw information from her husband's friend and well-known flirt, Major Fitz-David. Valeria records:

> [The chambermaid] came back with a box of paints and powders; and I said nothing to check her. I saw, in the glass, my skin take a false fairness, my cheeks a false colour, my eyes a false brightness – and I never shrank from it. No! I let the odious deceit go on; I even admired the extraordinary delicacy and dexterity with which it was all done. (57)

The example of Valeria Macallan gestures to a number of themes characteristic of sensation fiction: false appearances, wilful female characters and cautious men. This chapter will explore these themes, with attention to notions of identity and performance.

After Valeria is transformed, she remarks: 'I seemed in some strange way to have lost my ordinary identity – to have stepped out of my own character' (58). In sensation novels, the ability to 'step out of one's character' is often figured as a particularly feminine act. That is, sensation fiction frequently suggests that women's identities are more fragmented than those of their male counterparts, and that women are more skilled in the art of disguise and performance. Embodying a false identity can reveal possibilities of empowerment for female characters. However, sensation fiction also shows how false female identities are often the result of a desperate need for concealment, a need that lays bare women's precarious social position. The supposed malleability of female identity also affected views of sensational reading. For instance, it was common for Victorian reviewers to conflate sensation heroines with their authors, much to the disadvantage of female novelists. Further, conservative critics often worried that women readers would be unable to separate their own desires from those of sensation heroines: a concern that implied not only a naïve readership but also the uncanny tendency of women to somehow merge with other women, whether fictional or real. This chapter discusses such concerns, as raised by conservative commentators, and considers how sensation authors responded to debates about female (over)identification and reading practices in their novels.

While sensation fiction might be defined, in part, by its aggressive female characters, in contrast, many male characters seem less lively and self-aware. One reviewer complained in 1866 that 'the model husband of modern fiction' was '[a]t best a good-looking, good-tempered, wealthy dolt, who will not even raise a finger to interfere with his wife's crimes if she be criminally disposed'. This, he complained, was 'as unwholesome a type of manhood as could possibly be found towards which to direct the channel of feminine admiration'.[3] There exist many characters that fit such a description of the stagnant, easily duped husband: perhaps the best example is Sir Michael Audley in Mary Elizabeth Braddon's *Lady Audley's Secret* (1862), who marries a very pretty bigamist. Yet in addition to this model, sensation fiction frequently sees its young male characters, like Walter Hartright from Wilkie Collins's *The Woman in White* (1859–60) and Robert Audley from *Lady Audley's Secret*, spring into action. In other words, young male figures in these novels must, in the course of the narrative, step up and become men. This narrative of masculine development sees these characters embodying the proper identity of the professional, driven, middle-class gentleman, but it also places them in a position of surveillance that itself disrupts the notion of the home as the man's place of safety.

Female imposture and performance

Sensation fiction is filled with impostors who don false names, appearances and social positions. Jonathan Loesberg, who has identified a persistent concern with identity and its loss in sensation fiction, claims that the sensation novel locates anxieties about identity via its legal and class aspects rather than any psychological aspect.[4] While class identity may indeed motivate the majority of sensation plots, most novels interrogate a variety of identity categories. Valeria Macallan's notion that a simple change in appearance makes her lose her 'ordinary identity' is striking. It is often, in fact, the disjunction between outward appearance and inward psychology that the sensation novel emphasises as most troubling. The slippage between appearance and reality became such a common trope that in 1863 Henry Mansel claimed that he was 'thrilled with horror' to think that the 'man who shook our hand with a hearty English grasp half an hour ago – the woman whose beauty and grace were the charm of last night ... how exciting to think that under these pleasing outsides may be concealed some demon in human shape, a Count Fosco or a Lady Audley!'[5] In contrast, Margaret Oliphant, an author critical of the sensation genre, questioned the assumption that 'a stratum of secret vice underlies the outward seeming of society'. Her neighbours, she writes, 'are very good sort of people, and we believe unfeignedly that our neighbour's neighbours resemble our own'.[6] Yet it was the very difficulty of knowing one's neighbours that the sensation novel relied upon and exploited. Further, the revelation that a 'demon in human shape' might lie behind a respectable disguise had very different implications for men and women. The portrayal of female imposture was seemingly more threatening as it exposed the ideal of the 'good Victorian wife' as a façade and women's hidden desires as very real.

The sensation novel frequently details how women's familiarity with elaborate clothing and cosmetics make them naturally gifted in the act of imposture. In *Lady Audley's Secret*, Lucy Audley tells her maid, Phoebe, 'you *are* like me ... Why, with a bottle of hair-dye, such as we see advertised in the papers, and a pot of rouge, you'd be as good-looking as I, any day.'[7] In another servant–mistress switch, Magdalen Vanstone from Collins's *No Name* (1862) asks her maid to dress up like a lady, while she poses as a servant; she reassures her maid that a lady is simply 'a woman who wears a silk gown, and has a sense of her own importance'.[8] And Valeria's transformation in *The Law and the Lady*, despite the overtones of prostitution inherent in her 'false colour' and 'false brightness', allows her to charm Major Fitz-David and to uncover her first important piece of evidence. While Lucy Audley's masquerade as the perfect Victorian wife is threatening,

Valeria's is admittedly less so, and she reveals the way in which Victorian women constantly falsified their appearances, whether for sensational purposes or for everyday interactions. While the scene I began this chapter by quoting registers the ambiguity of Valeria's transformation – the chambermaid who helps her is like a witch, whose 'wicked forefinger' points to the glass when she is finished – Valeria comes to value cosmetic improvements throughout the novel. As the chambermaid claims, 'Ah, what a thing pearl powder is, when one knows how to use it!' (57).

Although the benefits of cosmetic enhancements are somewhat innocuous in Valeria's case, this is only one example of *The Law and the Lady*'s larger engagement with female masquerade. The novel exposes the manner in which Victorian femininity itself is a performance. Sara Macallan, Eustace's first wife, died of arsenic poisoning. During the trial, the prosecution argues that Eustace gave Sara the poison in her tea, while the defence – correctly – argues that Sara overdosed on arsenic herself. Arsenic was sometimes used in the Victorian period to improve women's skin and Sara is known to have had 'defects in her complexion' (169). However, the very secrecy of women's enhancements makes it difficult to prove the defence's case, as even Eustace is unable to attest to Sara's use of the poison. The entire trial thus turns on women's falseness:

> Does my learned friend actually suppose, that women are in the habit of mentioning the secret artifices and applications by which they improve their personal appearance? Is it in his experience of the sex, that a woman who is eagerly bent on making herself attractive to a man, would tell that man, or tell anybody else who might communicate with him, that the charm by which she hoped to win his heart – say the charm of a pretty complexion – had been artificially acquired by the use of a deadly poison? The bare idea of such a thing is absurd   From first to last, poor creature, she kept her secret; just as she would have kept her secret, if she had worn false hair, or if she had been indebted to the dentist for her teeth. And there you see her husband, in peril of his life, because a woman acted *like* a woman.   (180–1)

The defence thus argues that falseness and secrecy are embedded in normative female behaviour. Sensation novelists relied upon cultural anxieties surrounding the permeability of class distinctions and women's changing social roles in order to create threatening examples of false, upwardly mobile impostors like Lucy Audley and Lydia Gwilt from Collins's *Armadale* (1866); nonetheless, many novels also expose, with varying degrees of sympathy, the masquerade that women are encouraged to embrace each day.

This more nuanced notion of masquerade exposes the need for women to constantly perform their identities, often under strained circumstances. For instance, in Braddon's *John Marchmont's Legacy* (1863), the cold Olivia Arundel, a latter-day Edith Dombey, marries the dull John Marchmont in order to escape her monotonous life as a rector's daughter. 'O my God!' she exclaims early in the novel, 'is the lot of other women never to be mine? Am I never to be loved and admired; never to be sought and chosen? Is my life to be all of one dull, grey, colourless monotony [?].'[9] Olivia never reveals her desires publicly; to those around her, she appears 'grave, reserved, dignified' (83). Braddon emphasises that Olivia, despite her unhappiness with her social limitations, is 'patiently employed in the strict performance of her duty' (83). It is a performance that she insists in enacting but it is one that is exhausting and debilitating. After her husband's early death, Olivia remains under male control. She becomes the puppet of Paul Marchmont, a man whose own acts of imposture are characterised by the narrator as 'diabolical artifice' (291). Under Paul's influence, and encouraged by her self-inflicted performance of duty, Olivia becomes 'a human automaton' who is left 'malleable to his skilful hands' (397, 405). Though Braddon offers some sympathy for this character, the narrative consistently presents authenticity and candidness as desirable qualities for both men and women, and so Olivia's behaviour, despite her vulnerability, emerges as anti-social. The example of Olivia reveals that the performance of femininity has its limitations. While Valeria's performance is exciting and allows her to influence others, Olivia's performance necessitates a painful suppression of feelings and desires.

Despite her resistance to sensational narratives, Margaret Oliphant wrote a sensation novel, *Salem Chapel* (1863), which details a similarly pained performance of femininity. Rachel Hilyard (actually Rachel Mildmay) lives in hiding from her abusive husband and under an assumed name. Midway through the novel, she shoots, and nearly murders, her husband. When describing her mysterious past to her minister, Arthur Vincent, Rachel gestures to the way in which she has reinvented herself: 'Some people die two or three times in a lifetime, Mr. Vincent. There is a real transmigration of souls, of bodies, or both if you please. This is my third life I am going through at present.'[10] Rachel does not don a dramatic disguise for her 'third life', but simply performs the part of the reserved, quiet and respectable woman. She is largely secluded in her home and her disguise, if it may be called that, is invisibility. In crafting Rachel, Oliphant seems to have drawn on Collins's depiction of the spectre-like Anne Catherick in *The Woman in White*, who is 'a thin, dark, eager shadow'.[11] While Rachel's existence makes Vincent feel 'how insignificant are the circumstances of life', Rachel's sister-in-law, Lady Western, responds, 'I think, when I see her, oh, how important [circumstances] are! and that I'd rather die than live so' (64). Rachel thus warns Lady Western of the precariousness of women's circumstances and she stands as a reminder of women's social vulnerability.

This, too, is a theme prevalent in Collins's *The Woman in White*. In a highly sensational example of 'the transmigration of souls, of bodies', Laura Glyde's money-hungry husband switches her with the deceased Anne Catherick, a woman who looks suspiciously like Laura. In an argument that would also be applicable for Olivia or Rachel, Tamar Heller argues that Anne 'embodies the social invisibility that renders women blank pages to be inscribed by men'.[12] Yet many sensation heroines inscribe these 'blank pages' themselves. The sensation novel thus details how acts of imposture can be empowering performances of self-creation on the one hand, and acts of violent erasure on the other. These performances suggest a complex and sometimes contradictory understanding of what it means to enact womanhood.

Sensational reading and overidentification

Sensation fiction's transgressive female characters not only registered contemporary anxieties about what it meant to be a woman, they also prompted debates about the relationship between fictional characters and real women. Frequently, conservative reviewers worried about how naïve female readers would respond to the world around them after reading sensation fiction. One reviewer insisted that husbands and fathers should 'scrutinize the parcel that arrives from Mudie's' since 'young ladies are led to contrast the actual with the ideal we see worked out in popular romance'.[13] Francis Paget, in the afterword to his satirical sensation novel, *Lucretia* (1868), expressed unease about the 'kind of follies, scrapes, and difficulties' into which a girl might fall 'who should take the sensational novel as her guide in the common-place events of everyday life'.[14] These writers express concerns that young women reading sensation fiction would become dissatisfied with the commonplace world around them and that they would be unable to distinguish between fiction and reality. The sensation novel thus risked carrying its female readers away: they not only read of worlds curiously like their own, they somehow inhabited these texts. Implied in such anxieties about sensational reading was the notion that women readers would in fact *become* the characters they read about.

The discourse surrounding the sensation novel thus took for granted an uncanny ability for women to merge with other women. Margaret Oliphant remarked that in these novels an 'eagerness of physical sensation ... is represented as the natural sentiment of English girls, and is offered to them ... as the portrait of their own state of mind'.[15] What Oliphant describes is more than the experience of feeling sympathy for a character; instead, the notion that a woman could locate her 'own state of mind' in the mind of the sensation heroine, that she could read of others' experiences as though they were her own, suggests a process of overidentification. Overidentification and overinvolvement are terms used by film theorists to describe women's traditional relationship to film in Western culture, which is marked by passivity and proximity, rather than distance. The female viewer, more than the male, was thought to give in to the fascinations of the cinematic image, to view the cinematic spectacle with a pleasure that was somehow more intense. As Mary Ann Doane describes, 'there is a certain naïveté attached to women in relation to systems of signification – a tendency to deny the processes of representation, to collapse the opposition between the sign (the image) and the real'.[16] This process is comparable to how women supposedly related to sensation fiction; yet with both twentieth-century cinema and the Victorian sensation novel, the notion of female naïveté and overidentification was not taken for granted by all cultural commentators. In fact, the ability for women to merge with other women was detailed, and problematised, in sensation novels themselves.

The earliest sensation novels exploited this trope: again, *Lady Audley's Secret* relies on the physical similarities between Lucy Audley and her maid, and in *The Woman in White*, Laura Glyde looks so much like Anne Catherick that Sir Percival and Count Fosco can successfully place her in an asylum as Anne. Laura, wearing Anne's clothing and marked with Anne's name, almost becomes Anne. The nurse in the asylum tells her, 'Look at your own name on your own clothes, and don't worry us all any more about being Lady Glyde. She's dead and buried' (436). Anne and Laura seem to meld into a single body: Walter finds that the 'outward changes wrought by the suffering and the terror of the past had fearfully, almost hopelessly, strengthened the fatal resemblance between Anne Catherick and [Laura]' (442). While Laura's experience in the asylum is terrifying, Anne's falsified death is an even more violent act undertaken by the novel's male characters. Anne is simply a placeholder for Laura's body and identity as her name is covered by Laura's even in the moment of her death. Though the novel devotes more attention to the recovery of Laura's identity, it also reveals how the social and psychological identities of these two women are both so fragile that they merge strangely into one being. This process of overidentification is not marked as liberating but as violent and frightening.

Many novels explicitly comment on women's reading practices and the process of identification. Perhaps the most overt engagement with women's sensational reading is Mary Elizabeth Braddon's *The Doctor's Wife* (1864), a rewriting of Gustave Flaubert's *Madame Bovary* (1857). The novel was an attempt by Braddon to move away from popular sensational fare to something more literary; yet, in doing so, she critiques the sensation novel and sensational reading extensively and the novel is, perhaps ironically, her most sustained commentary on the genre and its effects on women readers. At the centre of the novel is Isabel Gilbert, the novel-hungry, daydreaming heroine who regrettably marries a commonplace country doctor, a man utterly unsuited to her romantic tastes. Isabel 'wanted her life to be like her books; she wanted to be a heroine, – unhappy perhaps, and dying early. She had an especial desire to die early, by consumption, with a hectic flush and unnatural luster in her eyes.'[17] She imagines herself to be a heroine from the novels of Dickens or the Brontës, such as Edith Dombey or Jane Eyre: 'Oh, to have been Jane Eyre, and to roam away on the cold moorland and starve, – wouldn't *that* have been delicious!' (98). Isabel is thus the embodiment of the kind of woman that many critics worried about: she is carried away by her books, and feels the ordinariness of the real world to be unsatisfying and dull compared to her fictional world. Further, the girl's masochistic, suicidal tendencies betray her fantasies as dangerous, rather than simply light-hearted, romantic desires. Braddon plays with Isabel's expectations, as well as those of the reader, by not allowing her heroine a romantic early death, but instead permitting her to live a long, commonplace life, as the men around her die dramatically. Isabel ends the novel, transformed from 'a sentimental girl into a good and noble woman', and, after a botched affair and the death of her husband, she learns valuable lessons about reading and fantasy (402–3).

Amelia B. Edwards is another sensation novelist who focused on the position of the female reader of sensation fiction; in novels such as *Hand and Glove* (1858) and *Barbara's History* (1864), she shows that reading passionately and uncritically can be damaging, especially for inexperienced female readers. An early sensation novel, *Hand and Glove*, details how Marguerite Delahaye's fascination with her town's new minister, Xavier Hamel, causes her to turn to fictional models that are misleading. Like Isabel Gilbert, who imagines her lover Lansdell to be 'the hero of a story-book' (214), Marguerite sees Hamel as 'a hero of romance'.[18] Furthermore, Edwards links the seductive Hamel to seductive reading. While Marguerite's English companion encourages her to read novels by Dickens, Maria Edgeworth and Walter Scott, Hamel offers Marguerite 'the early productions of George Sand'. This, the narrator claims, is 'a class of literature which, however admirable in its way, deals too largely with feeling to be quite healthy reading for the inexperienced and the young' (112). Further, Hamel urges Marguerite to surrender herself to the world of the novel, insisting, 'the author should hold you captive, and the people of his book should become your own familiar friends. A novel is then an ideal world, which, while it lasts, seems no less real than our own' (107). Yet, as in *The Doctor's Wife*, such submissive reading has its risks. Edwards thus links dangerous men and dangerous books, emphasising the similar feelings that both could evoke, and she encourages her reader to maintain the critical distance that Marguerite seems incapable of maintaining herself.

She continues to disapprove of women's overidentification in her most popular novel, *Barbara's History* (1864), by juxtaposing the affective, fantasy-prone heroine with her more pragmatic aunt, who chides her for following sensational scripts. The young heroine, Barbara, leaves her husband suddenly when she thinks he is a bigamist. She escapes to the Continent with her maid, takes on an assumed name and gives birth to a child, presumably out of wedlock. Yet, months later, Barbara and the reader learn that her husband was not in fact previously married. Her aunt, who discovers her in Italy, chastises Barbara, telling her, 'you acted like a fool, and ran away. I dare say you thought it very fine, and heroic, and dramatic, and all that sort of thing. Nobody else did.'[19] Aunt Shandyshaft's humour deflates the sensational scenario and Edwards shows the dangers in allowing sensational scripts to dictate real life circumstances, especially for vulnerable women.

Sensation novels, then, do not deny the possibility of women identifying with sensational characters. Yet many writers, like Braddon and Edwards, urge their female readers to abandon naïve and uncritical reading practices. Abandoning oneself to the world of the novel comes dangerously close to losing one's identity in the manner of Anne Catherick or Laura Glyde. Laura's realisation that she is in Anne's clothing and covered with Anne's name may be regarded as a model for dangerous reading practices, in which the female reader is consumed by the story. In turn, a positive model of female imposture, where women may, like Valeria, 'step out of their own character', but be able to step back in, may offer a positive model of controlled female readership.

Masculinity and the villain-finder

While female sensation characters were donning disguises, escaping from asylums and running off to the Continent, what, we might ask, occupied the male characters of these novels? Just as female figures in sensation fiction are often opposing types – the wicked sensation heroine versus the innocent, wronged woman – male characters, too, were often opposites. On the one hand sits the easily duped husband, who is unaware of his wife's evil behaviour. George Gilbert, the commonplace country doctor who marries Isabel, the would-be consumptive in *The Doctor's Wife*, is a typical example of this figure. Isabel wants to marry a man like Henry Esmond or James Steerforth, but instead George is 'the very incarnation of homely, healthy comeliness, the archetype of honest youth and simple English manhood' (64). Furthermore, he is completely oblivious to her desire for Roland Lansdell. The gullible husband had become such a common trope that, by 1869, Florence Wilford, in her novel *Nigel Bartram's Ideal*, could have one of her characters position himself against this model. The titular character, Nigel, insists to his wife, 'I am not the model husband of a sensation novel, a poor blind tool in the hands of less scrupulous people.'[20]

On the other hand, and in contrast to this static figure, is the sensation villain, who may attempt to seduce, imprison or rob the sensation heroine. This figure is perhaps best represented by the captivating Count Fosco from Collins's *The Woman in White*, who conspires, with Sir Percival Glyde, to steal Laura's inheritance. Many of Collins's disreputable men are intriguingly complex figures who push the boundaries of appropriate masculinity, such as the half-man, half-machine that is Miserrimus Dexter in *The Law and the Lady* and Laura Fairlie's selfish and disengaged uncle, Mr Fairlie, who claims to be 'nothing but a bundle of nerves dressed up to look like a man'.[21] These melodramatic men are sensation versions of the gothic villain who imprisons his victim in remote a European castle and takes advantage of her naïveté and vulnerability.

Yet perhaps the most significant development in male characterisation in the sensation genre is a third type: the amateur detective. In *Lady Audley's Secret*, Robert Audley disrupts his leisured existence to right the wrongs done to Sir Michael Audley and George Talboys, and, no less significantly, to commit Lucy Audley to an insane asylum. In another well-known example, from *The Woman in White*, Walter Hartright must support his wife Laura and her sister Marian with his artwork, while attempting to help Laura reclaim her identity and inheritance. E. S. Dallas claimed that sensation fiction was structured around the dynamic between the 'villain and a villain-finder': 'The villain is the hero, and the villain-finder is set like a sleuth hound on his path.'[22] The narratives of these 'villain-finders' amount to more than simply an interplay between villain and sleuth, however: they are narratives of manhood and professionalisation. Robert and Walter's stories end with them married to suitable heroines and employed in professions that allow them to support their wives and families. Their adoption of the role of the detective is the first step in this narrative of masculine progression. Playing detective, then, offers these characters tools that are vital to personal and professional fulfilment.

Like the female impostor or double, the male detective has a complex relationship to notions of identity. These characters are positioned in opposition to sensation villains, who are typically characters whose hidden past or previous identity needs to be unearthed. They are thus excavators of identity: they are also the figures who decide what constitutes a 'true' identity or a performance. Dallas suggests that the 'acuteness of the villain-finder is preternatural. He sees a hand you cannot see, he hears a voice you cannot hear.'[23] These figures are watchers – they are attuned, in particular, to the feminine art of masquerade. The amateur detective often sits in contrast to the outmoded style of masculinity typified by the gullible, unknowing husband; the sensation hero, the husband of the future, these novels imply, must be watchful, self-aware and attuned to the demands and desires of women.

The hero of Ellen Wood's *St Martin's Eve* (1866) is a latter-day Robert Audley. Frederick St John is watchful of the woman, Charlotte Carleton, who hopes to marry his half-brother, and he is instrumental in committing her to an asylum. Although a reviewer of the novel claimed that '[n]o amateur detective or briefless barrister is set in motion to trace out [Charlotte's] crime and bring her to justice', Frederick is the epitome of the amateur detective.[24] Early in the novel, Charlotte marries Frederick's cousin George and she is later responsible for the death of her stepson, Benja, who dramatically burns to death. In addition to murder, Charlotte's social crimes are manifold: she does not love her stepson as she does her own son; she is passionate, angry and thus unwomanly; and, after the death of her husband and both of her children, she hopes to marry Isaac St John, Frederick's brother and the recipient of George's fortune. Even without knowing her murderous tendencies, Frederick senses that Charlotte is mad and he hopes to keep her from his family's money. Frederick begins the novel as an idle man without real aim or occupation. In fact, the reader is first introduced to him when he is arrested for unpaid debts and reprimanded by his more responsible brother. Frederick's role as detective thus changes the course of his future as it not only offers him a useful pastime, but allows him to protect his brother's – and his own – personal happiness and financial stability.

When Charlotte enters their home as a guest, Frederick watches her closely: 'As to Frederick, he was apparently leading a very idle life: but in point of fact he was silently busy as ever was a London detective. He was watching Mrs. Carleton. He had been watching her closely, not seeming to do it ... now three weeks ago, or more, and he persuaded himself that he detected signs of incipient madness.' Frederick seems to possess the preternatural abilities that E. S. Dallas finds characteristic of the amateur detective, as he is the only character who can see how much Charlotte hates her romantic rival, Georgina Beauclerc. He sees the wild look that Charlotte gives Georgina when she passes by, and the narrator notes, 'it all passed in a moment and was imperceptible to general, unsuspicious observation: but Frederick was *watching*'.[25] His watching comes with recompense: Charlotte is finally locked away in a mental institution and Frederick will one day inherit his brother's money and estate. He uncovers the supposed madness lying under Charlotte's respectable façade and is rewarded with a happy marriage and a hopeful future. Yet Wood, despite her reputation as a conservative sensationalist, leaves the reader feeling somewhat uneasy about her hero's motives and motivations. In a review of Wood's earlier *East Lynne* (1861), Margaret Oliphant remarked that it is the adulterous heroine, Isabel Carlyle, 'alone in whom the reader feels any interest', rather than the innocent Barbara Hare.[26] Again, in *St Martin's Eve*, reviewers remarked with surprise that Wood sympathised with her immoral heroine: 'Mrs Wood stands by her heroine ... she speaks of her in terms of pity, and even modified approval.'[27] While the reader is encouraged to delight in the happy ending afforded to Frederick and the other characters, the narrator's sympathy for Charlotte seems a blemish on an otherwise happy ending. This ambiguity also suggests that the line between the amateur detective and the sensational villain, both of whom dictate the futures of the female characters and protect their own interests in doing so, may be rather thin.

Margaret Oliphant's *Salem Chapel* documents male watching and detection with a similar ambiguity. In this instance, it is the hero himself who questions what he has learned and gained through his detection. With Arthur Vincent, Oliphant complicates the easy progression from amateur detective to productive, happy member of society. Arthur arrives in the quiet town of Carlingford as the new dissenting minister and his sensational detection gets in the way of his sacred duties. Initially, he embodies fully the role of sensation sleuth: he rushes off to despatch telegraphs and races around the country on trains. Yet his detection does not pause on 'the day of rest' during which he is 'rushing wildly along distant railways' (236). Sensational watching thus interrupts Arthur's carefully planned existence:

> To think that this day, with all its strange encounters and unexpected incidents, was Sunday, as he suddenly remembered it to be – that this morning he had preached, and this evening had to preach again, completed in Vincent's mind the utter chaos and disturbance of ordinary life. It struck him dumb to remember that by-and-by he must again ascend the pulpit, and go through all his duties. Was he an imposter, doing all this mechanically? (331)

Arthur's encounters with female and male impostors – Rachel Mildmay, posing as Rachel Hilyard, and her husband, Colonel Mildmay, posing as Herbert Fordham – lead him into a world of confusion and chaos. Ordinary life is no longer understandable or without disturbance, and Arthur, the young idealistic minister, even questions whether *he* is in fact an impostor. Though Arthur, like most villain-finders, ends the novel happily, poised to marry Rachel's daughter, his sensational detection disturbs his tranquil world. He leaves the ministry and the novel's happy conclusion cannot entirely clear away the sense of 'the utter chaos and disturbance of ordinary life'. While detection does indeed make a man of Arthur, robbing him of his naïveté and innocence, in this case, it comes at a cost.

With its emphasis on gender identity and performance, the sensation novel thus exposes contemporary gender norms, as well as the machinations and expectations of the Victorian novel. Narratives of personal and professional progress, even those of the villain-finder, are put into question because they are mimed so convincingly by villains and impostors. The impostors with whom Arthur is thrown into contact destabilise his former sense of the world, leaving him to ask, 'which was the criminal? which was the innocent?' He is thrown into a 'wild confusion of sin and sorrow, of dreadful human complications, [and] misconceptions' (305). The sensation novel's playful engagement with human complications and misconceptions, however, made it an ideal form in which to disrupt gender conventions and challenge stable notions of identity. While women's seeming predilection for imposture leads to innovative representations of female desire and identity formation, the need for male watchfulness, even in the family home, gestures to fissures in masculinity and domestic security.

NOTES

1. E. S. Dallas, review of *Lady Audley's Secret*, *The Times* (18 November 1862), 4.
2. Wilkie Collins, *The Law and the Lady*, ed. Jenny Bourne Taylor (Oxford University Press, 1992), 54. Further references to this edition will be given in the text.
3. Unsigned, 'Novels Past and Present', *Saturday Review* (14 April 1866), 439.
4. Jonathan Loesberg, 'The Ideology of Narrative Form in Sensation Fiction', *Representations* 13 (1986), 115–38 (117).
5. Mansel, 489.
6. ON, 259–60.
7. Mary Elizabeth Braddon, *Lady Audley's Secret*, ed. David Skilton (Oxford University Press, 2008), 58.
8. Wilkie Collins, *No Name*, ed. Mark Ford (London: Penguin, 1994), 503.
9. Mary Elizabeth Braddon, *John Marchmont's Legacy*, ed. Norman Page and Tori Saski (Oxford University Press, 1999), 68–9. Further references to this edition will be given in the text.
10. Margaret Oliphant, *Salem Chapel* (New York: Virago Press, 1986), 93. Further references to this edition will be given in the text.
11. Wilkie Collins, *The Woman in White*, ed. John Sutherland (Oxford University Press, 1996), 11. Further references to this edition will be given in the text.
12. Tamar Heller, *Dead Secrets: Wilkie Collins and the Female Gothic* (New Haven, CT: Yale University Press, 1992), 112.
13. Unsigned, 'Art VII', *Christian Remembrancer* 46 (1863), 208–36 (234).
14. Francis Paget, 'Afterword', *Lucretia; or, The Heroine of the Nineteenth Century* (London: John Masters, 1868), 308.
15. ON, 259.

16. Mary Ann Doane, *The Desire to Desire: The Woman's Film of the 1940s* (Bloomington: Indiana University Press, 1987), 1.
17. Mary Elizabeth Braddon, *The Doctor's Wife*, ed. Lyn Pykett (Oxford University Press, 1998), 28. Further references to this edition will be given in the text.
18. Amelia B. Edwards, *Hand and Glove* (Ontario: Rubicon, 2000), 123. Further references to this edition will be given in the text.
19. Amelia B. Edwards, *Barbara's History* (Ontario: Rubicon, 2000), 448.
20. Florence Wilford, *Nigel Bartram's Ideal* (London: Wells, nd), 208.
21. Collins, *The Woman in White*, 356.
22. Dallas, review of *Lady Audley's Secret*, 4.
23. *Ibid.*
24. Unsigned review of Ellen Wood, *St Martin's Eve*, *Saturday Review* (31 March 1866), 387.
25. Ellen Wood, *St Martin's Eve*, ed. Lyn Pykett, in *Varieties of Women's Sensation Fiction: 1855–1890*, ed. Andrew Maunder, 6 vols. (London: Pickering and Chatto, 2004), vol. III, 357.
26. OSN, 567.
27. Unsigned review of Ellen Wood, *St Martins' Eve*, 387.

11

TATIANA KONTOU

Sensation fiction, spiritualism and the supernatural

Henry James commented in his 1865 review of Mary Elizabeth Braddon's novels that part of the novelty of sensation fiction was the contemporary, domestic setting of the novels and accredited Wilkie Collins with single-handedly modernising thrilling tales by

> having introduced into fiction those most mysterious of mysteries, the mysteries which are at our own doors ... Instead of the terrors of Udolpho, we were treated to the terrors of the cheerful country house and busy London lodgings. And there is no doubt that these were infinitely the more terrible. Mrs Radcliffe's mysteries were romances pure and simple; while those of Mr Wilkie Collins were stern reality. ... Modern England – the England of to-day's newspaper – crops up at every step.[1]

James perceives the gothic as obsolete, outmoded by the new sensation novels which engage their readers' interest and spur their imagination by substituting castles and faraway places with contemporary landscapes and modern settings. Mrs Radcliffe's employment of the supernatural is, according to James, not an altogether unproblematic narrative device. It might titillate her readers but the supernatural has to be neatly and naturally explained. For James, who wrote one of the most chilling ghost stories of the *fin de siècle*, only a well-wrought imaginative faculty could rise to the challenge of introducing supernatural elements without having to prosaically de-mystify them in the finale. Instead, James argues, Collins and Braddon need not stretch their imaginative faculties as they find creative stimuli in the everyday, drawing material from modern England, from newspaper reports and from their fellow humans. Ghosts might be terrible but so is human nature, and readers, James opines, can forge emotional connections to the country house but not the Apennines. The 'stern reality' is a powerful substitute for the romance plots of yesteryear.

Sensation novelists exchanged medieval castles for well-appointed London apartments and the maidens of yore for heroines who use the telegraph and travel by train, but did not outstrip their narratives from supernatural motifs. Most sensation novelists, such as Collins, Braddon, Ellen Wood, Rhoda Broughton and Florence Marryat, also contributed ghost stories to periodicals, a fact that bears testament not only to supernatural fiction's continuing popularity but also to the affinities between sensational and supernatural tales, as the readers of sensation novels did not find the transition from sensation to ghost story in any way forced. In addition, the emergence and widespread practice of spiritualism in the second half of the nineteenth century introduced a new way of thinking about ghostly and supernatural occurrences, as convinced spiritualists and sceptical scientists engaged in experiments aimed at providing natural explanations for seemingly supernatural phenomena. Although Henry James delineates sensation fiction's digression from its gothic predecessor, sensation did not become a substitute for ghostly and supernatural tales; instead, sensation novelists veined their novels with elements that veered towards the ghostly and the supernatural. In this chapter I will examine how, rather than being strange bedfellows, the supernatural and spiritualism offered new venues of expression for sensation novelists.

Spirits, Swedenborg and Sheridan Le Fanu

Modern spiritualism, the belief that the living can systematically communicate with the spirits of the departed, has a specific date of origin: 31 March 1848. This was when Margaret Fox and Kate Fox, two adolescent sisters from Hydesville, New York, claimed to have established contact with the spirit of a murdered pedlar in their family home. The sisters, in the presence of their mother, snapped their fingers and called on an invisible spirit to repeat the sounds. Soon they were asking questions and received answers through proto-telegraphic 'rappings'. The reputation of the girls soared and table-rapping was accepted as a manifestation of the existence of spirits. Later the Fox sisters were accused of being responsible for the raps by snapping their toe-joints; nevertheless, spiritualism had been consistently spreading in the States and across the Atlantic.

Fashionable and amusing for sceptics, awe-inspiring and proof of life after death for converts, spiritualism gripped the cultural imagination and pervaded both the literary and scientific circles.[2] Mesmerism, phrenology, physiognomy and developments in evolutionary biology, all of which had challenged religious faith in varying degrees, created a fertile ground for the development and popularity of spiritualism. There was no single, unified spiritualist movement as spiritualists drew on different aspects of utopianism, socialism, vegetarianism, Christianity and Buddhism to formulate their theories of the afterlife, while also adapting the vocabulary of evolution and often using the most advanced technological devices such as photographic cameras and typewriters to communicate with the discarnate spirits. Over the last fifty years of the nineteenth century, spiritualist phenomena included full-body materialisations, for which the medium would withdraw into a cabinet, fall into a trance and produce a materialised spirit, automatic writing and direct voice phenomena (writing and speaking through a medium). Manifestations varied, with physical materialisation being the most popular in the late 1860s and early 1870s and with more mental, psychological aspects of communication taking precedence in the 1880s, partly due to the Society for Psychical Research's (founded in 1882) extensive investigations and discredit of physical mediumship.

Some spiritualists embraced the philosophical writings of Emanuel Swedenborg (1688–1772), who claimed that a person's actions and spiritual awareness, while on earth, would determine which of the spheres he or she would reside once passing over to the next world. There were seven spheres, according to Swedenborg, which represented the various levels of light and happiness that each person was fitted to reside. He also believed that guardian spirits and angels would assist the dying to make the transition to the other side and claimed to have communicated with the spirits of the departed. For sensation authors, Swedenborg, séances and mediums offered tropes for exploring what James called the mysteries at 'our own doors'. Households in Britain were experimenting with spirit communication and the practice pervaded both the parlour and the drawing-room, bringing the mysteries of death and the other world within the domestic sphere. The Irish author Sheridan Le Fanu (1814–73) used references to Swedenborg and clairvoyance in his 1864 novel *Uncle Silas*, whose eponymous hero tries to murder his orphaned niece, Maud Ruthyn, and inherit her fortune.

Wilkie Collins's *The Woman in White* (1860), Mrs Henry Wood's *East Lynne* (1861) and M. E. Braddon's *Lady Audley's Secret* (1862) had set the tone for the sensation novel deploying the *Doppelgänger* to explore the shortcomings of the legislation system in relation to women's property, divorce and bigamy. Gothic tropes threw into relief social concerns and taboos. Sensation was peaking, attracting a varied readership as well as the contempt of the critics. Le Fanu was anxious to position his novel as a direct descendant of the 'tragic English romance' shaped by Sir Walter Scott and did not wish to be associated with the 'degrading term' of 'sensation fiction'.[3] However, the innocent young heiress, the satanic uncle, the ferocious governess, the attempted murder, even the references to spirits, were characteristics all too readily identified as hallmarks of sensation fiction; the novel contradicted the author's romance intentions by becoming one of his most popular sensation tales.

Uncle Silas is narrated by Maud Ruthyn, who relays her journey from innocence to experience; it is a study in *Bildungsroman* where the young heroine evolves from youthful, passive girlhood to maturity, and the many references to Swedenborg and spirits seem all too natural when the reader considers Maud's upbringing. Maud's father had left the Church of England and later converted to Swedenborgianism, yet Maud is not brought up according to her father's new faith but feels that alongside these 'hazy notions of these sectaries [Swedenborgianism] there was mingled a suspicion of necromancy, and a weird freemasonry, that inspired something of awe and antipathy' (11). Maud's own narrative hints that the antipathy and awe have morphed into a repository of ghostly imagery through which Maud will relate the story of how her uncle tried to poison her. The supernatural is introduced early on in the novel as Maud reminisces on an episode of clairvoyance shortly after the death of her mother. One of her father's friends and fellow Swedenborgian takes young Maud for a walk, and through his powers of second sight describes a cottage and children playing shortly before they see it with their own eyes. The man goes on to explain to Maud that just as she was not able to see the cottage and the children from a distance as she was far away and does not have the gift of second sight, she is unable to see, equally, that her mother is in a 'beautiful landscape, radiant with wondrous light, in which, rejoicing, my mother moved along an airy path' (23). Whether this story is offered as consolation to a mourning child or whether it is truly believed is unclear; Maud's descriptions of herself as 'sensitive and melancholy' (9), as once having been a 'nervous child' (27), make the presence of the supernatural more an interplay between her experiences and her imagination.

The interstice between reality and illusion is filled with spirits and ghosts for Maud. Soon after the clairvoyance episode she remembers her governess, Madame de la Rougierre, who had been dismissed by her father for mistreating Maud and is then employed by Silas to assist him in his plans. Maud's description of the first encounter with Madame de la Rougierre oscillates between the natural and the ghostly: 'On a sudden, on the grass before me, stood an odd figure – a very tall woman in grey draperies, nearly white under the moon, curtseying extraordinarily low and rather fantastically' (24). Maud later calls her 'an apparition' and uses the verb 'haunted' to describe Madame's presence in Maud's life. Madame de la Rougierre's name implies nature: blood, and artificiality: rouge. The grey clothes that she insists on wearing are a foil in a sense for her name, that is charged with life, death and deceit. She becomes a spectral presence not only because of her strange appearance but because she will manipulate Maud's fate so much as to be characterised by the latter as 'a shadowy Atropos' (426), the most ugly and ruthless of the Fates.

Like the gothic heroines of old, Maud also seems passive, unable to challenge her destiny. Interpreting a dream of her late father as his wish for her to reside with her Uncle Silas, she decides to live with him despite her relatives' pleas. Even Maud's imagination seems to be controlled by her uncle's presence, as she admits to 'something mesmeric in the odd sort of influence which, without effort, he exercised over my imagination' (352). On first meeting her uncle, Maud is so startled that she cannot fully describe Silas and resorts to calling him an 'apparition, drawn as it seemed in black and white, venerable, bloodless, fiery-eyed, with its singular look of power, and an expression so bewildering – was it derision, or anguish, or cruelty, or patience?' (201). In another moment, Silas becomes a mask with 'hollow, fiery, awful eyes!' (205). Madame de la Rougierre and Uncle Silas are portrayed as spectral and artificial because they subvert their behavioural expectations of a kind governess who protects her charge and of the uncle who loves his orphaned niece.

In order to make sense of the situation, Maud draws on her father's Swedenborgian readings to describe how Uncle Silas becomes a Mephistopheles, a sweet-talking goblin, with a 'phosphoric radiance covering something colder and more awful than the grave' (353). On the night she is almost murdered Maud finds herself drawn towards the spirit world: 'the people I saw dizzily, made of smoke or shining vapour, smiling or frowning, I could have passed my hand through them. They were evil spirits' (430).

Finally Maud is not saved by the interference of discarnate spirits but by two servants that act as her guardian angels. Eve M. Lynch has argued that 'like the ghost, the servant is *in* the house but not *of* it',[4] a comment that adds a social layer to the ways that ghostliness is used in sensation novels. In *Uncle Silas*, Meg, the young girl who lives in Bartram-Haugh, Uncle Silas's residence, and Tom, her lover who drives the carriage, observe and go unnoticed by Uncle Silas and Madame de la Rougierre. In the end, Meg and Tom manage to save Maud and inform her relatives of Silas's plans. *Uncle Silas* is heavily imbued with references to living characters as spectres, with laudanum-induced trance states, and features a heroine who morphs from a hysterical, nervous girl to a heroine capable of telling her own story. The references to spirits and Swedenborg allow Maud to draw on her childhood knowledge and emotional life in order to tell a story that seems more sensational despite Le Fanu's historical-romance aspirations.

Mediums, séances and Florence Marryat

In her study of the sensation novel, Winifred Hughes argues that one of the major transgressions of the genre was its tendency 'to undermine the prevailing Victorian world view, to alter the perception of "reality" and to revise its traditional meaning'.⁵ Hughes reads sensation as constantly challenging boundaries in terms of cultural norms and narrative forms. Instead of a realistic, mirror-image of life, sensation offers not an alternative but an enhanced reality. Similarly, spiritualism or involvement in séances produces the same effect. William James, president of the Society for Psychical Research between 1894 and 1895, wrote about spirit phenomena that 'it is pleasant to turn from phenomena of the dark sitting-room and rat-hole type (with their tragicomic suggestion that the whole order of nature might possibly be over-turned in one's own head, by the way in which one imagined oneself, on a certain occasion, to be holding a tricky peasant woman's feet) to the calm air of delightful studies'.⁶ Hughes's and James's comments bring sensation and spiritualism together as both identify the power that sensation and spirit materialisation had when it came to challenging given perceptions of reality and what constitutes the 'natural' world or 'natural world-view'.

Sensation calls attention to the empirical, affective understanding of the world; melodramatic tropes deployed in its narratives describe the physical gestures of characters, convey their emotions, provide detailed accounts of clothes, hair and objects as a means of calling attention to bodies within texts and to the bodies of its readers. Tellingly, the effect of reading sensation novels and the effect of the séance are described by critics of the genre and the movement in similar terms. In an often-quoted excerpt from Henry Mansel's 'Sensation Novels', the likes of Braddon's and Collins's texts are described as being of 'the galvanic-battery type' 'which carry the whole nervous system by steam' and intend to set the reader's 'hair on end or his teeth on edge'.⁷ In a satiric poem published in *Punch*, séance attendants experience a similar jolt as 'a causal finger-tap / seemed to vibrate through the system, / Like a sudden thunder-clap'.⁸ Furthermore, the use of electrical discourse to describe the physical sensation of reading is also adopted by spiritualists, as the séance room emulates a battery pattern with positive and negative sitters uniting their fingertips around a table. This fictional body (sensation fiction), which came into existence bit by bit in serial instalments, is akin to the spirit phenomena of the 1860s that, according to a sceptical critic, brought forth 'an entirely new-fashioned spirit, a different sort of ghost altogether, or ghosts in "piecemeal", only *bits* of spirits, *who never come of their own accord*, and have to be *squeezed* out of a table bit by bit'.⁹ The weekly instalment, like the partial spirit manifestations, carried the promise of wholeness and completion.

The sensation novel and the materialised spirit acquire a strange physicality that is both unbelievable and threatening. Mansel goes so far as to attack the physical appearance of the sensation novel published in volume form: 'a phase internally that of the grub, with small print and cheap paper, externally that of the butterfly, with a tawdry cover, ornamented with a highly-coloured picture, hung over like a signboard, to give the promise of the entertainment to be had within'.[10] Eerily, the description resembles that of the cultural configuration of the prostitute, a painted night moth promising pleasure but not without the danger of contamination. The textual body of sensation is in Mansel's view an eroticised body entered by the reader's gaze and entering the reader's mind. Pamela K. Gilbert discusses the compound discourses of sensation and prostitution and finds that novels of the 'mass market' are permeated by the metaphor of authorship-as-prostitution; the novels are seen as a 'commodified body' and the critic as doctor or policeman.[11]

Discussing the set-up in the séances of the mediums Catherine Wood and Annie Fairlamb, Marlene Tromp offers a similar view of spiritualist practices:

> Note the all male composition of the room of sitters and the semi-prone form of the medium, who exhibits herself from behind a curtain, just as Yolande [the materialised spirit] peeked from behind her veil. Like a scene in a brothel or an erotically charged freak show, the performance offers the reclining Fairlamb to the consumption of the viewers.[12]

Furthermore, the procuring of spirits, sometimes of spirit children, from mediums who had accepted money or gifts for their work, resonates with ideas of prostitution but also with the image of supply and demand that brings together discourses surrounding the sensation novels, materialised spirits and prostitution in the latter half of the nineteenth century.

The emphasis on the description of physical bodies is accentuated in both sensation novels and spiritualist accounts of séances. Margaret Oliphant, somewhat begrudgingly, comments on the detail sensation authors deploy to describe heroines' hair. She bestows on Braddon the title of 'inventor of the fair-haired demon of modern fiction'[13] and continues thus:

> We note, in glancing here and there through the luscious pages, that there is always either a mass of glorious hair lying across a man's breast, or a lady's white and jewelled fingers are twined in the gentleman's chestnut or raven curls – for 'colour' is necessary to every such picture. Our readers will have remarked that, even in the crisis of her misery, the poor little heroine of 'Cometh Up as a Flower' could not refrain from throwing her hair in 'splendid ruddy billows' over her lover's shoulder . . . Hair, indeed, in general, has become one of the leading properties in fiction. The facility with which it flows over the shoulders and bosoms in its owner's vicinity is quite extraordinary. In every emergency it is ready for use. Its quantity and colour, and the reflections in it, and even the 'fuzz', which is its modern peculiarity, take the place of all those pretty qualities with which heroines used to be endowed. What need has a woman for a soul when she has upon her head a mass of wavy gold?[14]

However critical Oliphant appears of the description of hair in sensation fiction she, too, seems to yield to the ekphrastic power of hair and physical characteristics as she goes on to discuss hair tints favoured by each prominent sensation author. She might be critiquing the authors' lush descriptions of hair but it seems that sensational hair has the magical power to fix her gaze on a survey of the textual manes found in sensation novels. She discusses the amber and golden hues of Braddon's and Ouida's characters in great length, almost fetishising the hair and the fingers or surfaces that touch it while at the same time she attempts but eventually fails to stop lingering on curls.

It seems somehow paradoxical that so much of spiritualism would similarly rely on the physicality of spirits and on descriptions of their bodies. Spiritualist and prolific sensation author Florence Marryat authored *There is No Death* in 1891, detailing descriptions of the séances she had attended in the past two decades, when mediums like Florence Cook, who materialised the spirit of 'Katie King', were in their heyday.

Marryat describes 'a profusion of ringlets falling to her waist that night', referring to 'Katie King'. Elsewhere, 'I turned to the form in my arms, and what was my amazement to see a woman, fair as the day, with large grey or blue eyes, a white skin and a profusion of golden, red hair.'[15] Marryat describes the hair and stature not only of the spirits but of the mediums too – perhaps in order to dispel any doubts about the medium's duplicity. If she elaborately distinguishes the differences between medium and spirit then sceptics might rest assured that the phenomena are authentic: 'Miss Florence Cook, who is brunette, of a small slight figure, with dark eyes and hair which she wore in a profusion of curls' (83). Another spirit is described as having hair 'of which she appears to have an immense quantity' falling 'down her back and over her shoulders' (88). Oliphant's rhetorical question concerning a woman's substitution of a soul for a profusion of hair may well apply to the materialised spirits at séances. If in Oliphant's world a heroine's hair substitutes for her soul, in spirit circles a profusion of hair comes to stand as proof of the psyche surviving death.

Marryat employs séances and materialised spirits in her sensation novel *Open! Sesame!* (1874–5), serialised in the *London Society* magazine, which she was then editing. Following the death of his beloved father, Lord Valence attempts to contact him through séances. Although Valence's experiments in automatic writing are in earnest, the hero is critical of 'spirit-rapping and table-turning [which] had just come into fashion – a strange term to use for what was either a great lie or an immortal truth'.[16] Although Valence has seen authentic proof of spirit communication, he calls the fashionable practice of 'table-turning' a 'pleasant past time', void of any serious emotion or awe, as

[t]he movements of the table were accompanied by shrieks of laughter; the silliest questions were answered at random; and it was only now and then that something startling occurred, and was generally followed by the more serious sitters declaring they would never have anything to do with table-turning again. The majority ridiculed it as folly; a few believed it to be by some agency of the devil; but no one ever seemed to derive any satisfaction from meddling with it. I was not, and I never have been, in the habit of mixing with society; but I heard all this from friends, and it disgusted me. I could not imagine any one with the least claim to common-sense wasting his time over such an employment. If table-turning proceeded from the mere force of animal magnetism, it was less instructive than the simplest game; if from the power of the spirits of evil, it was more dangerous than the most open sin. (vol. III, 135–6)

Perhaps Marryat is using Valence here as her medium, to articulate her own aversion to treating the other world as entertainment. Marryat does not include a fraudulent medium as her major sensational trope but portrays instead a fake materialised spirit, 'Isola'. Isola is brought into existence through the cunningness of Agatha, Valence's sister-in-law, who manipulates Valence and wishes to convince him that he should take his own life so that she can inherit from him. Marryat does not critique spiritualists or mediums but shows how spirits and believers may fall into the hands of unscrupulous non-believers. Agatha, whose name implies innocence, is anything but as Isola appears to Valence:

Slight and small in figure, and draped in some white, soft, cloudy material, that hangs loosely about every part, and yet seems to envelop all, 'Isola' is the embodiment of what a fanciful imagination might conjure up as the appearance of a visitant from the other world. Her golden hair ripples loosely to her knees; her features are not so distinct as Bulwer would wish to have them, because her head and shoulders seem to be covered with a veil that looks like black *crepe*; but her bare arms are deadly white, and bloodless-looking; and in one hand she bears a small antique lamp, the dimly burning wick of which just shows sufficient light upon her person to render it mysteriously unrecognizable except as a whole. (vol. III, 231–2)

The appearance of Isola draws on expectations of what a spirit should look like, she is described as the 'embodiment of what a fanciful imagination might conjure up' complete with rippled golden hair. Yet the language uncovers the truth that Isola is the crude embodiment of Agatha's imagination of how a spirit should look. At the end of the novel, when Agatha's masquerade is revealed, Valence decides to continue with his pursuit of spirit communication; he has proven a powerful method of automatic writing and a musical method of mediumship. Marryat seemingly warns her readers not against spiritualism but against the obsessive pursuit of spirit communication and against family members who might wish to exploit spiritualist affiliation for their own benefit. Perhaps Marryat's conversion to spiritualism and adamant belief in the authentic communication between the living and the dead prevented her from exploring fraudulent mediumship, masquerading spirits and fake séances more extensively. It was not until 1999 with Sarah Waters's *Affinity*, that sensation fiction and fraudulent mediumship came together in the blonde, angelic heroine Selena Dawes.

There are many links between the theatricality of the séance and the sensation novel, from melodramatic tropes (employed in the narrative to heighten the emotional currency of a scene) to masquerading spirits, and Marryat was aware of the relationship between the stage and the séance. The theatrical ambience of the séance is often evoked in *The Spirit World*, which she published in 1894. Marryat argues that, besides the gifts or limitations of a particular medium, the success of a séance is directly related to its setting. Spirit manifestations will occur if the room is aired daily, if the medium sits on a simple wooden chair and the correct light is maintained. Tellingly, her description of lighting a séance reminds us of stage equipment as opposed to simple domestic lamps and it seems to be influenced by the coloured plates used in the theatre of the time, which were coincidentally named 'mediums'. The device consisted of 'one pane of glass [which] was red, one blue, one orange, and one plain white. The lamp revolved and the spirits chose which colour they desired to use, according to the atmosphere or the party assembled, or other conditions known only to themselves.'[17] As for music, the 'solemn tunes of the harmonium' were deemed 'more appropriate to a spiritual gathering than any other', as they 'blend admirably with the human voices' (288). The desired atmosphere was one of seriousness – merriment was not becoming 'when interviewing those dear ones whose loss caused us to shed such bitter tears' (291).

It is very clear then that Marryat's guide to the invocation of spirits can be interpreted in terms of domesticated stage directions, as technical notes for 'set-design' and 'performances' that constituted the séance experience. The séance becomes a ghostly private theatrical; the manipulation of light and the music are entertaining for the sitters but also help to de-familiarise the séance room, transforming it from a drawing-room to a proscenium.

Family curses and apparitions in Ellen Wood

With a title like *The Shadow of Ashlydyat* (1863), Ellen Wood pointed her readers towards gothic and supernatural expectations. The eponymous shadow, formed of a bier accompanied by mourners and appearing in the Ashlydyat grounds, is a portent of death but also an anachronistic example of Freud's 'return of the repressed'. The 'Wicked Godolphin' has brutally murdered Richard De Commins and buried him in the grounds. The family fortunes of the Godolphin family fluctuate and by the time the novel is set, the current heir, Thomas Godolphin, is the unfortunate spectator of the bier:

> He had turned the corner, to the front of the grove of ash-trees, and stretching out before him was the Dark Plain, with its weird-like bushes, so like graves, and – *its Shadow*, lying cold and still in the white moonlight. Yes! there surely lay the Shadow of Ashlydyat. The grey archway rose behind it; the flat plain extended out before it, and the Shadow was between them, all too distinct. The first shock over, Thomas Godolphin's pulses coursed on again. It was very palpable. The bier, as it looked, in the middle, the mourner at the head, the mourner at the foot, each – as a spectator could fancy – with bowed heads. In spite of the superstition touching this strange shadow, in which Thomas Godolphin had been brought up, he looked round now for some natural explanation of it. He was a man of intellect, a man of the world, a man who played his full share in the practical business of every-day life: and such men are not given to acknowledge superstitious fancies in this age of enlightenment, no matter what may have been given to their minds in childhood. Therefore Thomas Godolphin ranged his eyes round and round in the air, and could see nothing that would solve the mystery. 'I wonder whether it be possible that certain states of the atmosphere should give out these shadows?' he soliloquized. 'But – if so – why should it invariably appear in that one precise spot; and in no other? . . .'
>
> He walked on towards Ashlydyat, his head turned sideways always, looking at the Shadow. 'I am glad Janet does not see it! It would frighten her into a belief that my father's end was near,' came the next thought.[18]

This passage throws into relief Thomas Godolphin's struggle to reconcile his family history, brought to him through the form of superstition and the age of enlightenment which he feels part of. The Shadow is definitely visible to him but instead of lapsing into hysterics, as he implies Janet Godolphin will do if she sees it herself, he tries to interpret the sign as a natural effect of the atmosphere rather than as a message of his own father's imminent end.

Finally, once the house has been sold and the grounds completely renovated in the attempt 'to do away entirely with its past ill character and send this superstition to the winds' (vol. 1, 225) the bones of the unfortunate De Commins are found and he is finally laid to rest. The legend has it that as long as the bones remain unfound the bier will appear and so, at the end of the novel when the renovation has taken place, complete with landscaped gardens and summer house, the Shadow disappears. It is up to the reader to accept in the supernatural or to see the effect as a product of garden landscaping. But the novel resists a completely natural conclusion. As Janet Godolphin says:

> A great deal of this story, The Shadow of Ashlydyat, is a perfectly true one; it is but the recital of a drama of real life. And the superstition that encompasses it? ten thousand inquisitive tongues will ask. Yes, and the superstition. There are things, as I have just said, which can neither be explained nor accounted for: they are marvels, mysteries, and so they must remain. Many a family has its supernatural skeleton, religiously believed in; many a house has its one dread corner which has been fully enclosed to the right light of day. Say what men will to the contrary, there is a tendency in the human mind to court the in-creeping of superstition. We cannot shut our eyes to things that occur within our view, although we may be, and always shall be, utterly unable to explain them; what they are, where they spring from, why they come. (vol. I, 175–6)

Interestingly in this extract the supernatural is linked to family secrets and the superstitions are talked of in such a way that points towards the heavy freight of a family past. Writing in 1863, at a time where séances were commonly practised in British households, Mrs Wood resists seeing supernatural and spiritualist effects in terms that demonstrate their veracity or fraudulence. Rather, as Janet Godolphin says, she asks her readers to consider the human mind's love of the marvellous and the secrecy surrounding occult and ghostly occurrences.

Whether used for dramatic effect, as metaphor for social concerns or as a way of exploring troubling family histories, spiritualism and the supernatural flirted outrageously with sensation fiction so that rather than stripping their novels of ghostly and occult references, authors used superstition, clairvoyance, spiritualism and the ghostly to examine modern, literary and social concerns.

NOTES

1. Henry James, 'Miss Braddon', The Nation 1 (1865), 593–4 (594).
2. For a history of spiritualism see Janet Oppenheim, The Other World (Cambridge University Press, 1985).
3. Sheridan Le Fanu, Uncle Silas, ed. Victor Sage (London: Penguin Books, 2000), 3. Further references to this edition will be given in the text.
4. Eve M. Lynch, 'Spectral Politics: The Victorian Ghost Story and the Domestic Servant', in The Victorian Supernatural, ed. Nicola Bown, Carolyn Burdett and Pamela Thurschwell (Cambridge University Press, 2004), 67–86 (67).
5. Winifred Hughes, The Maniac in the Cellar: Sensation Novels of the 1860s (Princeton University Press, 1980), 51–2.
6. William James, 'Presidential Address', PSPR 12 (1896), 2–10 (6).
7. Mansel, 487.

8. Anon., 'At Home with the Spirits', *Punch* (18 April 1863), 159. The 'home' of the title might allude to one of the most prominent Victorian mediums, Daniel Dunglas Home.

9. George Cruikshank, *A Discovery Concerning Ghosts; with a Rap at the 'Spirit Rappers'* (London: Frederick Arnold, 1863), 21. Emphasis in original.

10. Mansel, 485.

11. Pamela K. Gilbert, *Disease, Desire, and the Body in Victorian Women's Popular Novels* (Cambridge University Press, 1997), 26–7.

12. Marlene Tromp, *Altered States: Sex, Nation, Drugs and Self-Transformation in Victorian Spiritualism* (Albany: State University of New York, 2006), 103.

13. ON, 263.

14. *Ibid.*, 269.

15. Florence Marryat, *The Spirit World* (London: F. W. White, 1894), 144; 142. Further references to this edition will be given in the text.

16. Florence Marryat, *Open! Sesame!* 3 vols. (London: Chatto and Windus, 1875), vol. II, 134. Further references to this edition will be given in the text.

17. Florence Marryat, *The Spirit World* (London: F. W. White, 1894), 286. Further references to this edition will be given in the text.

18. Ellen Wood, *The Shadow of Ashlydyat*, 3 vols. (London: Richard Bentley, 1863), vol. I, 146. Further references to this edition will be given in the text.

12

LILLIAN NAYDER

Science and sensation

Surveying 'the history of chemistry' and its 'present state' for his students in Mary Shelley's 1818 novel, Professor Waldman delivers a lecture that proves a turning point for Victor Frankenstein. 'The ancient teachers of this science ... promised impossibilities, and performed nothing', Waldman asserts, before detailing their successors' triumphs:

> The modern masters promise very little; they know that metals cannot be transmuted, and that the elixir of life is a chimera. But these philosophers, whose hands seem only made to dabble in dirt, and their eyes to pour over the microscope or crucible, have indeed performed miracles ... They have acquired new and almost unlimited powers; they can command the thunders of heaven, mimic the earthquake, and even mock the invisible world with its own shadows.[1]

Synthesising miracles as they mimic God's powers, these modern chemists set the precedent for Frankenstein, whose attempt to create life ends disastrously, mocking the divine.

The daughter of Mary Wollstonecraft, author of *A Vindication of the Rights of Woman* (1792), Shelley grounds her critique of science in a wider critique of gender politics and patriarchal abuses of power. The aims and assumptions of science and those of patriarchy are inseparable in *Frankenstein*; in a violation akin to sexual assault, scientists 'penetrate into the recesses of nature, and shew how she works in her hiding places' (28). Shelley's eponymous hero not only pursues nature but destroys her, dismembering the partly formed Eve he has constructed for his Adam, fearful that she will 'refuse to comply' with his desires (114), and he destroys his wife as well. He appears to do so inadvertently, misunderstanding the creature's threats and leaving Elizabeth unprotected on their wedding night. Yet the creature's homicidal meaning is clear enough to readers, who easily foresee Elizabeth's fate, one common among the beleaguered wives of gothic fiction.

Well versed in Shelley's writing, Wilkie Collins enjoyed 'horrifying' relatives by reciting 'the most terrible portions of ... Frankenstein' as a teenager.[2]

His fiction, like other works of the 'sensation school', is heir to the gothic and to *Frankenstein* particularly. Tamar Heller and Jenny Bourne Taylor see Shelley's influence in Collins's use of narrative framing to provide alternative perspectives,[3] and in the 'monstrous . . . social outcast[s]' central to his social criticism.[4] But as we will see, Collins's debt to Shelley, like that of Mary Elizabeth Braddon and other sensation novelists, is also evident in his gendered representations of science.

Critics generally agree that sensation fiction destabilises social categories, treating identity as fluid and obscuring differences in class, race and gender. Among the sensation novels of Collins and Braddon, for example, a Caucasian man becomes a dark-skinned other because of medical treatment (*Poor Miss Finch* (1872)), lady's maids change places with their mistresses or serve as uncanny doubles (*The Dead Secret* (1857), *Lady Audley's Secret* (1862)), and a baronet proves to have no more claim to his title than the lowliest stable hand (*The Woman in White* (1859–60)). Because Victorian science was understood to wield a 'democratizing power' and 'threaten traditional boundaries',[5] it provides one vehicle for the social transformations that characterise sensation fiction, challenging assumptions about authority and provoking anxieties about political change. In Collins's *The Moonstone* (1868), the lowly 'half-caste' Ezra Jennings scientifically reconstructs the theft of the Hindu gem, incriminating a gentleman and overcoming social prejudices, while John Herncastle, the English officer who initially stole the diamond, performs chemical experiments that signal his social and moral decline. 'Sometimes he was reported to be trying strange things in chemistry', Gabriel Betteredge recounts. 'Sometimes he was seen carousing and amusing himself among the lowest people in the lowest slums of London. Anyhow, a solitary, vicious, underground life was the life the Colonel led.'[6] Herncastle uses his will to establish 'a professorship of experimental Chemistry at a northern university' (70), fuelling the social changes scientific pursuits were believed to foster, particularly in the industrial north. Yet sensation fiction inverts the formula of industrial success literature, since the mobility catalysed by science leads gentlemen downward rather than bringing studious labourers into the middle class.

With its tendency to 'jumble ranks and utterly confuse . . . social standing', sensation fiction was recognised as 'a sign of the times' by Victorian reviewers, and understood to express 'a craving for some fundamental change in the working of society'.[7] Jonathan Loesberg argues more specifically that sensation writers responded to debate over political reform in the late 1850s and 1860s – to changing conceptions of class that led to the Second Reform Act (1867). The preoccupation with class identity in sensation fiction and the 'sensation response' typically triggered by images of its loss reveal underlying anxieties about a broadened suffrage and the social chaos it might create, Loesberg contends.[8]

Yet sensation fiction also traces its origins to mid-Victorian debates over marriage law reform and married women's property rights, and to the advent of civil divorce in the late 1850s. Responding to well-publicised details of marital conflict, sensation writers bring home to England gothic horrors, revealing 'those most mysterious of mysteries, the mysteries which are at our own doors'.[9] To this end, they domesticate gothic science. Isolated from his family, Frankenstein works in desolate regions and foreign lands (113). But the scientist in sensation fiction experiments in a laboratory adjacent to, or indistinguishable from, his home. He uses physiology, vivisection and chemistry – their techniques, powers and elixirs – to test, defend and/or transform domestic relations. For sensation novelists, the scientist and his triumphs illuminate and critique the power that husbands wield over their wives while also enabling women to resist and subvert that power. Weapons in marital strife, the methods and products of science become means of committing and punishing social transgression and provide ways to address anxieties raised by marriage law reform and civil divorce, the latter commonly represented in sensation fiction as the crime of bigamy.

Victorians often touted their age as one of social and moral progress, attributing many perceived advances to scientific achievement. Articles published alongside sensation novels serialised in Dickens's *All the Year Round* celebrated Victorian scientists and their discoveries. The volumes in which Collins's *The Woman in White* and *No Name* (1862–3) first appeared included articles that represented scientists setting 'the world in a blaze with a new light', building organic compounds and demonstrating, as Pasteur did, that microscopic life was 'in the air', and that outlined the wonders of the hospital laboratory, in which physicians 'magically' identified poisons in corpses and transformed the grave 'into the damning witness of . . . crime'.[10]

Insofar as sensation novelists represent science as a source of progress, they usually do so through such wonders – in depicting forensics, which enables their scientists to accomplish what the police often cannot. What Ronald R. Thomas observes of *The Moonstone* is sometimes true of other sensation novels: 'science is the sanctioning authority . . . superseding and eventually collaborating with that of the law to reveal the truth'.[11] As a writer in the *Examiner* remarked in 1856, responding to the use of toxicology to convict Dr William Palmer, 'we do not remember any case exemplifying so remarkably the great advance made in our time by science . . . as a power bearing witness against crime . . . The dead woman has spoken, and science has presented itself as interpreter.'[12] Scientists could make 'speaking bodies' from uncooperative suspects as well as from murder victims. Thus Ezra

Jennings succeeds where Sergeant Cuff fails, uncovering the truth of the Moonstone's theft by means of a laboratory experiment that transforms 'the body of the suspect' into a legible 'text'.[13]

More often than not, however, Collins and his fellow sensation writers use science to question the law, not to supersede or reinforce it – to dramatise and challenge the nearly absolute power it grants to men over their wives. 'Throughout Victorian fiction, scientific professionals of various kinds are on trial', John Kucich observes, and reflect 'great anxiety about the conjunction of scientific knowledge and social power'.[14] Sensation novelists use this conjunction in their marriage law critiques, casting oppressive suitors and husbands as scientists who employ their expertise to deprive women of agency and will – at times, to suppress or eradicate their very identity or being.

Mid-Victorian debate over marriage law led Members of Parliament to pass the Divorce and Matrimonial Causes Act (1857) and the first Married Women's Property Act (1870), limiting the common law principle of coverture.[15] Coverture denied legal identity and property rights to wives, presumably protected by the 'cover' their husbands supplied. 'The very being or legal existence of a woman is suspended, or at least it is incorporated ... into that of the husband, under whose wing, protection and cover she performs everything', Sir William Blackstone writes in *Commentaries on the Laws of England* (1765–9), his description still valid in the mid-1800s.[16] Sensation novelists prove eager to examine the meaning and consequences of coverture, and stage the wrongs legally inflicted on wives by means of that principle, drawing on material aired in Parliament, in the press and in such works as Caroline Norton's *English Laws for Women in the Nineteenth Century* (1854) – sources depicting the private sphere as a place of strife and suffering. 'In consequence of the imperfect state of the law, I have suffered bitterly', Norton writes of her home life, identifying her husband as her 'deadliest foe'.[17] As Walter Hartright tells us in *The Woman in White*, referring to the former Laura Fairlie, 'the commonest consideration for Lady Glyde's safety' forces her friends to 'remov[e] her at once from the place of all others that was ... most dangerous to her' – 'her own home'.[18]

In *The Woman in White*, Collins brings the powers of chemistry to bear on coverture through a conspiracy launched against Laura, an orphaned heiress whom Sir Percival Glyde marries for her money. With her separate settlement of property, administered under the law of equity, Laura would seem to be protected against the exploitation sanctioned by common law. But the terms of her settlement reinforce her vulnerabilities as a 'covered' woman. Against the family lawyer's protests, her guardian allows Sir Percival to be named the beneficiary of the settlement, giving her husband 'an interest of twenty thousand pounds in [her] death' (143).

Instead of murdering his wife, Sir Percival plots an elaborate fraud with Count Fosco, 'one of the first experimental chemists living' (199). Married to Laura's aunt Eleanor, a feminist whom he has 'tamed' (195), Fosco stands to benefit from their niece's death, since his wife will inherit ten thousand pounds if Laura predeceases her, a fortune to which coverture entitles him. Glyde and Fosco plan to stage Laura's death by substituting her illegitimate and dying half-sister, Anne Catherick, for Laura herself. Half-witted, Anne has escaped from a lunatic asylum. Should Anne survive beyond the period required for their scheme, Fosco will use his 'vast chemical resources' to 'open ... the doors of the Prison of Life' and 'release' her (561, 570). Anne dies a captive in Fosco's home one day prematurely; she is identified and buried as Laura, while Laura is identified as Anne and 'returned' to the lunatic asylum. Only through the counterplotting of Marian Halcombe, Laura's legitimate half-sister, and Walter Hartright, whom Laura loves and marries after Sir Percival's death, is she freed from confinement and ultimately acknowledged as her 'real' self.

The Woman in White is a study in marriage, and all of the husbands central to it suppress and/or exploit the women in their care. Sir Percival is most clearly brutal in his treatment of Laura, while Walter Hartright is most subtle in his oppression, 'kindly' infantilising her. Of the three, Count Fosco appears most extraordinary, calling science to his aid in his mastery of women. Yet Fosco's use of chemistry not only links him to Sir Percival and Hartright but comes to represent the marital norm. Artificially suppressing women's cognitive abilities, he realises the assumptions underlying coverture and illustrates its social consequences.

'Chemistry ... has always had irresistible attractions for me, from the enormous, the illimitable power which the knowledge of it confers', Fosco asserts. He goes on to explain: 'Mind ... rules the world', the body 'rules the mind', and the chemist – 'that most omnipotent of all potentates' – rules the body; thus science puts 'great men' in his power. With chemistry, he could make Nero mild, Alexander the Great cowardly and Shakespeare a 'driveller' (560). Yet Fosco's examples obscure his central aim: to reduce *women* to a state of near imbecility and subvert their potential for greatness.

Fosco's transformation of his wife, a 'once wayward Englishwoman' whom he has 'tamed' (195), testifies to his abilities as master. Once an ardent feminist who 'advocated the Rights of Women', the former Eleanor Fairlie is now her husband's mute and deferential servant (210). 'Never before have I beheld such a change produced in a woman by her marriage', Marian remarks, attributing the transformation to the Count's domestic violence (200). Yet Fosco himself traces his wife's subservience to English common law and its 'marriage-obligations' for women (570), and while

Marian represents the change in Eleanor Fairlie as unprecedented, it is soon replayed in Fosco's chemical transformation of Laura, whose 'state of partially-suspended consciousness' (569) connects her not only to the half-witted Anne but also to Eleanor Fairlie and *any* Englishwoman defined by coverture.

'With my vast resources in chemistry, I might have taken Lady Glyde's life', Fosco boasts. 'At immense personal sacrifice, I ... took her identity instead' (571). While Laura's fictive death functions as a metaphor for her legal non-existence as a married woman, the 'suspended consciousness' that Fosco chemically induces in her mirrors the mental impairment 'required' of wives under marriage law. As Frances Power Cobbe observes in an 1868 essay, the law categorises married women 'with the "idiots" and the "minors"', excluding them 'from many civil, and all political rights in England', on the grounds of their alleged 'feebleness' in mind and body, which justifies their enforced dependence.[19] 'I will sign with pleasure', Laura tells Sir Percival when he demands her blind consent, 'if you will only treat me as a responsible being' (223). The incapacity her husband attributes to her is a legal fiction, Laura insists, yet Fosco uses chemistry to realise it, rendering her the 'confused' and 'sadly incoherent' creature that common law claims her to be (569, 390). 'They have tried to make me forget everything', Laura recounts after her liberation from Fosco and the asylum, 'her mind clouded' and her intellect shaken in the manner presumed by law (380–1, 388).

Like Collins, Braddon includes a chemist in her 1860 sensation novel, *The Trail of the Serpent* (first published as *Three Times Dead*). A tale of murder, attempted murder and bigamy, it is Braddon's first response to the advent of civil divorce and the debate over married women's property. Her chemist plays a pivotal role in the plot's twists and turns but proves a surprisingly benevolent figure. A marriage counsellor of sorts, Laurent Blurosset uses his chemical research to save a marriage, secretly preventing a wife from murdering her husband and ultimately reuniting the estranged couple.

Braddon seems to advocate for marriage law reform at the outset of her novel. Her anti-heroine, Valerie de Cevennes, is blackmailed into a union (later revealed to be bigamous) with the adventurer Raymond Marolles, who encourages her to poison her first husband, and she protests against the law that transfers a woman's property to her husband and thus makes matrimony a matter of financial 'speculation'.[20] 'You have the command of my fortune', Valerie bitterly remarks to Marolles on their wedding day:

> But if you think the words whose sacred import has been prostituted by us this day have any meaning for you or me ... you neither know me nor my sex. My fortune you are welcome to. Take it, squander it ... But dare to ... approach me

so near as to touch but the hem of my dress, and that moment I proclaim the
story of our marriage. (179–80)

Granting the wife power over her body at a time when marriage law denied
the possibility of spousal rape, Braddon challenges the current state of the
law and a husband's claims to ownership – of his wife as well as her
property. Although Marolles asserts that their union 'may be as happy as
many other[s]', this is so only because what should be a sacred bond has
been utterly degraded, a 'thrice-sacred sacrament, ordained by an Almighty
Power for the glory and the happiness of the earth . . . profaned and changed
into a bitter mockery or a wicked lie' (180).

But while an unhappy marriage resembles 'a chain no time has power to
wear' (180–1), Braddon does not use her novel to champion divorce or
judicial separation. Although she writes it in the wake of the 1857 Act, she
fails to acknowledge the legislation, instead marking the Act's passage with
the crime of bigamy. Valerie commits bigamy unknowingly but Marolles's
father, the Marquis de Cevennes, does so purposely, deserting his poor
English wife to marry a wealthy French widow. In response to the 'prostitution' of marriage, Braddon employs her chemist and his quasi-divine powers
to reclaim its status as an indissoluble and 'holy' sacrament (180–1), although
Valerie's attempt to kill her husband at the novel's outset casts the sanctity of
their bond into doubt.

Initially, Blurosset appears to help Valerie murder her first husband, Gaston
de Lancy, an opera singer whom she marries secretly for love. He provides
Valerie with a compound she believes will kill de Lancy, whom Marolles has
tricked her into believing is unfaithful. Eager to gain Valerie's wealth, Marolles
stages an 'ocular demonstration' of de Lancy's alleged affair. When Valerie
gasps for 'a pistol or a dagger' at the sight (144), Marolles brings her to
Blurosset for 'a lesson in chemistry' (153), expecting him to give her a more
discreet weapon, 'something which will change a glass of wine into a death-
warrant, but . . . defy the scrutiny of a college of physicians' (153).

Instead of complying, Blurosset thwarts their scheme. An inscrutable figure
(149), he sees through his visitors while evading scrutiny himself. His scientific endeavours are tinged with mysticism, and he understands the past and
shapes the future, giving Valerie what he identifies as 'a slow poison' (153)
that is, in fact, an opiate that temporarily suspends animation and allows the
chemist to 'raise the dead' (311). Exercising powers that mimic Christ's or the
devil's, Blurosset seems to resurrect Valerie's first husband while assuring her
that 'the dead never rise again in answer to the will of mortal man' (311).
Priest-like, he enables her to suffer and repent, de Lancy to pity and forgive,
and both to acknowledge their marriage as sacred and indissoluble (404).

'There never was but one being on earth whose good opinion I valued or whose bad opinion I feared', Valerie confesses to the chemist, while dismissing her second union as 'a marriage only in name' (309, 307). Reunited with de Lancy, Valerie embraces coverture, eager 'to bestow . . . on the husband of her choice' the 'immense fortune' of which she is 'once more mistress', only too glad to find in him 'a guiding hand' and 'supporting arm' (405, 323). Blurosset makes possible the realisation that marriage law itself is not the problem but rather its abuse by failed patriarchs such as Marolles.

More literally than Braddon's chemist, George Eliot's scientist, Charles Meunier, resurrects the dead in *The Lifted Veil* (1859) – at least temporarily – reviving a corpse by transfusing it with his own blood. Instead of salvaging a marriage, however, the medical researcher inadvertently exposes a wife's plot to poison her husband, as the servant whom he returns to life survives long enough to denounce her mistress as a would-be assassin.

The Lifted Veil is narrated by Latimer, a 'fragile, nervous' man with a poetic sensibility.[21] He sees into the future and hears others' thoughts, an unwanted power he develops after an illness. Despite his poetic leanings, Latimer is 'schooled in science'[22] – forced to study zoology, botany, electricity and magnetism by his father. Yet for scientific expertise, Latimer defers to Meunier, his intimate schoolmate, whose medical genius earns him great celebrity.

Overshadowed by his half-brother Alfred, who is engaged to marry Bertha Grant but dies accidentally, Latimer succeeds to Alfred's fortune and engagement. Although Latimer foresees the misery of his union with Bertha and glimpses her 'barren selfish soul' (62), she is the one person whose thoughts are veiled to him and he marries her against his better knowledge. He soon discovers that she cares only for power and social status, and plans to make her husband her slave (93). Proving powerless in her marriage, she despises Latimer and desires a separation, 'meditat[ing] continually how . . . she could be freed from this hateful bond' (96–7). But Latimer refuses to part from her, despite their mutual repulsion (95). His reasoning underscores his prerogatives as a husband: 'I never thought of taking any steps towards a complete separation, which would have made our alienation evident to the world. Why should I rush for help to a new course, when I was only suffering from the consequences of a deed which had been the act of my intensest will?' (97–8). He claims that 'the rich find it easy to live married and apart' (98) but Bertha remains unhappy with their arrangement and plots to poison him, confiding in her lady's maid, Mrs Archer.

Meunier uncovers her scheme during a visit to the couple. With Latimer's consent and assistance, Meunier conducts a medical experiment on the corpse of Bertha's maid, dead from peritonitis. 'I want to try the effect of transfusing blood into her arteries after the heart has ceased to beat for some minutes', Meunier explains. 'I have tried the experiment again and again with animals that have died of this disease, with astounding results, and I want to try it on a human subject' (113). Agreeing that 'there are always insuperable difficulties with women in these matters' (114), the men withhold their plans from Bertha, who is vigilantly watching over Mrs Archer, the latter struggling 'to say something which pain and failing strength forbid her to utter' (116). After her death, Meunier opens an artery in her neck and transfuses blood from his arm into her body while Latimer 'keep[s] up the artificial respiration' (120). Life returns long enough for Mrs Archer to level her accusation, with Bertha hearing herself denounced: 'You mean to poison your husband ... the poison is in the black cabinet ... I got it for you ... you laughed at me, and told lies about me behind my back, to make me disgusting ... because you were jealous ... are you sorry ... now?' (121). Rather than bring Bertha to justice, Latimer swears Meunier to silence, and husband and wife live apart, 'she ... the mistress of half [their] wealth' and generally 'pitied and admired' (123).

The Lifted Veil has been understood to indict female nature – because of the malice conveyed by Mrs Archer's last words. As Mary Jacobus argues, Meunier's experiment shows women as 'morally debased, loving neither men nor each other', their 'unredeemable' nature 'persist[ing] even beyond death'.[23] Yet Eliot underscores more specifically Bertha's animosity as a wife – one who would rather kill her husband than accept her powerlessness – examining the grounds, dynamics and consequences of an ill-matched union and a woman's desire for separation or divorce. Criminalising Bertha's attempts to separate from Latimer, Eliot suggests the danger of empowering wives under the Matrimonial Causes Act. Eliot complicates matters by means of science, however – through the experiment that unveils Bertha's treachery. That proceeding illuminates not only Meunier's trespasses as a scientist but also Latimer's abuse of power as a husband, and reminds us that his perspective alone is presented in the tale.

Pondering Bertha's 'hard features', Latimer doubts that she was 'born of woman' (118–19). Yet he is the one who, with Meunier, circumvents mother nature and, Frankenstein-like, engages in paternal birthgiving. While Eliot models Meunier's transfusion on those performed by James Blundell and Charles-Édouard Brown-Séquard between 1818 and 1858,[24] she uses it to restore sexual dominance to her threatened male figures. Meunier's transfusion is less sexually explicit than those in Bram Stoker's *Dracula* (1897), in which all four of Lucy Westenra's blood donors can claim her as their bride, her 'polyandry' strengthening patriarchal ties.[25] But Meunier's aversion to using 'a medical assistant from among [Latimer's] provincial doctors' and his concern that 'a disagreeable foolish version of the thing might get abroad'

(113–14) suggest the scandalousness of his procedure, as does his seeming courtship of Bertha, who is 'much struck' by his 'fascinations', 'put[s] forth all her coquetries' in response, and 'apparently ... succeed[s] in attracting his admiration' (109). Although Mrs Archer, not Bertha, receives Meunier's blood, the lady's maid, with her 'bold, self-confident coquetry' and contempt for Latimer (102), serves as Bertha's double. The transfusion suggests Meunier's intimacy with the women yet also signals his control over them and defuses the threat of adultery. The experiment supplants heterosexual pairings with a homosocial '*tête-à-tête*', Meunier 'pour[ing] forth' to Latimer 'wonderful narratives of his professional experience' (109) and the two working together over the body of Mrs Archer, now utterly objectified.

Eliot is far from celebrating their triumph, however. Mrs Archer's behaviour contributes to the horror of the finale (123) but so do the methods and assumptions of the scientists. Meunier claims that his postmortem transfusion 'can do [the maid] no harm – will give her no pain' (113) but the heaving breast, gasping voice and haggard face of the reanimated corpse cast doubt on his assurances and remind us that the subject herself had no say in the matter. 'Latimer gives Meunier permission' to experiment, Richard Menke notes, but 'the consent of the maid herself' is neither discussed nor obtained.[26] For Kate Flint, this subversion of female agency lies at the heart of Eliot's critique. In the image of Mrs Archer revitalised, granted a 'new power of speech' by means of male expertise and 'the intake of *male* blood', Eliot conveys her own tenuous agency as 'a woman author writing with masculine authority'.[27] Yet Eliot curtails male authority even as she acknowledges it, with Bertha finally obtaining her separation, her reputation intact, and Meunier temporarily 'paralysed' by the story's denouement (122). Although 'the case' had been 'taking precisely the course [Meunier] expected', Latimer notes (115), its results point beyond his understanding: 'life for that moment ceased to be a scientific problem to him' (122–3).

Like Eliot, Collins considers the use of women as experimental subjects in *Heart and Science* (1883), a work dedicated to the anti-vivisection cause but responsive to the second Married Women's Property Act (1882), which put an end to coverture. It centres on the cruelty of Dr Benjulia, who claims to perform harmless chemical experiments while engaging in the 'horrid cutting and carving' of living creatures.[28] His subjects of study include dogs, cats and monkeys but also the heroine, Carmilla Greywell. A young woman with a hysterical complaint, she is engaged to her cousin Ovid Vere, a doctor who travels for much of the story. Instead of treating Carmilla's potentially fatal illness, Benjulia allows it to progress to observe its symptoms, and his patient is only saved when her fiancé returns and uses the discoveries of an anti-vivisectionist to cure her; they marry and have a child while Benjulia, defeated and exposed, liberates his animals, burns his laboratory, and commits suicide. The plot is complicated by the machinations of Mrs Gallilee, Ovid's mother, an amateur scientist who masters her husband, gets into debt and falsely alleges that Carmilla is illegitimate to obtain her inheritance.

In *Heart and Science*, Dr Benjulia's brother objects to his experiments because 'man is [as much] an animal' as a dog; if the law protects living men from dissection, it should protect other animals too (176). Yet Collins focuses on a different inequity – that between men and women, the latter nearly as vulnerable to abuse as the lower animals and as readily 'caged' or domesticated in service to men. He juxtaposes a visit to London's Zoological Gardens and its 'creatures in prison' with a discussion of hysteria as a diagnosis, suggesting that Carmilla's illness, one commonly attributed to the weakness of female physiology, is due to social restrictions unfairly imposed on women and girls (75).

Their connection with imprisoned animals proves double-edged, however, at times reinforcing stereotypes of 'primitive' female nature and working against Collins's ostensive theme; women *lend* themselves to scientific study, he implies. Thus Carmilla's nurse, Teresa, defends her 'cub' as a tigress would, using her 'lean brown fingers' like claws against Mrs Gallilee (250), while Dr Benjulia's 'wild' cook, thwarted romantically, 'snatche[s] up a knife' to attack him 'in an outbreak of fury' (211–12). Who can blame her master for wanting to study 'the brain of an excitable woman', Collins seems to ask, or for 'looking (experimentally) at the inferior creature seated before him … as he looked (experimentally) at the other inferior creatures stretched under him on the table' (210)?

Collins reinforces this counter-theme with his portrait of Mrs Gallilee, the woman scientist who proves pathologically unfeminine and poses an even greater danger to Carmilla than Dr Benjulia does. Her fate – incarceration in a lunatic asylum – reveals the dangers of a woman's pursuit of male interests and prerogatives. Writing his novel as coverture was finally abandoned, Collins conveys his regrets over its loss, confirming assumptions about female weakness, claiming science as an exclusively male domain and representing the need for husbands to exert their authority, claim their children and keep wives in place. Coverture may have failed them, he implies, but child custody remains. 'Don't distress yourself about your children', the attorney kindly assures Mr Gallilee. 'Thank God, we stand on firm ground, there … No matter what [your wife] may say … the father is master … You have only to assert yourself' (270).

Critical of gender inequities but wary of women's empowerment, *Heart and Science* is characterised by contradictions – in form as well as theme. Jessica Straley notes that its anti-vivisection message conflicts with its sensationalism, since sensation fiction was 'the aesthetic counterpart to vivi-section' in the effects it allegedly produced. As Straley puts it, 'vivisectors exposed the brains of immobilized animals, boiled their skins, and galvanized their spinal cords, while Sensation writers stood likewise accused of "Harrowing the Mind, making the Flesh Creep ... [and] Giving Shocks to the Nervous System" of the captive reader'. In pairing sensation fiction with *anti*-vivisection, Straley argues, Collins 'reflect[s] ... on the conventions of his genre', grapples with 'the pejorative connotations of "sensation"' and com-pares the 'experimental subject' with his own reader.[29]

But if sensation writers resemble the vivisectionists in their stories, they also resemble the chemists depicted there: among them, Louis Trudaine in Collins's 'Sister Rose' (1855), who discovers a formula that makes texts disappear. For his 'remarkable improvements in chemistry', Trudaine is offered a professorship at the Academy of Sciences in Paris.[30] When he and his sister Rose are betrayed by Rose's husband and condemned to death during the Reign of Terror, their ally Lomaque uses the formula to erase their names from the death list and save them from the guillotine. As Lomaque describes it, the compound 'remove[s] writing from paper, and leave[s] no stain behind' (208). To the gaoler who sees the original text and then puzzles over what is missing, Lomaque offers some advice: 'keep your head on your shoulders, by troubling it about nothing but the list there in your hand. Stick to that literally, and nobody can blame you' (217). While literal readings are perhaps safest in times of political upheaval, Collins suggests, he acknowledges their inadequacy here, and sensation readers should take heed. Despite its reputation for subversion, sensation fiction is a compound mix-ture, as reactionary as it is radical, with texts split from subtexts and words forced from view in either case. Those who understand its science will search for its 'erasures' and the 'stains' that mark them (210, 208), never wholly eliminated from the page.

NOTES

1. Mary Shelley, *Frankenstein*, ed. J. Paul Hunter (New York: W. W. Norton, 1996), 27–8. Further references to this edition will be given in the text.
2. Wilkie Collins to William Collins, RA, 24 August 1842, *The Letters of Wilkie Collins*, ed. William Baker and William M. Clarke, 2 vols. (New York: St Martin's Press, 1999), vol. 1, 13–14.
3. Jenny Bourne Taylor, *'In the Secret Theatre of Home': Wilkie Collins, Sensation Narrative, and Nineteenth-Century Psychology* (London: Routledge, 1988), 24, 92.
4. Tamar Heller, *Dead Secrets: Wilkie Collins and the Female Gothic* (New Haven, CT: Yale University Press, 1992), 36–7.

5. Clare Pettitt, '"Cousin Holman's Dresser": Science, Social Change, and the Pathologized Female in Gaskell's "Cousin Phillips"', *Nineteenth-Century Literature* 52:4 (1998), 471–89 (481, 475).

6. Wilkie Collins, *The Moonstone*, ed. J. I. M. Stewart (London: Penguin, 1986), 64. Further references to this edition will be given in the text.

7. Unsigned, 'Our Female Sensation Novelists', *Christian Remembrancer* 46 (1864), 208–36 (210).

8. Jonathan Loesberg, 'The Ideology of Narrative Form in Sensation Fiction', *Representations* 13 (1986), 115–38 (117, 121).

9. Henry James, 'Miss Braddon', *Nation* (9 November 1865), quoted in Norman Page (ed.), *Wilkie Collins: The Critical Heritage* (London: Routledge and Kegan Paul, 1974), 122–3.

10. Unsigned, 'Inventors and Inventions', *All the Year Round* 2 (1860), 356; unsigned, 'Sugar and Milk', *All the Year Round* 7 (1862), 497–8; unsigned, 'The Modern Alchemist', *All the Year Round* 8 (1862), 384.

11. Ronald R. Thomas, '*The Moonstone*, Detective Fiction and Forensic Science', in *The Cambridge Companion to Wilkie Collins*, ed. Jenny Bourne Taylor (Cambridge University Press, 2006), 65–78 (71).

12. Unsigned, 'Science in the Witness Box', *Examiner* (19 January 1856), quoted in Ian A. Burney, 'A Poisoning of No Substance: The Trials of Medico-Legal Proof in Mid-Victorian England', *Journal of British Studies* 38:1 (1999), 59–92 (73).

13. Thomas, '*The Moonstone*, Detective Fiction', 68, 71, 67.

14. John Kucich, 'Scientific Ascendancy', in *A Companion to the Victorian Novel*, ed. Patrick Branlinger and William B. Thering (Oxford: Blackwell, 2002), 119–36 (134).

15. See Mary Lyndon Shanley, *Feminism, Marriage, and the Law in Victorian England* (Princeton University Press, 1989).

16. Sir William Blackstone, *Commentaries on the Laws of England*, quoted in Lee Holcombe, *Wives and Property: Reform of the Married Women's Property Law in Nineteenth-Century England* (University of Toronto Press, 1983), 25.

17. Caroline Norton, *English Laws for Women in the Nineteenth Century*, in *The Disempowered: Women and the Law*, ed. Marie Mulvey Roberts and Tamae Mizuta (London: Routledge/Thoemmes Press, 1993), 1–3.

18. Wilkie Collins, *The Woman in White*, ed. Harvey Peter Sucksmith (Oxford University Press, 1991), 396. Further references to this edition will be given in the text.

19. Frances Power Cobbe, 'Criminals, Idiots, Women, and Minors: Is the Classification Sound?', in *'Criminals, Idiots, Women, and Minors': Victorian Writing by Women on Women*, ed. Susan Hamilton (Peterborough, ON: Broadview Press, 1995), 110, 118–19.

20. Mary Elizabeth Braddon, *The Trail of the Serpent*, ed. Chris Willis (New York: Modern Library, 2003), 173. Further references to this edition will be given in the text.

21. George Eliot, *The Lifted Veil and Brother Jacob* (Leipzig: Tauchnitz, 1878), 41. Further references to this edition will be given in the text.

22. Kate Flint, 'Blood, Bodies, and *The Lifted Veil*', *Nineteenth-Century Literature* 51:4 (1997), 445–73 (459).

23. Mary Jacobus, *Reading Women: Essays in Feminist Criticism* (New York: Columbia University Press, 1986), 269.

24. See Flint, 'Blood, Bodies, and *The Lifted Veil*', 464–7, and G. H. Lewes, *The Physiology of Common Life*, 2 vols. (London: Blackwood, 1859), vol. 1, 276–7.
25. Bram Stoker, *Dracula*, ed. A. N. Wilson (Oxford University Press, 1992), 176.
26. Richard Menke, 'Fiction as Vivisection: G. H. Lewes and George Eliot', *ELH* 67:2 (2000), 617–53 (630).
27. Flint, 'Blood, Bodies, and *The Lifted Veil*', 470.
28. Wilkie Collins, *Heart and Science* (Phoenix Mill: Alan Sutton, 1994), 178. Further references to this edition will be given in the text.
29. Jessica Straley, 'Love and Vivisection: Wilkie Collins's Experiment in *Heart and Science*', *Nineteenth-Century Literature* 65:3 (2010), 348–73 (350, 351–2).
30. Wilkie Collins, 'Sister Rose', in Collins, *After Dark* (New York: Collier, 1900), 138–9. Further references to this edition will be given in the text.

13

GRAHAM LAW

Sensation fiction and the publishing industry

In considering the perils to which our language is exposed, the constant influence of corruption from colonial sources must not be overlooked . . . There seems . . . to be an unhealthy passion for adoption on the part of the public. Two or three years ago nobody would have known what was meant by a Sensation Novel; yet now the term has already passed through the stage of jocular use . . . and has been adopted as the regular commercial name for a particular product of industry for which there is just now a brisk demand.[1]

A commercial atmosphere floats around works of this class, redolent of the manufactory and the shop. The public want novels, and novels must be made – so many yards of printed stuff, sensation-pattern, to be ready by the beginning of the season . . . Various causes have been at work to produce this phenomenon of our literature. Three principal ones may be named as having had a large share in it – periodicals, circulating libraries, and railway bookstalls.[2]

The two quotations above are both taken from unsigned articles in prestigious intellectual quarterly magazines, which, despite their different ideological platforms, were united in the mid 1860s in mounting a reactionary critical assault on the fiction of sensation. The first, from the *Edinburgh Review* with its pronounced Whig tendencies, was merely a passing gibe in the course of a denunciation of current abuses of the English language penned by the barrister Matthew Brickdale, who nevertheless implied that the enjoyment of sensation fiction itself should be treated as an 'unhealthy passion'. The second appeared in the Tory *Quarterly Review* and was by Henry Mansel, then a Cambridge don and shortly to be appointed Dean of St Paul's Cathedral; though formally a review of two dozen novels, including works by Braddon, Collins and Wood, it in fact constituted a broadside attack on the febrile, ephemeral nature of sensation fiction. Both centre on provocative comments on developments in the mid-Victorian publishing industry, which are nevertheless prone to distortion on account of the elitist ideological position each periodical espoused. This chapter will thus take the form of a contextualised commentary on the points raised in these two quotations from the quarterlies, focusing first on the issues concerning the local origins and brand value of the term 'sensation novel' raised by Brickdale, before turning to the three distribution channels associated with the genre by Mansel, that is, circulating libraries, periodical publications and railway bookstalls.

'Corruption from colonial sources'

Although Brickdale's remarks are open to challenge on more than one count, he is right to see the term 'sensation novel' as originating elsewhere in the English-speaking world and only recently introduced to Britain. Noting that 'vast quantities of printed matter now pour in daily from the very outskirts of civilization',[3] Brickdale clearly intends the word 'colonial' in a broad, derogatory sense. The evidence in fact points unmistakably towards the United States as the source of the attributive use of 'sensation', with the earliest instances found from the later 1850s in notices of stage melodramas. The *Oxford English Dictionary* finds its earliest example in an 1860 journal entry by Emilie Cowell, wife of the comic singer Sam Cowell, during his concert tour of America, where at Cincinnati she attended a 'new "sensation Drama"' which she found 'full of strong and immoral situations'.[4] However, the recent proliferation of digital editions of nineteenth-century newspapers allows us to cast the net rather more widely. Advertisements and reviews of contemporary works at demotic Broadway venues such as Wallack's Lyceum, Barnum's Museum or Laura Keene's Varieties, touting the attractions of 'sensation' dramas, plays, pieces or scenes, are not difficult to find by late 1857 in popular New York weeklies such as *Spirit of the Times* and *Frank Leslie's Illustrated Newspaper*, or dailies such as Horace Greeley's *Tribune* and James Gordon Bennett's *Herald*. Indeed, a report from an early 1857 issue of the *Herald*, covering a political scandal concerning Russian agents in the State Department, jokes that this offers a golden opportunity 'for the young dramatists of New York to write a sensation play',[5] thus suggesting that the term may have been current rather earlier. Certainly well before the end of the decade the phrase was common in press notices of stage performances in cities throughout the Union.

The globe-trotting Irish actor-playwright Dion Boucicault was often considered responsible for introducing the term to Britain by contemporary commentators, including Henry Morley who, in noting in his theatre diary for December 1861 that *The Colleen Bawn* was still being performed 'in all directions' after opening in London at the Adelphi in the autumn of 1860, described ' "sensation" scene' as 'the new term in theatrical slang, which Mr Boucicault imported for us from the other side of the Atlantic'.[6] It was while starring at Wallack's Theatre, New York in the late 1850s, in works such as *Jessie Brown* (set during the Indian mutiny) and *Brigham Young* (on a number of Mormon scandals), that Boucicault became aware of the remarkable profits to be made by recycling contemporary news stories as sensationally staged theatrical scenes. Yet the Irish playwright does not bear sole responsibility. By 1859, more than a year before Boucicault returned to Britain, the widely read London weekly theatrical paper the *Era* was regularly citing notices of 'sensation' plays, and so on, from a range of American journals. Indeed, as early as the autumn of that year, the paper printed what must have been among the first occurrences of the term 'sensation novel' in the home country. This was in a report of the shows appearing at Barnum's Museum, lifted from the *Spirit of the Times* of 8 October, where it was reported, with reference to the English clergyman H. G. Jebb's *Out of the Depths* (1859), the story of a repentant prostitute, that the theatre had 'already dramatized and produced the latest sensation novel … a work of somewhat dubious character'.[7] Well before then, the American press had clearly begun enthusiastically to transfer the epithet from the drama to a wide range of other activities, including journalism, politics and, of course, fiction. The phrase 'sensation-novel style' can be found in the review columns of the *New York Times* as early as February 1858 (noticing *Fifteen Years Among the Mormons* from Scribner),[8] while advertisements from publishing houses for the latest 'sensation novel' appear regularly in New York and other cities from around the same time.

What is important here is that, while American uses of the term 'sensation' are predominantly affirmative and constructive, in the case of fiction at least, there emerges a significant difference in usage as we cross the Atlantic. This point is made vividly in a leading article in Bennett's typical popular-nationalist vein in the *New York Herald* in autumn 1860. This was written in praise of both domestic 'sensation journalism', which 'depicts passing events exactly as they impress themselves upon the masses of the people', and domestic 'sensation drama', as witnessed by the 'thoroughly American' performances of *Hamlet* by Edwin Forrest at Niblo's Garden, which expose 'the very age and body of the time'. Yet the author notes that 'our British cousins' still find such contemporary modes of expression distasteful, though they may be expected to 'know better by-and-by'.[9] Indeed, despite Brickdale's assertions, throughout the 1860s and beyond, while sales of Collins, Braddon, Wood and others were undoubtedly flourishing, there is remarkably little evidence of the concept being put to work by British publishers, booksellers or librarians as a brand identity for such goods, though plenty of the phrase still being used with comic and ironic intent by novelists, reviewers and critics alike.

Generic subtitles such as 'A Domestic Novel', 'A Romance', or 'A Story of Real Life', were commonly employed during the later nineteenth century to alert potential customers to new wares in an increasingly crowded marketplace for fiction. However, a search on comprehensive book-title listings such as the British Library Catalogue comes up with no similar cases of the use of 'A Sensation Novel' or the like in the mid-Victorian decades: ironically Edmund Yates's first full-length novel *Broken to Harness* (1864), a great hit on account of its sensation scenes, was subtitled 'A Story of English Domestic Life'. The only positive example I have found is a short serial aimed at a proletarian readership, the anonymous 'Golden Gap: A Sensational Novel', appearing in the January 1870 issues of John Dicks's weekly penny fiction journal *Bow Bells Magazine*, but apparently never reprinted in book form. (The adjectival form 'sensational' tended to gain ground in Britain steadily over the course of the 1860s.) Similarly, combing the extensive booksellers' advertisements in the columns of *The Times* over the relevant period suggests how reluctant publishers were to exploit the publicity value of 'sensation' as a generic marker. Throughout the 1860s, I have found only a dozen or so instances, most decidedly deconstructive, like the notice for Francis Paget's parody *Lucretia; or, The Heroine of the Nineteenth Century* from the house of J. Master, quoting the *Pall Mall Gazette* in praise of the author's exposure of 'the mischiefs of the sensational novel'.[10] Among the few affirmative examples were Mrs C. J. [Emma] Newby's *Wondrous Strange* from the notorious fiction house of T. C. Newby, apparently no relation, 'the best written sensation novel that has been submitted to our notice' according to the *Athenaeum*;[11] and Meta Fuller's *The Dead Letter*, touted in London as 'The Sensation Novel in America' from J. A. Berger of Catherine Street, following its stellar success in the USA in both magazine-serial and dime-novel form from the house of Beadle.[12] Both of these are, of course, marginalised works from decidedly minor publishers. The foremost London fiction houses, like Bentley, who managed Ellen Wood's list from *East Lynne* (1861) onwards, and Smith, Elder, which took over Wilkie Collins's repertoire in 1865, studiously avoided the sensation label in their advertisements. It was not until Collins's copyrights were bought up in the mid 1870s by the enterprising new house of Chatto and Windus that the tune changed: *The Times* notice for *The Law and the Lady*, the first new Collins novel to be issued by Chatto, prominently describing the author as 'the greatest master the sensational novel has ever known', citing Yates's society weekly the *World*.[13]

This restraint was in stark contrast to the brash marketing of melodrama on the London stage from the early 1860s, including the many unauthorised dramatisations of popular sensation novels like *East Lynne* and *Lady*

Audley's Secret, when long files of placard carriers blocked the pavements of the West End to promote the latest show. There are around ten instances of the use of the 'sensation' tag in *The Times* theatrical notices for one among the publishers' advertisements, with Sadler's Wells Theatre, the Theatre Royal, Drury Lane and the Princess's Theatre all advertising extensively in this fashion. The first notable example, however, was Benjamin Webster's production of *The Colleen Bawn* with its extravagant water scenes at the New Adelphi, starring Boucicault and his wife Agnes, which, on achieving 100 performances in little over three months, began to be promoted as 'the great sensation drama';[14] eventually the show clocked up 230 nights before moving to the larger Astley's Amphitheatre, and helped to earn the couple over £20,000 within the year. Ironically, the only instance I have found of blanket publicity exploiting the phrase 'sensation novel' occurs in early 1871, when W. S. Gilbert's comic operetta of that title, satirising the absurdities of the school of sensation fiction 'in three volumes', opened with a fanfare of publicity at Thomas German Reed's Gallery of Illustration. Though the popularity of Collins's *The Woman in White*, to take a seminal example, was exploited to some extent for commercial purposes by its contracted publishers Sampson Low – after its success as a weekly serial in Dickens's *All the Year Round*, the initial three-volume edition was widely advertised, sold 1,350 copies within the week and received eight impressions in less than six months, while a single-volume reprint appeared within the year embellished with a signed likeness of the author – this paled in comparison with the efforts of unauthorised agents. Theatrical pirates were by no means the only commercial operators to cash in at the peak of the novel's popularity, when, as attested by advertising in papers like the *Illustrated London News*, 'every possible commodity was labelled "Woman in White". There were "Woman in White" cloaks and bonnets, "Woman in White" perfumes and … toilet requisites, "Woman in White" Waltzes and Quadrilles.'[15]

Even the sensation novelists themselves were reluctant to acknowledge the validity of the term or to claim it as a badge. We can recognise this in the jocular, self-conscious fashion that the term is handled by Braddon, for example, both through her fictional narrators and in her own voice in private correspondence. Among the novels, Braddon mocks the sensation brand most explicitly in *The Doctor's Wife* (1864), which includes several satirical scenes of authorship and publishing featuring the character Sigismund Smith, a cheerful bohemian who makes his living writing melodramatic fiction for the proletarian market, and who is introduced in the second chapter, entitled 'A Sensation Author': 'Sigismund Smith was the author of about half a dozen highly-spiced fictions, which enjoyed an immense popularity amongst the classes who like their literature as they like their tobacco – very strong.'[16]

Since we know that Braddon herself began her literary career writing not for circulating library subscribers but for the penny public, and can recognise in Smith's words echoes of her own comic letters to her mentor Bulwer Lytton on the qualities required in the production of the penny dreadful ('The *amount of crime, treachery, murder, slow poisoning*, and general infamy required by the Halfpenny reader is something terrible'),[17] it is difficult not to read this as self-deprecation. As though in compensation, the narrator later protests: 'This is *not* a sensation novel. I write here what I know to be the truth' (vol. III, ch. 9). In similar ways, Edmund Yates, in *Broken to Harness* (running simultaneously as a serial with *The Doctor's Wife* in the monthly *Temple Bar*), claimed tongue-in-cheek to be writing not 'a full-flavoured romance of the sensational order' but merely 'a commonplace story of every-day life',[18] while, as late as 1878, Wilkie Collins could refer, in a letter to a literary friend who requested the author's inscription in a copy of his latest novel, to 'that dreadful "sensational work" which you honour me by choosing as a birthday present for [your wife]'.[19] In this way, the lowly cultural status assigned to the sensation novel as a mass-market commodity encouraged the sensation novelists themselves to join in the chorus of mockery with which the genre was generally greeted by the critics.

The reluctance on the part of both publishers and authors to promote the novel of sensation can indeed be explained in part by the caustic nature of critical responses to the new genre. The elite intellectual quarterlies were, of course, roundly negative: besides those of Brickdale and Mansel, there were attacks alike in the radical *Westminster Review*, where 'Sensational Mania' was judged to 'afflict only the most poverty stricken minds',[20] and the broad church *North British Review*, which damned sensation fiction as one of 'the abominations of the age'.[21] Indeed, this is true of the British periodical press as a whole when it came to general critical articles discussing the phenomenon, though the tone ranges from mockery to moral outrage. In contrast, there was no shortage of enthusiastic reviews of individual sensation novels – the extensive, timely and laudatory notices in the columns of *The Times* of *East Lynne* ('the best novel of the season'),[22] and *Lady Audley's Secret* ('the work of a really clever authoress'),[23] for example, were extremely influential in attracting public attention not only to two hitherto unrecognised female authors, but also to a new mode of contemporary fiction. Nevertheless, Samuel Lucas and E. S. Dallas, the respective reviewers in question, managed to do so without once employing the term 'sensation'. Yet perhaps the only consolidated contemporary defence of sensation fiction was that offered in the columns of the monthly *Belgravia*, founded only in late 1866 and edited by Braddon herself. The key articles were not from her pen but that of George Sala, with a good deal of experience as literary editor and sensation novelist, but now increasingly occupied as a journalist on the popular *Daily Telegraph*. There Sala wrote aggressively in the face of the recent critical outcry, declaring Shakespeare and Dickens themselves forerunners in the art of sensation, and defining the form proudly as 'the contemporary novel of life and character and adventure – the outspoken, realistic, moving, breathing fiction, which mirrors the passions of the age for which it was written'.[24] To understand why Sala remained a lone critical voice in defending the sensation novel, and how, to adapt Brickdales's formulation, the term itself took so long to traverse 'the stage of jocular use' without ever being 'adopted as the regular commercial name for a particular product of industry', we must turn now to Mansel's comments, in order to study in more detail the conservative practices of the British publishing industry, which then functioned on very different principles from its American counterpart.

'So many yards of printed stuff, sensation-pattern'

The three main causes of the commodification of literature detected by Mansel in the sensation boom – circulating libraries, periodical publications and railway bookstalls – can all rather be seen as consequences of the British publishing industry's long-standing commercial policy of producing the latest works of imagination and ideas alike in luxury editions priced far beyond the reach of all but the wealthiest. Virtually throughout the Victorian period, the standard post-octavo volume was retailed for the lordly sum of half a guinea, more than the weekly wage of a manual labourer at the mid-century, while the guinea-and-a-half charged for the triple-decker set in which new bourgeois novels typically appeared was close to the monthly stipend of a Church of England curate or other gentlemanly professional at the lower end of the middle class. In this, the London book publishers were out of step not only with other metropolitan media industries such as news broadcasting and the performing arts, but also with their counterparts in rival industrial economies. As Matthew Arnold noted in 1880, both France and the United States, despite their contrary policies concerning intellectual property – the former favouring the rights of authors and the latter the needs of readers – were both far prompter in appreciating the advantages of a regime of inexpensive new books of decent quality than England with its 'highly eccentric, artificial, and unsatisfactory system of book-trade'.[25] Private lending libraries encouraging middle-class subscribers to borrow rather than purchase selected new books, serial publications offering advance copy of the latest works in economic instalments over a lengthy period and railway editions reprinting the most popular works in cheap and cheerful formats several years behind the times, each in its own way eccentric and artificial, were all attempts, imaginative, enterprising but not entirely satisfactory, to take advantage of or work around what was at bottom an 'absurd system of dear books'.[26]

Convicted by Mansel as 'the oldest offender of the three',[27] commercial circulating libraries were already flourishing by the mid-eighteenth century, rather ahead of cooperative subscription libraries. Both were middle-class institutions, the latter typically developed from male self-governing associations for the reading and discussion of non-fiction, while the former were the offshoots of stationery and bookselling businesses and mainly loaned novels to a female clientele. With the chronic inflation generated by the Napoleonic Wars, the price of books, along with other commodities, rose steeply in the new century, so that it is unsurprising that the number of circulating libraries nationwide jumped sixfold in the first two decades. What is more difficult to understand is that, even after the 1832 Reform Act and the phase of economic liberalisation that it heralded, new book prices remained prohibitive and the circulating library maintained its ascendancy as a distribution device, though in a significantly altered form. Until the early Victorian years, the circulating system was highly decentralised, with country libraries in market towns and spa and seaside resorts perhaps more active and influential than a host of small metropolitan lenders. Established in 1842, with its low subscription rates, efficient distribution mechanisms and ample but varied holdings (little more than one third fiction), Charles Mudie's Select Library rapidly obtained imperial control of the market, grabbing the lion's share of many print runs, pushing publishers to provide at steep discounts, and thus driving out or taking over many local rivals not only in the capital but in the provinces and colonies also. Transferring to larger and grander metropolitan premises twice during the 1850s, and in 1864 forming a limited liability company with major fiction houses like Bentley as the main shareholders, Mudie had a hegemonic hold on the distribution of new books by the time of the sensation boom.

The collusion between the central circulating library and the major publishers not only served to reinforce the foundations of the nation's 'absurd system of dear books', but also helped to create a delicate conservative mechanism of ideological control over the form and content of new writing, discursive as well as imaginative. Mudie's library was selective not only regarding the social status of its customers but also the moral standing of its books. Not that there was much call at first for direct censorship of the sensation novel, since the melodramatic mode tended to encourage veiled rather than explicit treatments of social and sexual transgression, while, as Mansel noted, the commercial library system generally tended to foster small editions of a large number of works regardless of quality, thus expanding the number of titles available. Yet the ideological tension became more overt with the rise of what Mansel refers to as sensation fiction 'with a didactic purpose',[28] by writers such as Reade and Collins. Twice during the 1870s, fascination with the theme of the reformed prostitute caused Collins to fall foul of 'that fanatical old fool Mudie',[29] who demanded a less provocative title for *The New Magdalen* (1873) and refused altogether to handle *The Fallen Leaves* (1879). However, it was not until the 1880s – under the threat of more overt representations of sexuality through the influence of Zola's naturalism on novelists such as George Moore, and with progressive new publishing houses challenging the Mudie monopoly by issuing original work in cheaper, more compact editions – that there were signs of outright battle between the librarian and the author.[30] Mansel's critique, of course, could not see so far, and indeed failed entirely to recognise the impact of the Mudie revolution, instead assuming that the function of the circulating library had changed little since it supplied 'the light reading of our grandmothers',[31] that is, the fashion for gothic romances at the turn of the nineteenth century.

Mansel also failed to acknowledge that periodical publications had an even more lengthy and varied history than circulating libraries, with formats such as the news coranto dating back to the early seventeenth century. Branding them with the commercial character of 'goods made to order', holding only 'an ephemeral interest' and lacking 'coherence in their parts',[32] the future dean of St Paul's provided a decidedly inferior estimation of the role of magazines and journals to his contemporary E. S. Dallas, who had recently declared 'the great event in modern history' to be '[t]he rise of the periodical press'.[33] Dallas asserted that the press represented 'not only the expression of public opinion and the index of contemporary history' but further that it was 'itself a great force that reacts on the life which it represents, half creating what it professes only to reflect',[34] thus anticipating Jürgen Habermas in identifying the periodical as a key agent in the formation of the bourgeois public sphere.[35] As Richard Altick argues, such an initial print context was particularly appropriate for sensation fiction, preoccupied as it was with the 'presence of the present', that is, the events and issues of the day.[36] In fact, the instalment publication of unified texts within magazines and newspapers, or as independent fascicles (numbered pamphlets), also goes back to the mid-eighteenth century and beyond. To begin with, such serial issue at regular intervals, typically weekly or monthly, and not just of novels but also of many kinds of literary, scholarly and reference work, was undoubtedly commercially motivated. Through such a mechanism, producers were able to spread the costs of manufacture, and consumers the price of purchase, painlessly over the lengthy period of issue, while either side could withdraw from a work that proved unsatisfactory. Yet, by the early Victorian decades its increasing prevalence indicates that serial fiction had also come to fulfill psychological needs, so that we then have to recognise the aesthetics of serial composition and consumption, as well the economics of serial production and distribution. Nevertheless, because of Britain's 'highly ... unsatisfactory system of book-trade', still in the mid-nineteenth century purchasing novels in instalments represented something of a bargain. Compared to the retail price of a triple-decker (31s. 6d.), a complete novel of average length could be purchased in independent numbers at 20s., or, along with a basket of other literary goods, for around 12s. if issued in a shilling monthly such as *Temple Bar*, but for only 6s. if in a twopenny weekly such as *All the Year Round*.

Indeed, the most significant trend in the serial publication of fiction at the time of the sensation boom was the shift from the dominance of monthly to that of weekly issue. As is well known, Dickens had a good deal to do with the popularising of serial issue, with his first two novels both appearing in monthly parts, *Pickwick Papers* in fascicles (1836–7) and *Oliver Twist* in the columns of *Bentley's Miscellany* (1837–9). In the early decades of the Victorian period, weekly issue of fiction was still 'connected with publication of the lowest class – small penny and halfpenny serials that found in the multitude some compensation for the degradation of their readers', as E. S. Dallas put it in the *Times* review of *Great Expectations*.[37] Thus Dickens's first weekly miscellany, *Master Humphrey's Clock* (1840–1), was a relative failure, despite featuring both *The Old Curiosity Shop* and *Barnaby Rudge*. Yet, after the mid-century there was a rapid proliferation of respectable weekly formats, including both pictorial journals like the *Illustrated London News* and family miscellanies like *All the Year Round*. Since, as Mansel argued, 'circumstances of production naturally have their effect on the quality of the articles produced',[38] it is not surprising that the weekly instalment encouraged narrative of fast pace, relying a good deal on the mechanics of enigma and suspense, with a striking opening to the serial as a whole and 'climax and curtain' closures to each instalment. Thus, in the final paragraphs of his article, Mansel identifies the 'bloods' issued in penny parts or penny papers for a proletarian readership as 'the original germ' of the bourgeois sensation novel,[39] just as J. R. Wise in the *Westminster Review* represented 'Sensational Mania' as a 'virus ... spreading in all directions from the penny journal to the shilling magazine, and from the shilling magazine to the thirty-shilling volume'.[40] In contrast, the issue in *All the Year Round* of novels by Collins, Dickens and Lytton, each in its own way of a sensation bent, led Dallas to the conclusion that 'the weekly form of publication is not incompatible with a very high order of fiction'.[41] While Collins, Wood and Braddon also had quite a bit of experience writing serials for literary monthlies, their more formative training was in the cheap weeklies, particularly the twopenny *Household Words*, the penny *Quiver* and the *Halfpenny Journal*, respectively. Moreover, Braddon and Collins went on to make a significant contribution to the syndication of fiction in provincial weekly newspapers, the major innovation in serial publication of the 1870s.

If the serial and the circulating library were both distribution channels of long standing that underwent major changes in the mid-nineteenth century, the railway bookstall was a strikingly modern institution, like the railway network itself. Already in 1850, though, there were over 60 million passengers travelling over 6,000 miles or so of track at speeds of up to 60 miles per hour.[42] The station stall had begun early in the Victorian era as a local affair, rather like the commercial library, with the early holders typically either retired railway employees or the owners of bookselling businesses in nearby towns. But in 1848, when it was put out to tender, the bookstall contract for the entire London and Northwestern line from Euston to Manchester was awarded to W. H. Smith, the powerful wholesale newspaper distributor, and within little more than a decade the firm had control of stalls on virtually the whole of the English network. Still at the time of the sensation boom and indeed long after, the most visible and profitable function of the railway bookstalls was the sale of newspapers and journals, though the holders were by then also offering a range of other goods, including food, travel requisites and cheap editions of popular fiction. It was these that most concerned Mansel, who, in describing the stall-holders as aping the refreshment-rooms in 'offering their customers something hot and strong',[43] was perpetuating a myth of the pornographic railway novel that was long out of date. In fact, W. H. Smith was then already earning a reputation as a guardian of readerly morality on a par with Mudie, who in 1858 had indeed been offered the franchise to operate a circulating library from Smith's stalls. In refusing, Mudie had encouraged Smith to start the business himself and thus gradually become a major competitor as a commercial lender of books.

However, the main books on offer at the railway stations were 'yellow-backs', typically popular works sold at a couple of shillings, printed from stereotype on brittle paper and flimsily bound in strawboards covered with glazed yellow paper with a striking illustration on the front and a prominent advertisement on the back. Though original work was occasionally issued in this format, the yellowback was developed by houses specialising in cheap reprint fiction, with the prototype, lacking the pictorial cover and tinted in green rather than yellow, appearing from the mid-century in the 'Railway Library' of George Routledge. Well before the end, this library included over a thousand titles, to begin with mainly unprotected or out-of-copyright works (by Fennimore Cooper or Austen, for example), though soon the firm was in a position to pay large sums for the residual rights to the novel lists of, notably, Ainsworth or Lytton. The more familiar form emerged around 1854 with the

'Select Library of Fiction' from Chapman & Hall, who in 1859 joined with W. H. Smith to create a distinctive series for the latter's railway stalls. By the 1860s, major houses specialising in original work for the circulating libraries, like Smith, Elder and Bentley, were employing the same format for the least expensive editions on their backlists. Thus, by the time Mansel was writing, the railway book represented the final stage under the British book trade's long-standing policy of 'tranching down'. As analysed by William St Clair, this economic model emerged during the later eighteenth century under a copyright regime privileging the interests of booksellers at the expense of both writers and readers, and took the form of a steep demand curve, whereby publishers with monopoly rights maximised financial returns over time by gradually issuing larger runs of books in smaller formats at cheaper prices, thus steadily accessing discrete reading constituencies lower down the social hierarchy.[44] Decisively rejected in a post-independence America, which preferred an extremely flat demand curve giving common readers fast, unrestricted access to current knowledge and ideas, the British book trade policy came at a considerable social cost, hindering the development of those industrial and democratic practices crucial to modernisation. Ironically, because of the lengthy time lag dictated by the practice of tranching down, none of the seminal sensation novels – *The Woman in White, East Lynne* and *Lady Audley's Secret* – had as yet appeared in yellowback format at the time that Mansel launched his attack on the 'temporary excitement' offered by such works to the railway reader 'to relieve the dulness of a journey'.[45]

At the turn of the nineteenth century, the British publishing industry was still concerned predominantly with supplying luxury goods in limited editions for an elite readership. By the turn of the twentieth century, the focus had shifted in the main to the manufacture of inexpensive items in large print runs for a mass reading public, an uneven process that Richard Altick has described as 'the democratizing of reading'.[46] Such a development was inevitably accompanied by a range of long-term, socio-economic changes – most notably advances in communications technology, regulatory reform affecting both taxation and censorship and the expansion of institutions of popular education. In terms of mode of production, to employ Marxian terminology, petty commodity production thus gradually gave way to commodity production over the course of the century. The moment of the mid-Victorian sensation boom was an important one in this transition, not because the sensation novel itself was produced for or consumed by a mass audience, but rather in the sense that it represented an intrusion into the bourgeois literary sphere of commodity forms that had hitherto been associated with a discrete proletarian marketplace. This, above all, was what aroused the disgust, derision and dismay of the cultural establishment represented by the likes of Brickdale and Mansel.

NOTES

1. M. I. F. Brickdale, 'The Queen's English', *Edinburgh Review* 120 (1864), 39–57.
2. Mansel, 483.
3. Brickdale, 'The Queen's English', 53.
4. See Emilie Cowell, *The Cowells in America: Being the Diary of Mrs Sam Cowell During her Husband's Concert Tour in the Years 1860–1861*, ed. M. Willson Disher (Oxford University Press, 1934), 36.
5. Unsigned, 'Affairs at the National Capital', *New York Herald* (10 January 1857), 1.
6. Henry Morley, *Journal of a London Playgoer from 1851 to 1866* (London: Routledge, 1866), 281–2.
7. Unsigned, 'American Theatricals', *The Era* (23 October 1859), 10.
8. Unsigned, 'New Books', *New York Times* (23 February 1858), 2.
9. Unsigned, 'The Latest Metropolitan Sensation', *New York Herald* (25 September 1860), 6.
10. *The Times* (4 March 1868), 12.
11. See *The Athenaeum* (6 August 1864), 178; cited in *The Times* (31 August 1864), 3.
12. *The Times* (30 October 1867), 13.
13. *The Times* (10 April 1875), 12.
14. *The Times* (4 January 1861), 6.
15. S. M. Ellis, *Wilkie Collins, Le Fanu and Others* (London: Constable, 1931), 29–30.
16. Mary Elizabeth Braddon, *The Doctor's Wife*, 3 vols. (London: John Maxwell, 1864), vol. I, ch. 2. Further reference to this edition will be given in the text.
17. Robert Lee Wolff, 'Devoted Disciple: The Letters of Mary Elizabeth Braddon to Sir Edward Bulwer Lytton, 1862–1873', *Harvard Library Bulletin* 22 (1974), 5–35, 129–61 (11).
18. Edmund Yates, *Broken to Harness*, 3 vols. (London: John Maxwell, 1864), vol. I, ch. 5.
19. Wilkie Collins to Frederick Locker, 12 February 1878, in BGLL, vol. III, 184.
20. J. R. Wise, 'Belles Lettres', *Westminster Review* 86 (1866), 270.
21. Rae, 203.
22. Samuel Lucas, 'East Lynne', *The Times* (25 January 1862), 6.
23. E. S. Dallas, 'Lady Audley's Secret', *The Times* (18 November 1862), 4.
24. George Augustus Sala, 'The Cant of Modern Criticism', *Belgravia* 4 (1867), 45–55, and 'On the Sensational in Literature and Art', Belgravia 4 (1868), 449–58.
25. Matthew Arnold, 'Copyright', *Fortnightly Review* 159 (1880), 319–34 (334).
26. *Ibid.*
27. Mansel, 484.
28. *Ibid.*, 487.
29. Wilkie Collins to George Bentley, 20 May 1873, BGLL, vol. II, 401.
30. See George Moore's diatribe against Mudie in *Literature at Nurse, or Circulating Morals* (London: Vizetelly, 1885).
31. Mansel, 484.
32. *Ibid.*, 483–4.
33. E. S. Dallas, 'Popular Literature: The Periodical Press', *Blackwood's Edinburgh Magazine* 85 (1859), 96–112, 180–95 (100).
34. *Ibid.*, 97.

35. Jürgen Habermas, *The Structural Transformation of the Public Sphere*, trans. Thomas Burger (Oxford: Polity Press, 1989).

36. Richard. D. Altick, *The Presence of the Present: Topics of the Day in the Victorian Novel* (Columbus: Ohio State University Press, 1991), 80–2.

37. E. S. Dallas, 'Great Expectations', *The Times* (17 October 1861), 5.

38. Mansel, 485.

39. *Ibid.*, 505.

40. Wise, 'Belles Lettres', 268.

41. Dallas, 'Great Expectations', 5.

42. Charles Wilson, *First With the News: The History of W.H. Smith, 1792–1972* (London: W. H. Smith, 1985), 88–90.

43. Mansel, 485.

44. William St Clair, *The Reading Nation in the Romantic Period* (Cambridge University Press, 2004), 19–42.

45. Mansel, 485.

46. Richard D. Altick, *The English Common Reader: A Social History of the Mass Reading Public, 1800–1900* (University of Chicago Press, 1957), 5.

14

PAMELA K. GILBERT

Sensation fiction and the medical context

> [T]he pleasure which we may conceive taken by the children of the
> coming time, in the analysis of physical corruption, guides, into fields
> more dangerous and desolate, the expatiation of an imaginative
> literature: and . . . the reactions of moral disease upon itself . . . have
> become the most valued material of modern fiction, and the most eagerly
> discussed texts of modern philosophy.[1]

John Ruskin, that temperamental commentator on the arts of his time, was
displeased with the general tendency of mid nineteenth-century literature to
focus on non-ideal physical and mental states. Within this trend, sensation
fiction was a genre particularly connected to current understandings of physiology and medicine. Its madwomen and nerve-wracked men existed in a
cultural context of acute interest in the body's relation to the mind and soul,
in which anti-social actions earlier attributed to evil and sin began to be
explained in terms of degenerate constitutions and maniacal obsessions.
This chapter will outline some of the background of medical history in the
period, and its specific resonance in sensation fiction, including the presence
of medical men as heroes and villains. A detailed reading of Wilkie Collins's
Armadale (1866) offers an example of the centrality of such themes to a novel
that, at first glance, might seem less clearly tied to medical history than many
other novels that have been so read.

Medical history and fictional form

The mid-Victorian period saw the rise of the modern medical profession. In
the early part of the century, there was a dramatic increase in the production
of medical knowledge, bringing a substantial break from earlier models of
medicine dating back at least to the Renaissance. The advent of morbid
pathology revolutionised surgery, as did the development of anaesthesia in
the mid-century. New instruments and optics expanded the range of physiological investigation in living tissue. Statistical technologies of health demo-
graphics, such as morbidity and mortality statistics in the public health arena,
and risk tables in the life assurance (insurance) industry shifted interest from

the individual sufferer to the broader population. New positivist approaches to medical evidence based on careful clinical examination became the standard for medical practice, and the old ideal of a doctor who interviewed a patient at length and knew him or her well as an individual was supplanted by an understanding of the clinician as an expert who relied on vision and non-verbal cues to interpret the condition of the patient, of which the sufferer might not even be aware, and was certainly incompetent to describe accurately. The patient as a unique subject was replaced by the model of the patient as a standardised bearer of constitutional and disease characteristics which were read as more important and telling than older notions of 'character'.

The novel, and, more specifically, the narrative mode of realism appropriates many of the techniques of the clinical medical gaze of this period: the focus on detailed and apparently objective description of minute but meaningful signs that must be interpreted by an expert (the author, and by flattering extension, the reader); careful cataloguing of physiological reactions (blushes, pallor, faintness); and a focus on the normative and everyday flawed, middle-class protagonist, rather than extreme or unusual situations and the heroic or villainous (often aristocratic) characters that marked the gothic or the romance. The quote by Ruskin with which this chapter begins refers not to sensation fiction by Braddon or Collins, but to the work of Dickens and Eliot. Literary critic and medical historian Lawrence Rothfield argues that the British and French nineteenth-century novel demonstrates that medicine and narrative realism take up 'similar strategies, construct similar kinds of subjects, [and] exert similar kinds of authority': novelists adopt not only 'a stock of characters but a set of quasi-artistic techniques, including, for example, a specifically symptomological semiology', as characters are embodied with particular pathologies and constitutions.[2] Realism's penchant for both detailed description and 'round' characters with complex interiorities, as well as fiction's preoccupation with the temporal and causal progress of events, means that the medical case study both models and mirrors the novel. In terms of literary history itself, the style and form of the novel seem to break from the romance's focus on the marvellous and unique; instead, it again shares some of the qualities of the case study, and something of the same purpose: through the narration of a singular but typical story, it seeks to reveal a larger truth applicable to everyday life.

Sensation novels at first glance might seem to repudiate this realistic mode of narration and offer a return to the gothic, with its emphasis on the unique and unrepeatable. Improbable coincidences, unusual situations and extraordinary emotional challenges abound. Instead of confronting the typical and quotidian, characters are thrust into extreme situations – and come up with equally extreme responses. On second look, however, sensation novels are deeply indebted to the realist tradition. The characters tend to be ordinary middle- to upper-class folk. Stories are set in the present or recent past, and in familiar locations. Their struggles have to do with ordinary Victorian challenges and the typical stuff of the novel – debt, bankruptcy, identity and the legitimacy of marriages, children and heirs. All of these themes relate to the larger question that critic Raymond Williams famously identified as central to the mid-century novel: the elaboration of a knowable community, responding to readers' desire to feel that a large group of people could be fully known and understood in relation to each other in the wake of the disorienting social changes wrought by the Industrial Revolution.[3] Sensation characters might best be said to experience realist challenges at an accelerated rate: whereas the realist protagonist has a detailed response to one or two of these conflict themes, sensation characters struggle with all of them in rapid succession. Their lives or case histories seem to be intensified and 'speeded up'.

The very notion of sensation itself is a physiological one, and its understanding by the critics and readers of its day was grounded in popular understandings of medicine and physiological psychology. As Henry Mansel disapprovingly said in 1863, sensation fiction 'preaches to the nerves'. Many reviewers voiced the concern that the (usually female) reader of sensation was experiencing – and would then become addicted to seeking – a physiological 'thrill' that bypassed her rational mind and, therefore, her ability to evaluate and respond morally to the text. 'Good' literature caused the reader to think carefully, sympathise with realistic responses to situations and make careful judgements. It was nourishing 'food' for the mind, rather than an inappropriately stimulating 'dram or ... dose'.[4] Sensation fiction was believed to develop a vitiated taste for ever more intense physiological stimulation.

The fiction itself focuses on physiology as well, alternately adopting a clinical view and challenging it for its materialist limitations. If the sensation novel is seen as acting upon the nerves, it is also preoccupied with the actions of other agents on the organism. Literary scholar Nicholas Daly notes that sensation thematised modernity through the actions of machines and modernity's reliance on new experiences of speed and shock associated with railways and telegraphs. (Likewise, sensation fiction was meant to be consumed – often by commuters on those railways – speedily, rather than slowly in a book-lined study.) Lady Audley is able to set her schemes in motion because she can run up to London quickly by rail and hardly be missed. Daly suggests that sensation novels provided a kind of 'temporal training' to inure people to the overstimulation of modern life.[5] Both plot and pace were attuned to modern experience of temporality: sensation is, he notes 'a *punctual* form, depending on accurate time-keeping and scrupulous attention to the calendar'.[6] Sensation fiction, then, contextualised human actions in an increasingly precise and mechanistic universe.

Medical history and fictional content

Some novels in the period depend for their principal interest on a particular physical condition: Collins's *Poor Miss Finch* (1872) relies heavily on detailed discussions of the medical condition of the blind heroine and the psychological issues resulting therefrom, as well as the secondary but rather more spectacular silver nitrate treatment that unfortunately turns her fiancé a permanent, unattractive blue. Madness, hereditary and otherwise, features as a significant plot point for novels throughout the period. However, it is more usual for the medical condition of the characters simply to underlie their motivations and reactions, rather than to drive the plot directly. The sensation genre's interest in extreme medical and mental states connects with the period's interest in evolution, degeneration, barbarism and the Other. Inherited disease – madness or the kind of degeneration associated with 'vice' – which in the 1890s come to be more directly articulated as infectious venereal disease and especially syphilis – in the 1860s is associated with similar but vaguer symptoms (paralysis, exhaustion, idiocy) which can be inherited but is rarely presented as infectious. The loss of 'vitality' over the generations from a 'vicious' parent or ancestor thus refers to ideas of degeneration. But geography or racial otherness can also carry the burden of this significance. In Collins especially, foreign characters are the bearers of dangerous physical states, and this is particularly true of mixed-race characters such as Ozias Midwinter in *Armadale* or Ezra Jennings in *The Moonstone* (1868).

While the form of the sensation novel evoked nervous stimulation and the threat of madness and addiction, the content of the sensation novel thematised the dangers of nervous disease. Physicians believed that the overstimulated nerve would progressively fail to respond to the same level of stimulus, thus requiring a stronger stimulus to achieve the same effect, until eventually the organism would collapse under the strain. The hermeneutic logic of the sensation form is obsessional: although one constantly discovers something surprising, the climax of ultimate discovery and closure in each case is deferred, demanding that the next revelation will be even more surprising. Obsession itself is structurally similar to addiction: both involve a craving that cannot be satisfied and indeed, that is only increased by being fed. Sensation fiction is particularly marked by its use of 'monomania', the Victorian term for obsession, as a theme, and this fascination dominates Dickens's fiction in the 1860s as well.

The connection between femaleness and madness has been often remarked by Victorian scholars, and has been understood to be foundational to the gender politics of the period since Elaine Showalter's groundbreaking study of hysteria, *The Female Malady* (1985). The term 'hysteria' refers to the womb, and women were thought to be particularly vulnerable to insanity due to their physiologies. Their reproductive systems were thought to be so delicately balanced that even the healthy woman was always on the verge of mental dysfunction. That said, the period also sees an exploration of male hysteria, addiction and obsession. In both sensation and realist novels, men succumb to the temptations of gambling and market speculation in terms redolent of the period's understanding of addiction. Characters are addicted to alcohol, opium and its derivatives, gambling and, of course, sensation novels. None of these things, it turns out, are good for the nerves.

Braddon's Robert Audley fears being a monomaniac; Reade's Dr Wycherly simply is one; and from Collins's hypochondriacal Mr Fairlie of *The Woman in White* (1859–60) to his nervous surgeon Dr Ovid and the sinister brain disease specialist Dr Benjulia in *Heart and Science* (1883) (who ultimately commits suicide, having become nervous himself), the insane male is the more sensational secret of many of these novels. After all, it was practically normal for a woman to be a little unbalanced, but the madman is a spectacle of horror as well as pity. More frighteningly, the madman (especially the monomaniac) seems to outsiders to function normally long after he is in fact quite ill. Braddon explores religious mania in her eponymous evangelical character Joshua Haggard, and, of course, Dickens's Eugene Wrayburn and Bradley Headstone in *Our Mutual Friend* (1865) are both obsessive stalkers, though Headstone is the more obviously mad in Dickens's culture's sense of the term, as he stalks another man with murderous intent, rather than a woman with amorous purposes. (His madness is also distinctly somatised, causing him to have frequent nosebleeds.) Miserrimus Dexter in Collins's *The Law and the Lady* (1875), one of the genre's many disabled characters, is burdened both with an absence of legs and an excess of nervous susceptibility, and is both mad and paralysed when he dies by the end of the novel.

Medical heroes and villains: the surgeon and the mad-doctor

After the clergyman, or minister of other denominations than the Church, who stands in such favour – and we are not at all jealous – with the real head of the family as the family doctor? . . .. Therefore, you have a power, an influence with men, and women too, in the middle ranks of life which none of us possess in the same degree.[7]

Given the importance of medicine in the Victorian novel, it is not surprising that medical professionals often feature as characters themselves, often as commentators who serve purposes of exposition in relating the condition of the main characters. The medical hero rose to prominence in the mid-century and was as frequently featured in sensation novels as his alter-ego, the lawyer (another rational middle-class professional). By the 1860s, doctors are everywhere in the fiction, but their uncanny ability to read symptoms and unearth secrets, as well as their drive to knowledge for its own sake, begins to have a darker side. In these novels, the legitimate doctor – often a surgeon – is akin to the novelist: a humane observer gifted with extraordinary perceptive abilities. The mad-doctor, however, may be mistaken in diagnosis, and even when he is legitimate and correct in his diagnosis, he is likely to suffer from a lack of humanity. The doctor, especially the doctor-scientist, becomes a frightening figure whose ability to sympathise with patients decreases as his brilliance increases: the doctor himself comes to have a god-complex, and if he is not mad in the strict sense, the latter-day Victor Frankenstein certainly becomes bad and dangerous to know.

Tabitha Sparks, in her recent study of the figure of the doctor in the Victorian novel, points out that as medical authority gained ground, the claim of the novelistic art to clarify the truth of the human condition waned, and fiction 'gradually loses the authority that medicine and science were claiming as the medical profession worked to locate the knowledge of human subjectivity in physiology',[8] but the novels she studies 'agree that the doctor's authority comes at the cost of his isolation from society and morality, exactly the ruling domains of the marriage-plot novel ... Fictional doctors increasingly become lonely bachelors or callous experimentalists.'[9] Several scholars have used Eliot's *Middlemarch* (1872) as an exemplar of narrative as a clinical case study, with the added bonus that it includes a protagonist who is himself a scientifically minded surgeon, up on the latest French techniques. But as Peter Logan has pointed out, Eliot also wryly points up the blindness of certain kinds of scientific attitudes, and Lydgate's noble ambitions are thwarted.[10] Generally, however, these surgeon-characters are heroic, such as the doctors in Dickens's *Little Dorrit* (1855–7) and *Bleak House* (1852–3), or in Charles Kingsley's *Two Years Ago* (1857). In Collins's *Man and Wife*, a surgeon, observing the physically splendid athlete Geoffrey, tells him he is in broken health. All observers around Geoffrey, and he himself, are incredulous: he is a prize-winning runner, oarsman and fighter. The surgeon alone is able to see that Geoffrey has dangerously depleted his strength, simply by observing his face at a distance.[11]

In short, the medical professional is able to read the inner truth of characters, even without a medical examination, and through his authority, we understand a reality that the other characters cannot accept because they cannot see what the surgeon perceives, even though – or especially because – they are observing Geoffrey in the same moment: 'The man who first declared that "seeing" was "believing" laid his finger (whether he knew it himself or not) on one of the fundamental follies of humanity. The easiest of all evidence to receive is ... the judgment of the eye' (219). The surgeon, of course, also relies on the judgement of the eye – however, he is gifted with the clinical gaze detailed by Foucault: a gaze which, though relying initially on visual inspection, sees more than the normal eye. It is important that the surgeon uses no instruments or tactile examination to perceive this truth. Because his gaze is uniquely trained, he can determine – with no more evidence available to him than to all the other characters – the truth that is invisible to them. In reading past the apparent truth of the individual to expose the universals of signs of disease, the doctor himself also in some sense transcends individuality, and is thus aligned with the novelist's ability to take in the whole of human experience.

The mid-century mad-doctor was a more ambivalent figure than the surgeon – perhaps in part because a surgeon rarely confined his patients (though he might well inadvertently kill them). Dr Francis Ainstie, in a plea for a more coherent system of medical expert testimony, observes that 'The practice of signing certificates for the committal of patients to houses of restraint is a very important matter ... because it has been made the ground of all kinds of suspicion against the candour and honesty of medical practitioners. The public has a chronic quarrel with "mad-doctors", as the pages of many a sensation novel will testify.'[12] And indeed, popular culture in the 1860s took up the theme of wrongful internment in madhouses with enthusiasm, as Charles Reade's *Hard Cash* (1863) dramatises. The protagonist Alfred Hardie is wrongfully committed by his father, who seeks to cheat him of his inheritance. Alfred becomes friendly with Dr Wycherly, the superintendent, only to discover that Wycherly is himself a (mostly asymptomatic) monomaniac. High-profile cases and physicians caught the public's imagination. The celebrated novelist, Edward Bulwer Lytton, incarcerated his troublesome wife Rosina, who appealed to the law for release and was avenged upon him when she published her autobiography with a detailed description of her wrongful imprisonment. As Jill Matus points out, the scene of Lady Audley's imprisonment contains dialogue similar to that reported by Lady Rosina, well calculated to recall her description to the mind of the reader.[13]

Braddon's Dr Mosgrave, the mad-doctor in *Lady Audley's Secret* (1862), is hardly jolly:

However powerful the science of medicine as wielded by Dr Alwyn Mosgrave, it had not been strong enough to put flesh upon his bones, or brightness into his face. He had a strangely expressionless, and yet strangely attentive countenance. He had the face of a man who had ... parted with his own individuality and his own passions at the very outset of his career.[14]

Dr Mosgrave is an ambiguous figure of authority. He aids Robert Audley, the reluctant 'hero' of the novel, but his own motives are questionable. Although he judges Lady Audley sane, and does not think she has committed murder, he is willing to permanently commit her quietly to a madhouse, where she will be, by his own statement, 'buried alive', on the strength of a twenty-minute interview:

If you were to dig a grave for her in the nearest churchyard and bury her alive in it, you could not more safely shut her from the world and all worldly associations. But as a physiologist and as an honest man, I believe you could do no better service to society than by doing this; for physiology is a lie if the woman I saw ten minutes ago is a woman to be trusted at large.   (381)

The ability to transcend individuality might easily slide into a repudiation of human subjectivity, and perhaps even a claim to a god-like right of judgement. Mosgrave judges Lady Audley 'as a physiologist' – that is, on the basis not of her actions, but of his expert observations of her body to determine actions of which he believes her capable – a standard which would hold in no court, and which equates her physiology to her soul. The 'expressionless' neutrality of scientific medicine, with its oracular ability to penetrate the secrets of the human heart, seemed almost supernatural in its abilities, but it could also seem inhuman and unsympathetic. Worse, doctors could be wrong.

In Collins's and Reade's novels mentioned above, the mad-doctors are not villains, but are simply deceived; still, their plots underscore the possibility that the mad-doctor is not a trustworthy diagnostician. As critic Peter Logan explains, it is a period in which definitions of insanity were rapidly changing – and expanding. By the mid-century, celebrated alienist John Conolly offered a definition of insanity in a court case that was quite inclusive, considering even socially inappropriate behaviours as markers of insanity. In short, what had been considered mildly eccentric or even normal behaviours were increasingly identified as insane. The new category of 'moral insanity', including monomania or insanity regarding a 'discrete topic', meant that insanity might be diagnosed even in a person whose behaviours and physical health were apparently normal.[15] The fiction of this period abounds with monomaniacs, and characters, who like Robert Audley, feared they might be becoming monomaniacal (though Dr Mosgrave, clearly having an opinion on Robert's mental health, keeps it to himself). And diagnoses of madness were certainly generally on the rise throughout the period. In 1824, there were eight madhouses with an average of 116 beds each; by 1860, there were 41 with an average of 386 – and the numbers continued to increase.[16] In 1881, the noted physician J. Russell Reynolds rather drily observed that, although the existence of specialists in mental illness was undoubtedly 'a most direct advantage to the profession and the public' the drawback of such a speciality is that the 'so-called "mad-doctor" fails, sometimes, to see anything from a sane point of view. The *mens sana* is a myth to him ... He may be right in regarding all people as somewhat mad, but he may be wrong in thinking that all men are so far mad as to require restraint.'[17] The sensation novel explored the frightening possibility that anyone in the reader's environment might be mad. But the only thing more frightening – and likely – than being mad was being diagnosed and treated for it.

By the end of the century, the medical scientist emerges in fiction as distinctly suspicious. Collins's beastly vivisector and specialist in nervous and brain disease, Dr Benjulia, genuinely believes that he is serving humanity with the scientific torture of animals and experimentation, even when he employs it on human patients. Benjulia is a sinister figure – as monstrous in his 'gigantic' and foreign 'gypsy' person as in his inhuman cruelty. He is a doctor interested in the nerves, in 'brain diseases'. By the end of the century, the evil scientist-doctor – or the anti-feminist, oppressive doctor – appears in both such 'medical gothic' and New Woman novels;[18] both are increasingly cast as threats to women. By 1896, Wells's Dr Moreau has been driven from Europe for his experiments, and becomes the cruel god of his own hapless little island in the South Seas until his creations finally rise against and kill him.

Armadale

Armadale offers a good example of many trends discussed in this chapter. First, the text is punctuated throughout by the appearance of doctors, who serve as independent observers and offer emotional and moral compass; however, they also represent the limits of materialist explanations of human experience and the frightening threat of the corrupt physician's access to the body and mind. The novel opens with a doctor in attendance on a dying man; the doctor represents the humane (and secular humanist) compassion that the other witness of the man's suffering, a deeply religious but uncharitable man, fails to demonstrate. Another kindly doctor at the centre of the novel uses medical frameworks to explain away a character's terrifying dream. A third humane surgeon met by chance on a journey warns the same character,

Midwinter, that 'Your face tells me more than you think ... If you are ever tempted to overwork your brain, you will feel it sooner than most men. When you find your nerves playing you strange tricks, don't neglect the warning – drop your pen.' Finally, Dr Downward, an abortionist turned mad-doctor (he founds an asylum for patients with 'shattered nerves'), is a criminal quack who joins forces with the unhappy villainness, Lydia Gwilt.

Dr Downward lacks the expressionlessness of Dr Mosgrave, but he is no less defined by his capacity for secretiveness: 'he was one of those carefully constructed physicians in whom the public – especially the female public – implicitly trust ... His voice was soothing, his ways were deliberate, his smile was confidential.'[19] The erstwhile abortionist reinvents himself as the alienist 'Doctor Le Doux, of the Sanitarium, Fairweather Vale, Hampstead' with a 'foreign Diploma (handsomely framed and glazed), of which the doctor had possessed himself by purchase, along with the foreign name'. He asserts that the asylum will always have patients: 'we live in an age when nervous derangement (parent of insanity) is steadily on the increase' (713). Smoothly charming as he is, Dr Downward is perfectly capable of murder, and conspires with Lydia Gwilt to commit it.

This dark parody of the legitimate doctor also has comments to make about the role of the novelist: when he is asked if his nervous patients are allowed to amuse themselves with novels, he responds:

> Only such novels as I have selected and perused myself ... Nothing painful, ma'am! There may be plenty that is painful in real life; but for that very reason, we don't want it in books. The English novelist who enters my house (no foreign novelist will be admitted) must understand his art as the healthy-minded English reader understands it in our time ... All we want of him is – occasionally to make us laugh; and invariably to make us comfortable.   (770)

But, of course, this is not how Collins sees his role: he believed that the role of the novelist was not merely to entertain, but to expose abuses and to incite change. In short, the novelist is the truer surgeon, whose job is to expose the hidden and complex reality that ordinary eyes miss; the surgeon's scalpel may be therapeutic, but it rarely 'make[s] us comfortable'. But Collins also warns us about the scientist who sees the emotions and imagination only as subordinate handmaidens to reason. It is novels and intuition that teach the dangers of the world; art that simply confirms or panders to existing prejudices without challenging the reader leaves the reader vulnerable to the quackery of a Dr Downward.

Even good doctors in *Armadale* unwittingly expose the limits of materialist views. When Ozias Midwinter reports a disturbing dream he believes to be prophetic, Hawbury, a sympathetic surgeon rationalises it. Midwinter retorts that, 'The view of a medical man, when he has a problem in humanity to solve, seldom ranges beyond the point of his dissecting-knife.' The doctor responds with a general positivist rule of evidence that natural explanations should always be sought first. He then turns to what readers will recognise as a case study method, drawing out a detailed explanation of the dream from the dreamer's recent experiences, and then framing it in this physiological theory of dreams: 'A dream is the reproduction, in the sleeping state of the brain, of images and impressions produced on it in the waking state; and this reproduction is more or less involved, imperfect, or contradictory, as the action of certain faculties in the dreamer is controlled more or less completely by the influence of sleep' (173–4). Jenny Bourne Taylor, in her thorough study of Collins's engagement with Victorian psychology, points out that Hawbury's presentation of dream theory represents a selective engagement: he focuses on the impact of recent experience on the individual self, whereas some Victorian psychologists also concerned themselves with the impact of more distant and transindividual past elements on the content of the dream. Collins, she argues, positions Midwinter's self as a palimpsest of recent and distant past experience, including that inherited from his father. He must learn to reinterpret the dream in order to free himself of his nervous, 'hysterical' sensibility in a process that is partly a psychological self-analysis and partly a religious reinterpretation. But, she also notes, the novel foregrounds uncertainty in determining the meaning of mental phenomena: 'Armadale … is never able to … reach a final interpretation of the dream, or offer a stable interpretation of itself to the reader.'[20] And, persuasive as the doctor's explanation is, Midwinter the 'mystic' is unconvinced, and the dream in fact does have predictive value, though Midwinter is able to change the doom he thinks the dream portends, giving the lie to his own terror of ineluctable predestination. The doctor here is kindly, but ineffectual, and ultimately incorrect.

Meanwhile, although Armadale contains that necessity of most popular sensation novels, a scheming villainess, Lydia Gwilt shows not even the most equivocal signs of 'nervousness', let alone insanity, until she falls in love. Under that influence, her nerves are affected, but not to madness. Her new sensitivity hampers her ability to commit crime; in effect, it makes her saner than she was before. On the other hand, the text abounds with men on the verge of a nervous breakdown. The tale begins with the first Allan Armadale's narration, from his deathbed, in the grip of nervous paralysis after 'a wild life, and a vicious life' (15) in the West Indies during slavery, and the damage to his nerves wrought by his own murder of a rival. His son, the protagonist Ozias Midwinter, is repeatedly told he must be careful of his nerves as they are apt to fail him. Even his other son, the model of manly English health Allan

Armadale, possesses a telltale 'nervous antipathy' (140): 'a nervous horror of the smell and taste of brandy' (681).

Further, the nervousness of the men undermines their moral fibre, rather than improving it, as Lydia's does. Old Mr Bashwood, whose crush on Lydia drives him to crime, is repeatedly described as a 'poor broken-down, nervous wretch ... now shrinking in the glare of the lamp, now wincing under the shock of Allan's sturdy voice' (279). His passion for Lydia Gwilt becomes obsession, and her death leaves him insane. Midwinter struggles to do right while consumed by a superstitious fear that he is fated to harm his friend and benefactor Allan. Midwinter's mixed-race ancestry (his mother was of mixed European and African heritage) enhances his tendency to superstition and hysteria, while making him repulsive to the nervous susceptibilities of the more healthy-minded Englishmen of the novel:

> If this man was honest, his eyes showed a singular perversity in looking away and denying it. Possibly they were affected in some degree by a nervous rest-lessness in his organization, which appeared to pervade every fibre in his lean, lithe body. The rector's healthy Anglo-Saxon flesh crept responsively at every casual movement of the usher's [Midwinter's] supple brown fingers, and every passing distortion of the usher's haggard yellow face. (73)

Although Midwinter's nervousness might be accounted for by his lifetime of abuse and hardship, the text repeatedly refers to his ancestry and physiology – a combination of his mother's African emotional susceptibility and the inheritance of a constitution vitiated by 'the sins of the father'. When he is angered by his wife's denial of their marriage, 'His eyes began to glitter; and the savage blood that he had inherited from his mother rose dark and slow in his ashy cheeks', but the incident ends, not with his enacting any savage violence, but in a disabling fainting fit (757).

What particularly drives Midwinter to behave 'hysterically' (other than the uncanny experience of repeatedly finding himself in situations anticipated in nightmare, which might well unsettle anyone) is the notion of fate embodied in the figure of modern clockwork that symbolises a mechanistic universe. The Major, a neighbour whose hobby is tending a scale model of the Strasbourg clock, demonstrates its workings. The machinery goes awry, so that although the figure of Time lowers and raises his scythe on cue, doors fail to open properly and so the other figures go through their motions in an untimely, ridiculous manner that elicits a hysterical fit of laughter in the susceptible Midwinter and thus offends the Major and his daughter.

If Midwinter is upset by the machinations of Time the Reaper who inex-orably brings fate and death, the failure of the other figures to go properly through their motions (exiting one door, crossing to and entering another) foreshadows the climactic scene of the long novel, when Lydia depends on perfectly timing a complex set of mechanical actions with the closing and locking of doors to kill her enemy by introducing poisoned air into his room. The suspense of the scene is heightened by the emphasis on the necessity to wait, watching the clock in the asylum, '[a] clock of the noiseless sort – incapable of offending irritable nerves' (779), in order to take each of the several actions necessary to accomplish the murder:

> Oh, the time! the time! If it could only have been begun and ended with the first Pouring! ... The first of the intervals of five minutes was endless. The time stood still. The suspense was maddening ... The fever-heat throbbed again in her blood, and flushed fiercely in her cheeks. Swift, smooth, and noiseless, she paced from end to end of the corridor, – her eye moment after moment on the clock. (802)

This time, all the machinery works perfectly, even the 'pacing' (a dual meaning here) figure of Lydia. But her husband Midwinter, sensing danger to Allan, has exchanged rooms with her intended victim as a precaution against any attempt on his life. Lydia is able to save Midwinter, and ends by taking her own life as restitution to him for her crimes. The clockwork, materialist view of human actions is again disrupted, this time by the power of imagination and sympathy represented by the warning of the supernatural dream, and the power of love to reform even a hardened evildoer such as Lydia. Human beings, Collins tell us, are not mere physiological mechanisms.

In this novel, doctors are not central to the plot: they are not principal characters, for example, and even Dr Downward holds a relatively small place in the overall length of the novel, as he does not play an important role until the last section. That said, doctors and medicine are vital to the novel's themes and structure: the entire novel is framed in the conflict between what Collins defines as a medico-scientific mode of understanding human experience and an intuitive, 'mystical' one. Moreover, the characters' actions and reactions proceed from a carefully defined physiological basis, even if their capacities ultimately transcend those limitations. Collins is careful to get his facts right about the actions of chemicals and illnesses on the body, and notes in his epilogue that, 'Wherever the story touches on questions connected with Law, Medicine, or Chemistry, it has been submitted before publication to the experience of professional men' (817). The final resolution of the epistemological conflict in the favour of the mystical, slyly proffered as a triumph of the novelist's art over a potentially spurious scientism, also reinscribes the value of science – in its place – by having the erroneous spokesperson for science be a quack. The recovery of Midwinter also functions as a kind of medical and artistic triumph, a validation of the organism's ability to regenerate itself under the direction of a human will: 'After causing some anxiety at first to the medical men … he [Midwinter] has rallied, as only men of his sensitive temperament (to quote the doctors again) *can* rally' (811). The imaginative temperament, finally, is materially stronger than materialism.

NOTES

1. John Ruskin, 'Fiction Fair and Foul', in *The Works of John Ruskin*, ed. Edward Tyas Cook and Alexander Wedderburn, 39 vols. (London: George Allen, 1903–12), vol. xxxiv, 264–399.
2. Lawrence Rothfield, *Vital Signs: Medical Realism in Nineteenth-Century Fiction* (Princeton University Press), xvii.
3. Raymond Williams, *The Country and the City* (London: Chatto and Windus, 1973).
4. Mansel, 268.
5. Nicholas Daly, *Literature, Technology and Modernity: 1860–2000* (Cambridge University Press, 2010), 46.
6. *Ibid.*, 47, emphasis in original.
7. The National Temperature League and the British Medical Association, *Medical Temperature Journal* 5–6:57 (1883), 24–34 (31).
8. Tabitha Sparks, *The Doctor in the Victorian Novel: Family Practices* (Aldershot: Ashgate, 2009), 7–8.
9. *Ibid.*, 8.
10. Peter M. Logan, 'Imitations of Insanity and Victorian Medical Aesthetics', *Romanticism and Victorianism on the Net* 49 (2008), [www.erudit.org/revue/ravon/2008/v/n49/017855ar.html#re1no1, accessed 15 January 2012].
11. Wilkie Collins, *Man and Wife*, ed. Norman Page (Oxford University Press, 2008), 218. Further reference to this edition will be given in the text.
12. Francis Ainstie, 'State Medicine', *Macmillan's Magazine* 11:64 (1864–5), 306–16 (312).
13. Jill Matus, *Unstable Bodies: Victorian Representation of Sexuality and Maternity* (Manchester University Press, 1995), 202.
14. Mary Elizabeth Braddon, *Lady Audley's Secret*, ed. Lyn Pykett (Oxford University Press, 2009), 374. Further reference to this edition will be given in the text.
15. Peter M. Logan, *Nerves and Narratives: A Cultural History of Hysteria in Nineteenth-Century British Prose* (Berkeley: University of California Press, 1997).
16. E. Fuller Torrey and Judy Miller, *Invisible Plague: The Rise of Mental Illness from 1750 to the Present* (New Brunswick NJ: Rutgers University Press, 2007), 94.
17. J. Russell Reynolds, 'An Address on Specialism in Medicine', *The Medical Press and Circular* (19 October 1881), 335–8 (337).
18. Sparks, *The Doctor in the Victorian Novel*, 13–14.
19. Wilkie Collins, *Armadale*, ed. John Sutherland (Oxford University Press, 2009), 410. Further references to this edition will be given in the text.
20. Jenny Bourne Taylor, *'In the Secret Theatre of Home': Wilkie Collins, Sensation Narrative, and Nineteenth-Century Psychology* (London: Routledge, 1988), 172.

15

GRETA DEPLEDGE

Sensation fiction and the New Woman

Later sensation fiction coincided with the increasing emergence of gender politics and brought a new breed of female sensation protagonists who engaged with emerging social debate. Ideas surrounding the New Woman were at the centre of much literary, social and political discussion in the last decades of the nineteenth century and these ideas are central to later sensation fiction.

While the New Woman was not named until 1894,[1] the appellation of 'New Woman' does have a wider literary and historical range. Lyn Pykett suggests: 'The beautiful (sometimes), self-assertive, quasi-adulterous heroine of the sensation novel became in the New Woman fiction, the destroyer and/or self-destructive seeker after truth, personal fulfilment and a measure of social and sexual equality with men.'[2] I am not arguing that writers of sensation fiction became New Woman writers but that traits of New Women and *fin-de-siècle* feminism can be seen in later works, with writers tackling issues central to the social purity campaigns of the late nineteenth century such as male sexual profligacy, the vivisection debate and the position of women in marriage. A review of fiction by Mary Elizabeth Braddon and Mrs Henry Wood in the *Spectator* in 1888 referred to 'feminine writers' who pander to 'the average novel reader'.[3] The implication is clear: the average novel reader, specifically of this type of popular novel, is likely to be female. The New Woman writers also needed to connect with the female reading population: 'New Woman fiction constitutes a direct, immediate and unequivocal appeal: for empathy with women, for gender solidarity, for political activism – for feminism. This is an appeal addressed, primarily, to women ... If New Woman fiction was to achieve its aim of reaching the widest possible audience of women, it had to hold popular appeal.'[4] Therefore, an approach that looks to the popular genre of sensation fiction for a representation of New Woman ideologies is invited by a theoretic framework which sees popular appeal as essential to any novel that raises issues surrounding the Woman Question, which later sensation fiction did.

Female characters who undertake private or profession sleuthing make for particularly rewarding study here. The need to detect, to solve, is indicative of a growing sense of autonomy and independence among women that bears no relation to the iniquitous acts of their earlier sensation sisters. Furthermore, sleuthing to unravel family secrets, enabling family peace or marital harmony, is not at variance with New Woman feminism. Just as the New Woman conformed to no one simple definition, neither did her views on marriage, although the need for reform in marriage was a regular feature of New Woman writing. Again, forging the link between New Women writers and sensation novelists, Lyn Pykett writes that:

> The New Women writers shared many of their predecessors' preoccupations. Chief among these was a common concern with women's marital and familial roles. Like Braddon and Wood, the New Woman writers of the 1890s focused minutely on the domestic space and, whether writing as feminists or as anti-feminists, engaged in a probing exploration and critique of marriage and the family.[5]

There are no binary oppositions of feminism versus subservience within marriage in later sensation fiction but an attempt to negotiate marriage as a union of mutual respect and understanding. Marriage is linked to all the sleuthing carried out in the novels to be discussed.

Any examination of the female sleuth in later sensation fiction has to acknowledge the debt owed to Wilkie Collins. However, the focus here is female writers. Mary Elizabeth Braddon and Florence Marryat engage with characters who perpetrate crimes and with those who seek to solve crime. What follows is a consideration of Marryat's *In Her Father's Name* (1876) and *In the Name of Liberty* (1897), plus Braddon's *The Fatal Three* (1888) and *Thou Art the Man* (1894). Despite the shift in *In the Name of Liberty* from personal sleuthing to a professional detective, Marryat does explore how women negotiated their place within marriage at the close of the nineteenth century.

Both Marryat and Braddon were redoubtable professional writers, publishing throughout the last four decades of the nineteenth century, and we see them embrace the issues that women were facing at this time of change. While the female protagonists depicted in the above novels end their stories being either happily married or having their momentarily threatened marriage restored, earlier ideals of romantic happy endings have not remained static. As we will see, the dynamics of gender relations have altered and women have entered or re-entered marriage with a shift in power being subtly but firmly displayed.

Marryat's *In Her Father's Name* provides an abundance of sensation themes: murder, mystery, cross-dressing, illegitimacy and hysteria. The heroine, Leona Lacoste, attempts to clear her father's name of a murder committed in England long before she was born. He stands accused of the murder of a clerk at the family's trading firm; fleeing the country on the night of the villainous deed seemingly confirms his guilt. He lives under an assumed name in Brazil for many years but his secret comes back to haunt him and he commits suicide. When Leona learns of her father's torment she sets off in pursuit of the truth, not before refusing a marriage proposal from her child-hood friend, Christobal: 'Am I not able to protect myself? No harm will come to me but of my own free will. But it must be free. I will shackle it with no man. Christobal, if you love me, as you say you do, you will never mention the subject of marriage to me again. I hate – I despise it.'[6] What is significant here is not only her assertion of independence and need to be in control of her own destiny, but also the awareness that in doing so she risks 'harm', but harm which will be of her own making. While her vehemence towards marriage is ultimately moderated, the institution, for now, is seen as one of limitation.

In her pursuit of truth Leona transgresses gender boundaries. She challenges ontological constructions of femininity and represents ideas of late nineteenth-century feminine discourse. Her need to establish her masculine believability while dressed as a man involves challenging another man to a 'duel', showing him(her)self to be capable of an act of 'male' aggression. However, she wounds her opponent, thus allowing Marryat to explore ideas surrounding traditional constructions of gender. When her opponent collapses, 'All the woman had come back to her in the idea that she might have killed her antagonist' (59). A retreat to feminine sensibilities means that Leona remains a sympathetic character and that her adoption of male attributes does not extend to her being at ease with killing. Leona can be practical and capable but she cannot be murderous. There is an evident shift here away from earlier sensation heroines like Lady Audley and Lydia Gwilt, whose transgressive behaviour is linked to crime. While Leona eschews gender boundaries by behaving and acting like a man: 'You know that I am somewhat of a mimic, and that I have lived among men long enough to make their manners sit on me almost as well as these loose suits of my poor father's do' (51), her feminine sensibilities remain close to the surface of her barely concealed identity: 'you betray yourself with every word you speak, ... if you do not show a little more reason in the matter, your sex will become apparent to the whole company' (60–1). Traditional frameworks of conventional femininity are utilised but Leona's cross-dressing, despite its ostensibly practical remit, does question these definitions. Christobal, who has travelled with her, fears her exposure, while others see her simply as a somewhat oversensitive young man. Vern Bullough and Bonnie Bullough, in their study of cross-dressing, argue that 'clothing helped determine one's gender'.[7]

There is no denying the freedom that women gained by pretending to be men, and we see this freedom explored later in the century in Sarah Grand's *The Heavenly Twins* (1893). While Marryat is not making a profound statement about sexual orientation or lifestyle choice in having Leona dress as a man, she is challenging established gender politics by showing the lengths a woman has to go to in order to pursue, not only an investigation, but also a modicum of autonomy and freedom.

The important point is that, dressed as a man, Leona is granted a freedom without any cultural anxieties about the propriety of a woman travelling alone and sleuthing. Furthermore, disguise and deception was, in earlier sensation fiction, often the strategy for the villain. This trend is reversed here: Leona is not trying to hide a secret or cover-up a crime but to solve one, so some of the stock-in-trade devices of earlier sensation fiction are now being used, within a sensation plot, as a device to ascertain truth rather than ensure obfuscation and deceit.

It is, of course, slightly ironic that she disguises herself as a man in order to clear her father's name, an investigation that other men, namely her father, his brother and their uncle, all singularly failed to even attempt. Leona proves herself to be mistress of more than one disguise, however. Later in the novel she also uses the cover of an old woman, adopting the masquerade in order to get a job taking care of her uncle's sickly daughter. Significantly, she disguises her eyes with the aid of spectacles: 'Leona had taken the extra precaution . . . of shielding her glorious eyes with a pair of spectacles' (244). This is reminiscent of Lady Isabel Vanc in Mrs Henry Wood's *East Lynne* (1861), who 'wears disfiguring green spectacles, or, as they are called, preservers, going round the eyes',[8] and by doing so manages to live undetected in the house of her husband and children. While this use of disguise does prefigure later crime fiction it also, perhaps, highlights the complexities of female autonomy in later sensation fiction. Women were able to achieve more by making themselves less conspicuous. This speaks to the increasingly vexed position of women at the *fin de siècle* and the trepidation, and indeed often hostility, that women who transgressed socially constructed gender boundaries faced.

Through all these machinations Leona does clear her father's name of the crime erroneously attributed to him. Furthermore, the novel closes with Leona accepting the marriage proposal of her childhood friend, Christobal. However, while this could be seen as a reversion to the traditional happy ending, I would suggest that Marryat offers us more than this with the narrative trajectory that involves Leona. It is clear that Leona enters her marriage with her independence and autonomy firmly established, not only in her own eyes but in the eyes of the man she marries. Leona's revelation of her father's innocence to his brother and extended family is also of interest.

She states that her father 'left me behind him to be a living witness of the purity of his life' (318). The use of the word 'purity' here reminds us of the social purity campaigns of the New Woman movement in the last decades of the nineteenth century. Purity in regard to Leona's father is somewhat ironic, however, as Leona has discovered that her uncle's daughter is, in fact, her father's illegitimate child. This sexual transgression can, seemingly, be overlooked but the stain of murder has been refuted absolutely. While ideas of sexual purity cannot be retrospectively applied to a previous generation in Braddon's 1888 novel, *The Fatal Three*, there is a tacit acceptance of the supposed sexual transgressions of a male parent, which does, then, influence the expectation for a higher standard of behaviour in a husband. What we see is a linear progression in how the sexual transgressions of a previous generation influenced and informed ideas of sexual and social purity for subsequent generations.

In *The Fatal Three* Mildred Greswold is confronted by the possible transgressions of two male relatives – her father and her husband. Mildred discovers that her husband's first wife is believed to have been the illegitimate daughter of her father, her half-sister Fay, who lived with her for a short period during their childhood. Fay died under supposedly mysterious circumstances; her suicide did, for a time, leave George under suspicion of her murder, leading to his mental collapse. All this took place before Mildred married him, and her subsequent discovery of this secret prompts her to leave him. As the law stood at that time, marriage with a dead wife's sister was illegal. That Fay was supposedly illegitimate means that there is no legal impediment to Mildred and George's marriage. But for Mildred such a marriage is deeply problematic because of her staunch religious beliefs.

However, while Braddon does use the novel to explore questions surrounding the *Deceased Wife's Sister's Bill* (1842), Mildred's acceptance of past sin is not straightforward. Like Leona she is prepared to overlook the supposed sexual transgression of the patriarch even if, for Mildred, this involves the dissolution of her marriage. She resigns herself to a life of isolation, and it is curious that she does not seek to detect the truth regarding Fay's parentage but accepts her father's guilt instead. The sexual transgressions of a previous generation are a *fait accompli*. Many New Women of the last decades of the nineteenth century supported social purity agendas so that another generation of wives and daughters would not be forced to live with the mistakes of their fathers. However, the suggestion that her husband is capable of murder inspires Mildred to act. 'I must know the worst . . . I must know all. I will take no step to injure my dear love.'[9] Mildred's combination of self-sacrifice with quiet determination is somewhat contradictory. She travels to Nice, to the scene of the supposed crime: 'She . . . had gone to the city by the sea, to try and trace out for herself the mystery of the past, to violate her husband's secret, kept so long and so closely, only to rise up after years of happiness, like a murdered corpse exhumed from a forgotten grave' (206). The language here speaks of transgression, with a woman actively seeking to 'violate' her husband's secrets. Like the New Woman who wanted disparity and equality in marriage, Mildred desires the truth, to know all, so she can absolve her husband from the sin of murder, even if her father's sexual transgressions mean, for her, that her marriage is over. The image of a murdered corpse rising up from the grave reminds us of sensation fiction's debt to the gothic tradition, utilising a traditional sensation trope while also indicating a feminist discourse of transparency within marriage.

Indeed, Mildred's decision to leave her husband is a potentially transgressive act but one that is in keeping with her strong religious beliefs. Mildred's act is similar to that of Evadne in Grand's *The Heavenly Twins*, and also speaks to social purity movements of the time. While Fay's illegitimacy means there is no legal impediment to George and Mildred's marriage, Mildred holds herself to a higher moral standard and puts the laws of the church above the institution of English law. As Jan Hewitt writes, 'Mildred's strength of purpose also has affinities with certain feminist stances in the late Victorian purity debates and, in her, the regenerative power of purity is both extolled and offered for scrutiny.'[10]

However, when Mildred discovers her father's innocence her previous willingness to accept his guilt haunts her: 'She had condemned her father ... upon evidence that had seemed to her incontrovertible. She had believed in a stain upon that honourable life' (309). That she so readily believed her father to be guilty of infidelity and fathering an illegitimate child is an implicit acquiescence of the sexual double standard of that generation, a problem that a new breed of women, the daughters of that generation, wanted to consign to history.

In her marriage Mildred acts independently and trusts to her own, arguably misguided, religious beliefs rather than acquiescing to her husband's. This movement towards some form of equality or, at the very least, forcing a husband's awareness of the wife's ability to act independently, is in keeping with New Women ideologies that were being increasingly vocalised at this time. Mildred cannot knowingly condone the guilt of a union she believes to be morally wrong. Sleuthing into her husband's past highlights her insistence on having knowledge of his life prior to their marriage: 'George, why did you not tell me ... that I was not your first wife? What reason could there be for concealment between you and me?' (83). The vulnerability of women within the marriage union, which New Women campaigned to eradicate, is evident in Mildred's position. It transpires that George had told Mildred's father of his previous marriage (though not to whom) and between the secrecy of her father and her husband she is placed in a position that is repugnant to her. While Mildred's spiritual advisor is clearly a bigot, unable to see that the laws of the medieval church to which he adheres, and to which he desires Mildred to adhere, are archaic and obsolete in late nineteenth-century England, in terms of New Woman ideals about equality within marriage, Mildred's vulnerability is first and foremost exploited by her father and her husband. Her father, doubtless happy to secure a seemingly good and comfortable husband for her, was 'generous enough to accept my confidence and to ask no questions' (117).

Real or supposed paternal 'crime' and daughterly obsequiousness is further explored in Braddon's 1894 novel *Thou Art the Man*. In this novel Braddon presents two female sleuths. Firstly, Lady Penrith, determined to discover if the scrawled note handed to her by a stranger indicates that her former lover, Brandon Mountford, is alive. Mountford was believed to have been drowned at sea as he fled from the charge of murdering Lady Penrith's half-sister (another illegitimate offspring of a philandering father), some ten years previously: a charge he could not refute because his severe epilepsy resulted in unconsciousness and memory loss. The actual murderer, Hubert Urquhart, the brother of Lord Penrith, forces his daughter, Coralie (our second female sleuth), to spy on Lady Penrith as she attempts to discover the secret behind the scrawled note. Urquhart has been responsible for having Mountford locked away as a lunatic for the past ten years.

It is Coralie who challenges gender stereotypes and embraces New Women ideologies, as she gradually detects her father's role in murder, her diary-keeping and recording of events helping her to emerge from under the powerful and destructive influence of her father. In the first instance Coralie spies on Lady Penrith at the request of her father, long before she is aware of his crime. However, a sense of disquiet about this task is evidenced by her decision to keep two diaries. Her duplicate diary keeping is a symbol of what is, at this stage, her duplicitous nature, but it is also evidence of her growing independence. Coralie does not conform to typical frameworks of conventional femininity. Her love of male company and male pursuits contrasts markedly with Lady Penrith's more typical femininity. She is advised: 'I think you ought to leave off being a jolly good fellow, Cora, and remember that you are a young lady, now your twentieth birthday is drawing near.' To which she replies:

> What, leave off cigarettes, and horsey talk, forego my morning fun in the stables and kennels – give the billiard-room a holiday – and take to embroidering window curtains and reading the last book of the Honourable Somebody's travels in Timbuctoo. So I would, Auntie, if I could only make up my mind

which line is likely to pay best in such a case as mine – the well brought up, stand-offish young lady, or the free and easy young person whom her male acquaintances talk of as 'good fun', or 'not a bad sort'.[11]

Coralie realises that, because the world works the way it does, marriage is her best option, but her obvious exuberance and the fact that she was 'brought up by a father instead of a mother [and] if her mother had lived she would have reared [her] in a state of guileless innocence' (99) indicates that she is potentially too modern to conform to the more traditional lifestyle of Lady Penrith. The lack of a maternal figure and subsequent lack of 'guileless innocence' means that Coralie is well aware that 'the ruck of young men prefer the society of a girl who is distinctly on their own level, a little below them rather than a little above. That is why chorus girls and barmaids often get on so well in the world' (9). As Ann Heilmann writes, 'by keeping middle-class girls and women ignorant of the physical side of marriage and of their husband's past, society condoned middle-class men's sexual exploits'.[12] Coralie is unlikely to go into marriage at the same risk of exposure to sexually transmitted diseases because of a husband's past life as we see Edith and Evadne exposed to in Grand's *The Heavenly Twins* (1893). The destruction of any girlish innocence, by her father, is arguably the best legacy he could leave her.

Many of Coralie's actions are seemingly at odds with the traditional aim of husband-catching. The masculine pursuits that she indulges in, such as cigarettes and billiards, hint at the negative constructs of New Womanhood that abounded in the press at the end of the century. Coralie wants out of the drawing room, and while not explicitly vocalising New Woman ideals, her behaviour demonstrates an independence of spirit, albeit one she does not completely understand:

> My regular rowdy speeches, forsooth! What is the use of having a sharp wit, which seizes the ludicrous aspect of everything? I fear I have been a little weak in letting them talk of French novels and sensational cases in the divorce court before me, and putting in my pert little tongue occasionally. But what can one talk of in this end of the century, if not sensational cases, when every new case goes beyond the old ones in sensational elements? There is a feeling in the air as if it were not the end of the century, but the end of the world. (200)

Coralie's independence is manifest here but she clearly does not know what to do with it. She is an example of a newly emergent, more worldly-wise young woman, whom social mores must, eventually, adapt to accommodate. Braddon presents her heroine on the cusp of change, not a fully emerged New Woman but an unsettled, dissatisfied Victorian girl. While Coralie had once believed that she saw herself 'ten years hence a spinster novelist, in a snug little house – in Mayfair' (273), a New Woman writer no less, she does ultimately end up married to a man with an estate and a good selection of hunters.

Lady Penrith correctly surmises that Coralie has discovered that her father murdered Marie Arnold. What nobody knows is that Coralie also witnesses her father kill Lord Penrith, invisibly watching him from the woods. Coralie hints to her father that she knows his secret. She tells him that he must no longer expect her acquiescence to his demands 'unless you choose to shoot me [to] make sure of my obedience' (307). By shielding her father from further guilt and shame she acts not dissimilarly from Jane in Marryat's *In the Name of Liberty* (1897). However, Coralie's knowledge becomes the power which liberates her from his patriarchal control. Jane's knowledge of her husband's 'crime', however, has a decidedly destructive influence. Her discovery of his actions while working as a professional detective takes crime away from a purely domestic setting, combining marital relations and international terrorism.

In 1889, an article on 'Queer Feminine Occupations' appeared in *Tit-bits* weekly magazine and discussed a detective agency which employed female detectives, stating that women were 'peculiarly qualified for the business'.[13] The female professional detective had made her appearance in English literature as early as 1860. Two early literary female sleuths were 'G' from Andrew Forrester's *The Female Detective* of 1864 and Mrs Paschal in the anonymous *Revelations of a Lady Detective*, also published in 1864. Some of the most well-known female detective stories from the nineteenth century are those by Catherine Pirkis, *The Experiences of Loveday Brooke, Lady Detective*, published in 1894. In these stories one character remarks that 'Lady detectives are a race apart and have a curious way of doing things!'[14]

Marryat's *In the Name of Liberty* is, in many ways, a classic sensation novel, despite its publication date of 1897; it contains illegitimacy, disguise, lost letters, inheritance issues, attempted murder and ill-fated love. Its modernity is indicated not only by the professional female detective but also by the added excitement of a couple of bombs. But through all this, Marryat explores a marriage that is challenged by, among other things, a woman acting independently, taking a job, and a job, furthermore, in a potentially dangerous profession. For much of this novel Jane exemplifies the New Woman of the period.

The novel begins with a married couple, Maurice and Jane, desperately poor – their infant child has just starved to death because the mother's milk has dried up – receiving help from a mysterious benefactor, who is depicted as regularly walking through the poorer areas of London indiscriminately giving aid to those in need. It is clear this mysterious figure is atoning for past sins. Maurice had been a journalist working for a very conservative paper.

However, he had been sacked for writing articles for a socialist paper. He has 'anarchist' sympathies. He falls back in with his radical friends and they persuade him to get involved with Fenian sympathisers who are agitating for home rule in Ireland and the establishment of an Independent Irish Republic. His first job is to go to America to liaise with sympathisers there, for which he will be handsomely paid, but he must go without further contact with his wife. Jane hears that her husband has been spotted on a boat leaving for America and assumes he has deserted her, and so sets about looking for a job to support herself. A close family friend, who happens to be a chief inspector in the police force, suggests that she work with him. Inspector Herschel tells her that he thinks she is 'eminently suited [for the work of a lady detective] both physically and mentally; added to which, the pay is good and the excitement and constant change of scene and action will divert your spirits at this crisis'.[15] She is placed with the unit investigating the anarchists, and is assigned specifically to protect a member of the aristocracy who has been repeatedly targeted because he owns land in Ireland. On her first job she realises that the earl she is protecting is the mysterious benefactor from the opening chapter of the novel. Unsurprisingly, her husband has been assigned the job of killing the earl, and one of the many dramatic moments of the novel sees Jane safely disposing of a bomb her husband was about to throw into the earl's house. Jane is torn between exposing her husband (she allows him to escape on that night) and her professional obligation. When her husband realises that the man he has been assigned to kill is the mysterious benefactor he tells his fellow anarchists he cannot go through with it, and is sentenced to death for being a traitor. The final twist is that the earl is his father – Maurice is the result of a foolish dalliance from the earl's misguided youth, during which he secretly married the maid who cleaned his rooms at college. She has a son, he comes in to his inheritance, goes to take up his new position, always meaning to bring his family together. Before this happens the earl hears that his wife and son have died. Just in time, the earl discovers that his son is alive; he saves him from the anarchists; Maurice is not charged for his anarchist activities; father and son are reunited; and so too are husband and wife. Jane's dereliction of duty in letting her husband escape on that fateful night is never discovered.

However, within this rather extravagant plot, Marryat does merge tropes that involve the female detective, amateur and professional, and looks to New Woman fiction of the period in its presentation of a woman embracing new opportunities for employment. Obviously the contrast between Jane and the amateur female sleuths is that Jane is a professional and the marital complication is given a twist – she becomes desperate not to reveal her husband's involvement in illegal activities. Marryat, in all of her fiction, repeatedly questions the role and function of women in marriage, and while her depiction of a professional detective is a nod to this very popular genre she does not allow this popular character type to restrict her from exploring the vulnerability of women within marriage. Jane takes up detecting because she believes herself to have been abandoned by her husband, but even when his activities compromise her newly established professional role she puts what she perceives to be her duty as a wife before her responsibilities as a detective.

What is crucial to Jane's success is her background. When she sees Maurice after she has discovered his involvement with the anarchists he does not understand why he has seen her at such a grand party, and because of the secrecy surrounding her role she is unable to tell him. She simply says 'you may remember that I come of a good family, and that it is nothing more than my birth entitles me to' (125). Her demeanour as a lady is crucial to Marryat's narrative trajectory. Early in the novel, despite her near starved appearance, we are told, 'She was a handsome young woman, with a graceful figure, and looked like a lady' (82). When she is first approached about being a lady detective, after thinking she would work for a milliner, Herschel says to her, 'I think I can find you something better fitted to your abilities and position in life. You mustn't forget what you sprung from, Jane' (87).

Marryat's emphasis on Jane's ladylike qualities is, of course, intended to prepare the reader for her station in society at the close of the novel but does also, I think, relate to social anxieties that surrounded the role of the working woman. Carla Kungl writes that: 'By creating feminine and upper-class detectives, women writers also found a way to preserve women's respectability despite their entrance into a professional world.'[16] When Jane is 'disguised' at a function of the earl's, working to sniff out potential assassins, a guest remarks that she is 'certainly more attractive in appearance than the generality of her sex ... not particularly beautiful; but ... essentially graceful, and had a foreign air about her' (92). This focus on her appearance is significant; she fits in; there is no sense that she does not belong. So despite the increasing professionalisation, a sleuth's femininity is still a useful tool. The female detective exploits her cloak of female invisibility, but challenges ideas of femininity and addresses the vexed problem of how women best fitted into a rapidly changing society where increasing numbers of respectable women needed to work.

Jane's femininity and larger anxieties over the potential destruction of female sensibilities relate to contemporaneous fears of New Women being involved in any profession. Fears were voiced that this new generation of women would become a barren race of over-educated, garrulous harpies. Jane's bravery seems decidedly unfeminine. On the night of the anarchist bomb attack we read that Jane 'sprang from her position and made straight for him, with no fear for herself, no thought but that she was the chosen agent to prevent a violent and bloody deed' (182). Marryat, however, reassures her readers that not all Jane's feminine sensibilities are lost. The next day, Jane says that

> The affair of last night has shaken my nerves. I couldn't answer for myself another time. The idea of hunting a fellow creature down to death or imprisonment is terrible to me . . . to hunt down a man, to lie in wait for him, and then to betray him into the hands of the police, Oh! It seems so mean, so crafty.   (224–5)

Jane's 'masculine' bravery is swiftly replaced with 'feminine' nervousness. Both Jessica Mann and Michele Slung discuss, in their respective works on female detective fiction, the inherent dilemma in creating a female detective who can combine innate female sensibility with dangerous and violent work. Mann writes that female detectives 'expect their femininity to be useful [but] it was important for these women not to alienate the interest of their readers. They were as feminine as contemporary prejudices required.'[17]

Michele Slung concurs: 'The authors themselves never seem to be quite certain of their creation, intent as they are on playing up the novelty of such a peculiar figure.'[18] These arguments can easily be applied to the dilemmas New Women writers faced with their New Women creations in general. Jane does have doubts about her profession, and Marryat combines the disparity of a professional role and female sensibilities with the crucial dilemma over her husband's involvement: 'If he elects to remain with those terrible Anarchists I can no longer be a detective. I cannot hunt my husband to his death' (278); a questioning, albeit under the most sensational of circumstances, of how marriage and a professional life combine. When Jane pleads with Maurice not to throw the bomb she appeals to him as a wife and mother. Her marriage prevents her from being a good detective because she cannot/will not? betray her husband. Marryat provides us with a female detective whose personal life throws her working life into turmoil and, when left alone to reflect on her husband's involvement, '[throws] herself back in the chair . . . and burst[s] in to a flood of hysterical tears – laughing and crying at the same moment . . . She was going on as incoherently as women generally do when under the influence of any strong feeling' (225). The ending of the novel is a disappointment, with Jane failing to fulfil her New Women potential but it is possible to read this as Marryat complying with a more conservative ending that is a feature of the sensation novel.

The female sleuth, moving from amateur to professional, provides us with an interesting character through which we may consider later sensation fiction. Arlene Young argues that the 'inconsistencies in characterisation that mark the fictional lady detective in many ways reflect the uncertainty of the middle-class woman's place in the nineteenth-century workforce'.[19] This also mirrors, more significantly, the role of the New Woman, moving from the more traditional domestic interior to embrace roles in the professional world. The female sleuths discussed in this chapter and other professional female detectives from the period embrace marriage at the end of their respective stories and, therefore, do not go on to have the extensive adventures of their male counterparts, such as Sherlock Holmes. Perhaps they reflect *fin-de-siècle* anxieties over women at the time and their retreat into marriage might seem to safely restore these women to a role reflective of earlier, ostensibly less transgressive and troubling times. Alternatively, we can see these figures as looking to moderate a path through the dilemmas of femininity, womanhood and gender constructions. They negotiate a new role for themselves within marriage, one where their foray into the wider world equips them to achieve a more equal status within marriage without having to resort to the dastardly acts and villainous ways of their earlier sensation sisters.

NOTES

1. Sally Ledger, *The New Woman: Fiction and Feminism at the Fin de Siècle* (Manchester University Press, 1997), 2.
2. Lyn Pykett, *The Improper Feminine: The Sensation Novel and the New Woman Writing* (London and New York: Routledge, 1992), 7.
3. Anon., *Spectator* 61 (1888), 1475.
4. Ann Heilmann, *New Woman Fiction: Women Writing, First-Wave Feminism* (London: Macmillan, 2000), 9.
5. Pykett, *Improper Feminine*, 143.
6. Florence Marryat, *In Her Father's Name*, ed. Greta Depledge (Brighton: Victorian Secrets, 2009), 37. Futher references to this edition will be given in the text.
7. Vern L. Bullough and Bonnie Bullough, *Cross Dressing, Sex and Gender* (Philadelphia: Pennsylvania Press, 1993), 159.
8. Ellen Wood, *East Lynne* (London: Everyman's Library, 1984), 397.
9. Mary Elizabeth Braddon's *The Fatal Three*, ed. and introduction Jan Hewitt (Stroud: Sutton, 1997), 202. Futher references to this edition will be given in the text.
10. Hewitt, introduction, xiii.
11. Mary Elizabeth Braddon, *Thou Art the Man*, ed. Laurence Talairach-Vielmas (Kansas City: Valancourt Books, 2008), 80. Futher references to this edition will be given in the text.
12. Heilmann, *New Woman Fiction*, 79.
13. Anon., 'Women as Detectives', *Tit-bits* (18 April 1891).
14. Catherine Louise Pirkis, *The Experiences of Loveday Brooke, Lady Detective* (Kila, MT: Kessinger Publishing, 2008), 153.
15. Florence Marryat, *In the Name of Liberty*, (London: Digby, Long, 1897), 87. Further references to this edition will be given in the text.

16. Carla Kungl, *Creating the Fictional Female Detective* (London: McFarland, 2006), 81.

17. Jessica Mann, *Deadlier Than the Male: An Investigation into Feminine Crime Writing* (Newton Abbot and London: David and Charles, 1981), 93.

18. Michele B. Slung (ed.), *Crime on Her Mind: Fifteen Stories of Female Sleuths from the Victorian Era to the Forties* (London: Penguin, 1977), 12.

19. Arlene Young, ' "Petticoated Police": Propriety and the Lady Detective in Victorian Fiction', *Clues: A Journal of Detection* 26:3 (2008), 15–28 (26).

16

LYN PYKETT

The sensation legacy

The persistence and dispersal of the sensation novel in the nineteenth century

In his important 1982 article 'What is Sensational About the Sensation Novel?' Patrick Brantlinger noted the brevity of the reign of sensation fiction, describing it as 'a minor subgenre of British fiction that flourished in the 1860s only to die out a decade or two later'. In fact, for Brantlinger, as, more recently, for Phillip Waller, the sensation novel did not so much die as 'burst apart into subspecies', living on in the 'adventure, thriller, detective, romantic, horror and fantasy fictions'[1] of the late nineteenth and early twentieth centuries, and, of course, as Brantlinger noted, in films. This chapter explores the dispersive trajectory of the sensation novel, and also looks at the rise of the neo-sensation novel in the late twentieth and twenty-first centuries. However, it begins by questioning whether the sensation novel's only or main legacy is to be found in these directions, and whether it was as short-lived a phenomenon as is sometimes claimed.

Despite the eagerness with which some mid-Victorian reviewers proclaimed the death of the sensation novel in the decade immediately following the one in which it had first sprung to prominence, it is clear that some of the sensation novels and novelists of the 1860s continued to exert their fascination on readers long after the initial sensation boom had passed. *Lady Audley's Secret*, *The Woman in White*, *The Moonstone* and *East Lynne* were all included in the *Daily Telegraph*'s selection of the 100 best novels of the nineteenth century in 1899. Four years later *T.P.'s Weekly* noted that it was 'no mean record for a book published nearly forty years ago to sustain as "Lady Audley" does, as strong a hold upon novel readers to-day as it promptly established when it appeared in its three-volume dress'.[2] Braddon, whose work had helped to define the sensation novel, continued both to produce sensation fiction throughout her long and productive career and to capitalise on her reputation as a sensationalist in order to market her fiction.

The term 'sensation novel' proved remarkably resilient in both the reviewing and marketing of fiction well into the 1890s and it was regularly used in advertisements for both new and reissued fiction.

As well as becoming dispersed into a range of sub-genres and informing a number of developments in fiction and other cultural forms at the end of the nineteenth and beginning of the twentieth centuries, the preoccupations and techniques of the sensation novel were taken up by many different kinds of fiction writers in the mid-Victorian period. Indeed, most mid-Victorian novelists worked with the same complex multiple plots which relied on coincidence and incident as did the sensationalists. Sensationalists and non-sensationalists alike engaged in a similar process of working with and reworking realism, and were concerned with the same issues of class, social change, sex, money, family, morals, manners and marriage and its alternatives. In short, sensation plots, sensation types, sensation themes and sensation machinery belonged to the general store of conventions on which all novelists drew. In this sense sensationalism was not confined to a sub-genre but was integral to mainstream fiction. Trollope, for example, although best known as the author of social and political novels in realist mode, believed that a good novel should be 'at the same time realistic and sensational'[3] and often relied in those novels on the sensation staples of crime, violence and sexual scandal. Trollope was also the author of a sensation novel and a parody of the genre. The first, *Orley Farm* (1862), includes the familiar sensation situations of a woman of high social rank and moral reputation who has a dark secret in her past, as well as plot complications arising from wills and codicils. The second, *The Eustace Diamonds* (1873), parodically rewrites *The Moonstone* by constructing a plot around a young woman who steals her own diamonds, as Cuff had erroneously suspected Collins's Rachel Verinder of doing.

Margaret Oliphant, a fierce critic of sensation fiction in her reviews for *Blackwood's Edinburgh Magazine*, was not averse to drawing on its subject matter and plotting in order to boost the sales of her own fiction. For example, halfway through its serialisation in *Blackwood's* (February 1862–January 1863), she sought to increase the popularity of *Salem Chapel* (the first of her 'Chronicles of Carlingford' series), a novel about the failed vocation of Arthur Vincent, a nonconformist minister, by embroiling the minister and his family in an elaborate sensational plot involving a woman with a secret past, the possibility of a bigamous marriage and a murder. The woman with a secret is Mrs Hilyard, an apparently widowed needlewoman and one of Vincent's parishioners, who is secretly being terrorised by her husband. The latter, in the guise of the mysterious Herbert Fordham, woos Vincent's teenage sister Susan who – perhaps in an echo of the famous Road murder case also used by Collins in *The Moonstone*, in which Constance Kent, a middle-class sixteen-year-old, was accused of murdering her brother – becomes the chief suspect when Fordham is shot. Another writer who deplored the melodramatic plots and unrealistic characters of the sensationalists, but was not averse to appropriating their methods, was George Meredith, the self-consciously high-brow novelist and an influential figure in nineteenth-century publishing through his role as a reader for the publishers Chapman and Hall. In *Evan Harrington* (1861) Meredith emulated Collins's sensationalism, deftly inverting aspects of *The Dead Secret* 'to serve his own idea of greater depths in psychological portraiture',[4] and a few years later, in an attempt to increase both his readership and income, he produced another sensation-influenced novel, *Rhoda Fleming* (1865), a tale of seduction and betrayal, bigamy and fraud.

Another high-brow novelist, George Eliot, doyenne of nineteenth-century realism, often deployed sensation effects and sensation machinery in her attempts to render the moral universe legible. The *Contemporary Review* was not alone in noting the indebtedness of *Felix Holt the Radical* (1866) to the sensation novel when it described Eliot's Mrs Transome – a woman with a secret, in this case a cross-class, adulterous affair which produced an illegitimate son – and Lady Audley as 'true twin sisters'. The *Contemporary* also accused Eliot of joining hands with Braddon in reversing 'the grand old idea of ... heroic behaviour, by cunningly eliciting our sympathy for individuals placed in doubtful circumstances, who fall into falsely tragical positions because of their weaknesses'.[5] Even *Middlemarch* (1871–2), the archetypal novel of high Victorian realism and moral seriousness, has its sensation elements: Raffles turns up as if from a sensation novel to provide the necessary plot machinery to expose the secret past of the ostensibly respectable banker Bulstrode, and there is a hint of adultery in the triangular relationships between Dorothea, Casaubon and Ladislaw and Rosamund, Lydgate and Ladislaw. The aesthetically ambitious *Daniel Deronda* (1876) includes such sensation elements as tangled intrigue, illegitimacy and other mysteries about parentage, women with secrets and other skeletons in cupboards. It also develops the psychology of sensation in its articulation of Gwendolen's moral character and development in terms of her nervous sensations.

Thomas Hardy, best known for his elegiac treatment of a dying rural world and doom-laden studies of modern life, launched his career with the anonymously published *Desperate Remedies* (1871), a novel he was later to dismiss as a 'sensational and strictly conventional narrative'.[6] In fact, Hardy's continued indebtedness to the sensation novel can be seen in his penchant for plots structured by the secrets of the past returning to shape the present and future lives of his characters, and his persistent focus on troubled marriages and the problematic nature of marriage as an institution. Hardy's indebtedness to sensation fiction can also be seen in the rhetorical excess of his style, particularly in his representation of female characters – for example, the Braddonesque 'Queen of the Night' passage on Eustacia Vye in *The Return of the Native* (which first appeared in *Belgravia*, a magazine noted for its sensational fiction, in 1878), and the anatomising of Tess Durbeyfield in *Tess of the D'Urbervilles* (1891).

To acknowledge both the persistence of the sensation novel beyond the 1860s and its dispersal into the mainstream and into novels which have come to form part of the canon of nineteenth-century fiction, is not, however, to deny the validity of Brantlinger's and Waller's claims that the sensation novel also dispersed into a range of new genres or sub-genres. Its narrative complicatedness and intricately constructed plots, as well as its concern with crime and detection clearly link the sensation novel to mid-century and *fin-de-siècle* developments in detective fiction. Indeed, from the outset, sensation novels were reviewed as examples of detective or crime fiction. Margaret Oliphant was one of the first to note the sensation novel's tendency to 'find its inspiration in crime, and more or less, make the criminal its hero', and also its creation of literary detectives: 'We have already had specimens ... of what the detective policeman can do for the enlivenment of literature,' she wrote in May 1862, 'and it is into the hands of the literary Detective that this school of storytelling must inevitably fall at last ... His appearance is favourable neither to taste or morals.'[7] Similarly, E. S. Dallas's review of *Lady Audley's Secret* in November 1862 described Braddon's novel as belonging to a new kind of fiction, in which as in Collins's *The Woman in White*, there 'is a secret, generally a crime, to be discovered'.[8] Some subsequent commentators on the genealogy of detective fiction have followed Oliphant and Dallas in acknowledging Collins as its progenitor, but have named *The Moonstone* as the novel which signals the birth of the genre. Thus, T. S. Eliot famously celebrated *The Moonstone* as 'the first and greatest of English detective novels',[9] and Dorothy L. Sayers concurred that judged 'by the standards of seventy years later ... *The Moonstone* is impeccable ... [It] set the standard, and ... it has taken us all this time to recognise it.'[10]

The Moonstone has also been claimed as the original country house mystery. Its outbreak of 'detective fever' provided a plethora of amateur and professional detectives, most importantly: Cuff, the fastidious, logical, deductive professional detective, 'for the last twenty years ... largely employed in cases of family scandal, acting in the capacity of confidential man',[11] who fails to solve the mysteries of the Verinder household; Franklin Blake, the dilettante with a taste for French novels and German philosophy, who deploys an eclectic and often conflicting range of methods in his quest to solve or resolve the mysteries of his own part in the disappearance of the diamond, Rachel's behaviour and his own identity and social role; the successful detective, Ezra Jennings – the mysterious and tortured outsider, a man of mixed race, dubious history and an opium addict – a highly sensitive subject, who uses his intuition, as well as his specialist scientific and personal knowledge to solve the mystery of the diamond's disappearance and of Franklin's role in it.

In some ways Jennings prefigures one of the most celebrated of fictional detectives, Sherlock Holmes, whose creator, Arthur Conan Doyle, has often been named as the true originator of British detective fiction. In fact, the characters and narrative structures of the Holmes stories are borrowed from earlier sensational novelists, just as the sensation novel skilfully plundered elements from earlier crime and detective fiction, such as the Newgate novel, G. W. M. Reynold's *The Mysteries of London* (1844–6) and proto-detective novels such as Dickens's *Bleak House* (1852–3). Certainly, the development of the detective science of Holmes, who made his first appearance in *The Study in Scarlet* in 1887, is anticipated in the sensation novel's depiction of ordinary citizens becoming detectives and developing the reading and forensic skills which transform an array of signs, circumstances, coincidences and documentary records into evidence which establishes a person's true identity and/ or their association with crime or wrongdoing. Moreover, the Holmes stories, like sensation novels, tend to deal with mysteries or irregularities in the family, which Holmes – like the amateur and professional detectives in the sensation novel – usually rectifies without having recourse to the law. Both the sensation novel and the Holmes stories appear to adhere to the belief voiced by Archibald Carlyle in Ellen Wood's *East Lynne*, that 'justice and law are sometimes in opposition'.[12]

Like the sensation novel, the development of mid and late nineteenth-century detective stories was associated with developments in the newspaper and periodical press. Drawing on newspaper reports of criminal cases for plot details, both forms of fiction also made use of the advertisement and personal columns of newspapers to propel their plots; wrong-doers place advertisements designed to defraud or dupe potential victims and detectives do so in order to entrap their suspects. Both forms of fiction were also products of the expanding market for family magazines, those weekly, fortnightly or monthly miscellanies which combined factual articles with stories and serialised novels. Whereas sensation narratives were designed to tantalise readers over many weeks or months of serial publication, and keep them returning to the magazine for the next episode, late nineteenth-century detective fiction contributed to and capitalised upon the growing vogue for short stories, and at the same time, redeployed the serial's capacity for building up reader loyalty through the development of a series format constructed around a particular detective.

Mid- and late nineteenth-century detective fiction also continued the sensation novel's concern with the modern and modernity. Some historians of nineteenth-detective fiction, such as D. A. Miller and Ronald Thomas, have attributed its development to 'the creation of the modern bureaucratic state'[13] and the discipline or self-policing subjectivity which it required. Others have seen the cultural preoccupation with detection as symptomatic of a specifically urban or metropolitan modernity. For example, the German social theorist Walter Benjamin argued that nineteenth-century detective fiction originated in the anonymity of modern city life, in the 'obliteration of the individual's traces in the big-city crowd'[14] and the universal suspicion with which modern city dwellers regard each other. Certainly class mobility, the increasing concentration of people in cities and their suburbs, as well as the return of people and objects from the outposts of Empire to the metropolitan centre or the heart of the English countryside are important elements of both sensation novels and detective fiction. So too is the focus on modern technology. In detective fiction, as in the sensation novel, the railway and the electric telegraph are repeatedly deployed by both wrong-doers and detectives.

The sensation novel's legacy can also be seen in the rise of the fictional female detective. Alongside women such as Collins's Marion Halcombe (*The Woman in White*) and Braddon's Eleanor Vane (*Eleanor's Victory*) who turn detective in order to solve the mysteries within their own and other families, the 1860s also saw the emergence of professional female sleuths such as Andrew Forrest's Mrs Gladden in *The Female Detective* (1864) and Mrs Paschal in the anonymously published (attributed to W. S. Hayward) *Revelations of a Lady Detective* (1864). Both early versions of the New Woman, Gladden and Paschal were harbingers of the fictional female detectives who gained a new prominence at the height of the New Woman debates in the 1890s in such collections as Catherine Louisa Pirkis's *The Experiences of Loveday Brooke, Lady Detective* (1894), George R. Sims's *Dorcas Dene, Detective* (1897), Fergus Hume's *Hagar of the Pawn Shop* (1899), L.T. Meades's and Robert Eustace's *The Detections of Miss Cusack* (1899–1900) and Grant Allen's *Miss Cayley's Adventures* (1899). Like many of the female protagonists in sensation novels, these female detectives invoke cultural stereotypes which associate femininity with duplicity and deceit: they are mistresses of disguise and impersonation who are able to insinuate themselves into the confidence of those whom they investigate. Similarly, the narratives in which they appear rework sensation fiction's focus on crime within the family and its preoccupation with household spies. Pirkis's Loveday Brooke, for example, is a professional detective who specialises in investigating robberies by entering households undercover in order to observe suspects at close quarters. This is seen by her employer as a particularly apt *modus operandi* for female detectives: 'the idea seems to be gaining ground in many quarters that in cases of mere suspicion, women detectives are more satisfactory than men, for they are less likely to attract attention'.[15] Like many of the female protagonists of sensation novels, Loveday transgresses conventional gender expectations in the way in which she adapts to the hand that life has dealt her: 'by a jerk of Fortune's wheel, Loveday had been thrown upon the world penniless and all but friendless', and 'had forthwith defied convention, and chosen for herself a career that had cut her off sharply from her former associates and her position in society' (402–3).

Independence and the transgression of traditional gender roles, not least through the pursuit of professional work outside the domestic sphere, were, of course, characteristics of the New Women of the 1880s and 1890s, and of their fictional representatives in New Woman novels. Despite initial appearances to the contrary there are in fact several similarities between the popular sensation novels of the 1860s and the 'modern women's books of the introspective type'[16] which appeared in the 1880s and 1890s, not least in their generic and stylistic hybridity. The New Woman novel takes up the sensation novel's preoccupation with exposing and exploring the contradictions of contemporary marriage and the domestic ideal. Like the sensation novel, New Woman fiction was produced by and intervened in current debates about conventionally prescribed social, familial and gender roles. There were also remarkable similarities in the terms of the critical debates which the two kinds of fiction generated. In many ways the critical debate on the New Woman novel picked up some of the main threads of the sensation debate, focusing on the (in)appropriateness of the fictional depiction of transgressive, independent heroines, and the representation of the female body and women's feelings.

Another late nineteenth-century legacy of the sensation novel is the *fin-de-siècle* revival of romance and tales of the fantastic, which, like sensation fiction, both articulate and represent a range of responses to that modernisation of the senses that accompanied the technological revolutions of the age. Such narratives include Robert Louis Stevenson's *The Strange Case of Dr Jekyll and Mr Hyde* (1886), Rider Haggard's *She* (1887), Oscar Wilde's *The Picture of Dorian Gray* (1891), Arthur Machen's *The Great God Pan* (1894), Bram Stoker's *Dracula* (1897) and Mary Elizabeth Braddon's vampire narrative 'Good Lady Ducayne' (1896), Marie Corelli's *The Sorrows of Satan* (1895), as well as H. G. Wells's scientific romances – *The Time Machine* (1895), *The Island of Doctor Moreau* (1896), *The Invisible Man* (1897), *The War of the Worlds* (1898), *When the Sleeper Wakes* (1899) and *The First Men in the Moon* (1901). One important link between the sensation novel and its mutations in *fin-de-siècle* romance and fantastic fiction is the use of layered, framed and embedded narratives including journal extracts and other ostensibly documentary records. As in sensation fiction, this narrative complicatedness works to create an illusion of verisimilitude, while, at the same time, dispersing narrative authority, disrupting narrative causality and problematising origins. Another legacy of sensation fiction is the way in which *fin-de-siècle* romance and fantastic fictions develop its preoccupation with colonial returns in narratives which figure a process of reverse colonisation in which the British metropolis is invaded by predatory alien forces. Some of these late-Victorian romances also develop what William Thompson, Archbishop of York, described as the sensation novel's attempt 'to persuade people that in almost every one of the well-ordered houses of their neighbours there was a skeleton shut up in some cupboard', and 'that their comfortable and easy-looking neighbour had in his breast a secret story which he was always going about trying to conceal'.[17] Stevenson's Jekyll, for example, is a fantastic version of the apparently conventional citizen with a dark secret, which, like so many of the secrets of the sensation novel, is produced by the role playing required in order to preserve Victorian social norms. As Jekyll puts it in his 'Full Statement of the Case':

> The worst of my faults was a certain gaiety of disposition . . . [which] I found . . . hard to reconcile with my imperious desire to carry my head high, and wear a more than commonly grave countenance. Hence it came about that I concealed my pleasures . . . I stood already committed to a profound duplicity of life . . . It was thus rather the exacting nature of my aspirations, than any particular degradation in my faults, that made me what I was, and, with even a deeper trench than in the majority of men, severed in me those provinces of good and ill which divide and compound man's dual nature.[18]

Another of the sensation novel's late nineteenth-century mutations is the political thriller. As the *Daily News*'s review of John K. Leys's *The Black Terror: A Romance of Russia* noted, although 'Nihilism may be a danger to the country at large', it forms 'a very effective motive for that important institution the sensation novel'.[19] The sensation novel also provided an important model for one of the most significant early twentieth-century novels about nihilism and terror, Joseph Conrad's *The Secret Agent* (1907). Conrad's indebtedness to the sensation novel was first noted in Edward Garnett's review of *The Secret Agent* in the *Nation* (28 September 1907), which commends the author for having 'brought clearly into our ken the subterranean world of that foreign London which, since the death of Count Fosco, has served in fiction only the crude purpose of our sensational writers'.[20] Conrad was in fact an avid reader of Collins, Wood and, his particular favourite, Braddon. *The Secret Agent* owes a great deal to both *Lady Audley's*

Secret and *The Woman in White*, all three narratives sharing a common preoccupation with women's struggles with their domestic lot and the capacity for discord and division within the secret theatre of home. In ending his novel 'with the disintegration of the domestic sphere ... [which] makes an ironic commentary on gender roles', Ellen Burton Harrington has suggested, Conrad is in effect 'referencing and re-envisioning the popular sensation novel and its themes of feminine frustration, the desire for liberation, and the dangers of degeneracy'.[21] Like the sensation novel, *The Secret Agent* exposes the contradictions and problems of women's traditional roles while remaining ambivalent or anxious about the political and social implications of increasing their autonomy.

Recycling the sensation novel: adaptations and appropriations

As Andrew Maunder has shown in chapter 5, sensation fiction has always had a complex relationship with the stage. Sometimes borrowed from the stage repertoire, the plots of sensation novels often returned to the stage, adapted by their authors (notably Collins) or by others. This stage legacy has been enduring, both with revivals of nineteenth-century adaptations and new adaptations in the twentieth- and twenty-first centuries. *Lady Audley's Secret* had at least four twentieth-century adaptations: Brian Burton's *Lady Audley's Secret or The Lime Tree Walk* (first performed at the Little Theatre, Leicester, 1966) and Constance Cox's one-act melodrama (published by Samuel French, 1976), in both of which Lady Audley commits suicide; Sylvia Freedman's (first performed at the Lyric Theatre, Hammersmith,1991), in which the heroine escapes from the asylum and adopts a new identity; and a musical version (music by George Goehring, book by Douglas Seale, lyrics by John Kunz), which had a short run at the Eastside Playhouse Theatre, New York in 1972. A musical version of *East Lynne* (by Robert Neil Porter and Jack Perry) was staged in the USA in 1972, and Lisa Evans's 1992 adaptation for the Birmingham Repertory Theatre has had several revivals. *The Woman in White* resurfaced as Tim Kelly's irreverent melodrama *Egad, The Woman in White* (1975), and, perhaps the most surprising recent example of the afterlife of the sensation novel, Andrew Lloyd Webber's musical extravaganza at the Palace Theatre, London in 2004 (lyrics by David Zippel, book by Charlotte Jones, directed by Trevor Nunn). This loose adaptation of Collins's novel foregrounds Marian, albeit as a lovesick woman pining for Walter's affection, and evokes the sensation drama's use of modern technology with its employment of shifting video projections for the novel's multiple settings.

As well as providing a generic model for modern mystery, detective and suspense films, sensation novels were also a direct source of the plots of early cinema. Collins's novels provided the plots of twelve silent films between 1909 and 1929: one based on *The Dead Secret* (1913), three on *The Woman in White* (1912, 1913 and 1929), one on *Armadale* (1916), three on *The Moonstone* (1909, 1911 and 1915) and four on *The New Magdalen* (1910, 1912, 1913 and 1914). *The Woman in White* provided a very loose basis for the British talkie, *Crimes at the Dark House* (1940), and a Warner Brothers's production (1947), starring Sydney Greenstreet as Fosco, also took liberties with Collins's narrative in an ending in which Laura finds fulfilment in mothering her child by Glyde, and Walter proclaims his love for Marian. Monogram's talkie of *The Moonstone* (USA, 1934) had a contemporary (1930s) setting and transformed Betteredge into a female housekeeper. The most recent film adaptation of Collins, Radha Bharadwaj's film of *Basil* (first shown on the American Movie Classics Channel in November 1998), gives its own version of Basil's earlier life and family situation and reconfigures some of the relationships between the characters. For example, Mannion is motivated by his desire to avenge his sister who has died from a botched abortion following her seduction and betrayal by Basil's brother.

Lady Audley's Secret was used for two American and one British silent film in 1912, 1915 (*The Secrets of Society*) and 1920. The latter (directed by Jack Denton for Ideal), updates Braddon's heroine by transforming her from girl of the period into a feisty, cigarette-smoking, bobbed-haired New Woman, but follows earlier stage adapters of the novel by making her a figure of pathos who dies by her own hand. Two silent film versions of *Aurora Floyd* were produced in the USA in 1912 and 1915. Film versions of *East Lynne* were based on nineteenth-century stage adaptations rather than the novel. Silent movies in 1916 and 1925 were followed by a lavish American-produced early talkie (1931), which received an Oscar nomination for Best Picture. Mack Sennett wrote the screenplay for Paramount's comedy *East Lynne with Variations* (1919) and in 1931 the popular British farce *East Lynne on the Western Front* depicted soldiers attempting to put on a production of a play based on Wood's novel.

Sensation novels have also been adapted for the modern cultural form that most closely resembles the nineteenth-century practice of family reading – the radio or television serial. Collins has been the most frequently adapted of the sensation authors. Radio adaptations of his work include: a two-part dramatisation of *Basil* (adapted by Robin Brooks, BBC Radio 4, 2006); a four-part dramatisation of *The Woman in White* (adapted by Martyn Wade, BBC Radio 4, 2001) and a reading in eight episodes (BBC Radio 4, 2004); a six-part adaptation of *No Name* (BBC Radio 4, 1973) and a two-part dramatisation by John Fletcher in 1989, as well as an earlier BBC Home service radio adaptation in 1952; a 1948 radio version of *Armadale* and Robin Brooks's three-part dramatisation for Radio 4 in 2009; a 1945 adaptation of *The Moonstone* for the syndicated American radio series 'The Weird Circle', and a six-episode dramatisation for Radio 4 in 1979.

The Woman in White was first dramatised for British television in 1957 as a short anthology piece in ABC Television's 'Hour of Mystery', and an American adaptation in 1960 was first aired as part of 'The Dow Hour of Great Mysteries'. A six-part adaptation by Michael Voysey followed in 1966. Perhaps influenced by the reinterpretation of the novel by feminist critics, Ray Jenkins's five-part adaptation for BBC2 in 1982 (shown in the USA in 1985) is notable for its representation of Laura and Marian as independent and spirited women. A two-part dramatisation of *The Woman in White* (a BBC, Carlton and WGBH Boston co-production) was broadcast at Christmas 1997, thus returning Collins to one of his original contexts as the producer (with Dickens) of special Christmas Numbers of *Household Words*. Tim Fywell's direction of David Pirie's adaptation focused on Marian, the first character seen and heard by the audience, who replaces Walter as the narrative's editor and shaper as it is her voiceovers which propel the narrative. This updated Marian is more active and more sexually knowing than Collins's original. So is Walter, whose transformation from spectator to actor is effected by his journeying into darkest London rather than grappling with the South American jungle. This adaptation also makes explicit the violence against and sexual exploitation of women, which is implicit in the social structure about which Collins writes, representing Laura as the victim of physical domestic violence and Anne as the victim of child sex abuse. In another updating of the novel's sensationalism Anne is presented as a tormented rather than distracted character whose final act of desperation is to commit suicide by jumping from a tower.

There have been three BBC TV dramatisations of *The Moonstone* to date – in seven parts (1959), five parts (1973) and two parts (Christmas, 1996). Kevin Elyot's screenplay for the 1996 adaptation relies heavily on Betteredge to convey essential plot information. It also emphasises the quirks of Collins's detective, Cuff (played by Antony Sher), reminding the modern audience just how much their favourite TV detectives owe to this nineteenth-century original. This adaptation also emphasises and reinterprets Collins's preoccupation with class, Empire and unusual mental states. In particular, Franklin's dream at the film's opening and dream-like sequences involving the Indians and the Shivering Sands at its close, invoke Empire as both a troubling component of the British psyche and as a material fact which underpins the comfortable lives of Franklin and Rachel and also remind the viewer of the troubled working-class girl Rosanna, who disappears from Collins's novel at an earlier stage in the narrative.

Braddon and Wood had to await their largely feminist-inspired rediscovery before being translated to television and radio. Television adaptations of *East Lynne* in 1976 and 1982 were followed by a radio dramatisation in seven one-hour episodes (by Michael Bakewell), first broadcast on BBC Radio 4 in 1987 to coincide with the centenary of Wood's death. *Lady Audley's Secret* was dramatised in two parts by Bryony Lavery for BBC Radio 4 in 1999, and a new version (directed by Julie Beckett and Fiona Kelcher) was broadcast as the Radio 4 Woman's Hour serial in 2009. Donald Hounam's adaptation of *Lady Audley's Secret* (directed by Betsan Morris Evans and first broadcast on ITV and US public Broadcasting in 2000), followed most nineteenth-century stage adaptations by omitting Clara Talboys and changing Braddon's ending. In this case, instead of dying of shock or by her own hand as in many earlier adaptations, a perfectly sane Lady Audley escapes from the asylum assisted by her stepdaughter Alicia, and is last seen – by an infatuated Robert – at a railway station accompanied by a man.

The sensation novel's currency in the form of radio and TV adaptations has no doubt exerted its influence on the plotting of turn-of-the-twentieth-century costume drama. Since the late 1980s the legacy of the sensation novel has also been evident in a growing number of neo-Victorian novels such as Sarah Waters's *Affinity* (1999) and *Fingersmith* (2002), James Wilson's *The Dark Clue* (2001) and Michael Faber's *The Crimson Petal and the White* (2002). *The Dark Clue* and *Fingersmith* are most obviously the heirs of the sensation novel: the former is presented as a sequel to *The Woman in White* and the latter fairly directly borrows both its dark atmosphere and plotting from Collins. *The Dark Clue* develops Collins's *ménage a trois* when Marian rescues Walter from his restlessness with his new life as a member of the landed classes by helping obtain a commission as J. M. W. Turner's biographer. Together they set out on a quest to unravel the secrets of the painter's double life, which takes Walter away from conventional upper middle-class society and his new role as a Victorian paterfamilias into the seamier side of London life. In the process of uncovering Turner's buried life both Walter and Marian discover something of their own buried lives and hidden desires. Dark desires and the criminal and sexual underworlds of nineteenth-century London are also the subject of Sarah Waters's *Fingersmith*. Like Collins, Waters delays the unravelling of her narrative's secrets and disperses narrative authority by dividing the narration between Sue, an orphan raised among thieves, who is involved in a plot to trick another orphan into marriage with the dashing criminal Richard Rivers, and Maud, the apparent victim of this plot. Virtually every character has at least one secret, and the plot, which, like

The Woman in White, involves the substitution of one woman for another in a lunatic asylum, has more twists than perhaps even Collins would have thought possible.

Beth Palmer has recently argued that the most significant and enduring legacy of sensation fiction is a 'self-consciousness about how the contemporary moment is constructed in and by print culture as it mediates the past', which is most clearly demonstrated in the 'self-reflexive interest in the materiality of print culture'[22] found in Waters's and Faber's knowing references to nineteenth-century sensation novels. For example, when Faber's prostitute-heroine Sugar fabricates the death of her lover's mad wife in order to save her from the lunatic asylum, the supposed death is reported in the form of reprinted newspaper article, which recalls Helen Tallboy's fake obituary in *Lady Audley's Secret*. In *Affinity*, Waters follows Collins in constructing her narrative from the diaries of the two female protagonists, Margaret Prior, the neurasthenic, middle-class prison visitor and Selina Dawes, the prisoner (and spirit-medium) whom she visits, and comes to desire. Both novelists also suggest that their characters have been shaped by their reading of sensation novels. Faber does this in knowing narratorial asides, for example, when Sugar suggests that her lover should employ a detective to search for his wife: '(She knows nothing about detectives beyond what she's read in *The Moonstone*, but she hopes the bumbling Seegraves outnumber the clever Cuffs).'[23] *Affinity* also invokes *The Moonstone* when Margaret attempts to explain the loss of her locket: 'perhaps I rose and seized the locket and placed it somewhere – like Franklin Blake in *The Moonstone*'.[24]

The numerous developments, adaptations, mediations and appropriations of sensation novels outlined in this chapter suggest not only the continuing appeal of sensation fiction, but also its adaptive capacity as it is reworked for the cultural imaginary and social and ethical concerns of the twentieth and twenty-first centuries.

NOTES

1. Patrick Brantlinger, 'What is Sensational About the Sensation Novel?' *Nineteenth-Century Fiction* 37:1 (1982), 1–28 (1); Phillip Waller, *Writers, Readers, and Reputations: Literary Life in Britain 1870–1918* (Oxford University Press, 2006), 667.
2. Edmund Downey, 'Miss Braddon and Her Work', *T.P.'s Weekly* (24 July 1903), 203.
3. Anthony Trollope, *An Autobiography*, 2 vols. (Edinburgh and London: William Blackwood and Sons, 1883), vol. II, 41–2.
4. Benjamin Fisher, 'A Genuine Gothic Exchange: George Meredith Pilfers Wilkie Collins's *The Dead Secret for Evan Harrington*', *Journal of the Georgia Philological Association* 1 (2006), 53.

5. H. A. Page, 'The Morality of Literary Art', *Contemporary Review* 5 (1867), 179.
6. Thomas Hardy, *Desperate Remedies* (1871; London: Macmillan, 1975), 37.
7. Margaret Oliphant, 'Sensation Novels', *Blackwood's Edinburgh Magazine* 91 (1862), 564–84 (580).
8. *The Times* (18 November 1862), 4.
9. T. S. Eliot, 'Wilkie Collins and Dickens', *Selected Essays* (London: Faber and Faber, 1932), 464.
10. Dorothy L. Sayers (ed.), *The Omnibus of Crime* (New York: Payson and Clarke, 1929), 29.
11. Wilkie Collins, *The Moonstone*, ed. John Sutherland (Oxford University Press, 1999), 163.
12. Ellen Wood, *East Lynne*, ed. Elisabeth Jay (Oxford University Press, 2005), 267.
13. Ronald R. Thomas, 'Detection in the Victorian Novel', in *The Cambridge Companion to the Victorian Novel*, ed. Deidre David (Cambridge University Press, 2001), 169–91 (169).
14. Walter Benjamin, *Charles Baudelaire: A Lyric Poet in the Era of High Capitalism* (London: Verso, 1973), 43.
15. Catherine Louisa Pirkis, *The Experiences of Loveday Brooke, Lady Detective* (London: Hutchinson, 1894), 581. A further reference to this edition will be given in the text.
16. Hugh Stutfield, 'The Psychology of Feminism', *Blackwood's Edinburgh Magazine* 161 (1897), 104.
17. *The Times* (2 November 1864), 9.
18. Robert Louis Stevenson, *The Strange Case of Dr Jekyll and Mr Hyde, and Other Stories*, ed. Jenni Calder (London: Penguin, 1979), 81.
19. 'Novels of the Day', *Daily News* (6 December 1899), 7.
20. Reprinted in Norman Sherry (ed.), *Conrad: The Critical Heritage* (London: Routledge and Kegan Paul, 1973), 56.
21. Ellen Burton Harrington, 'The Anarchist's Wife: Joseph Conrad's Debt to Sensation Fiction in the Secret Agent', *Conradiana: A Journal of Joseph Conrad Studies* 36 (2004), 51–63 (51).
22. Beth Palmer, 'Are the Victorians Still with Us?: Victorian Sensation Fiction and Its Legacies in the Twenty First Century', *Victorian Studies* 55 (2009), 86–94 (87, 92).
23. Michael Faber, *The Crimson Petal and The White* (Edinburgh: Canongate, 2002), 693, 677.
24. Sarah Waters, *Affinity* (London: Virago, 1999), 91.

FURTHER READING

Bachman, Maria K. and Don Richard Cox (eds.), *Reality's Dark Light: The Sensational Wilkie Collins*. University of Tennessee Press, 2003.

Baker, William (ed.), *Wilkie Collins's Library: A Reconstruction*. New York: Greenwood Press, 2002.

Baker, William and William M. Clarke (eds.), *The Letters of Wilkie Collins*. 2 vols. Basingstoke: Macmillan, 1999.

Baker, William, Andrew Gasson, Graham Law and Paul Lewis (eds.), *The Public Face of Wilkie Collins: The Collected Letters*. 4 vols. London: Pickering and Chatto, 2005.

Beller, Anne-Marie, *Mary Elizabeth Braddon: A Companion to the Mystery Fiction*. Jefferson, NC: McFarland, 2012.

Brantlinger, Patrick, 'What is Sensational about the Sensation Novel?' *Nineteenth-Century Fiction* 37:1 (1982), 1–28.

Carnell, Jennifer, *The Literary Lives of Mary Elizabeth Braddon: A Study of her Life and Work*. Hastings: The Sensation Press, 2000.

Clarke, William, M. *The Secret Life of Wilkie Collins*. London: Allison and Busby, 1988.

Costantini, Mariaconcetta (ed.), *Armadale: Wilkie Collins and the Dark Threads of Life*. Rome: Aracne, 2009.
  Venturing into Unknown Waters: Wilkie Collins and the Challenge of Modernity. Pescara: Edizioni Tracce, 2008.

Cvetkovich, Ann, *Mixed Feelings: Feminism, Mass Culture, and Victorian Sensationalism*. New Brunswick, NJ: Rutgers University Press, 1992.

Garrison, Laurie, *Science, Sexuality and Sensation Novels: Pleasures of the Senses*. Basingstoke: Palgrave Macmillan, 2011.

Gasson, Andrew, *Wilkie Collins: An Illustrated Guide*. Oxford University Press, 1998.

Gilbert, Pamela K. ed. *A Companion to Sensation Fiction*. Oxford: Blackwell, 2011.
  Disease, Desire, and the Body in Victorian Women's Popular Novels. Cambridge University Press, 1997.

Harrison, Kimberly and Richard Fantina (eds.), *Victorian Sensations: Essays on a Scandalous Genre*. Columbus: Ohio State University Press, 2006.

Heller, Tamar, *Dead Secrets: Wilkie Collins and the Female Gothic*. New Haven, CT: Yale University Press, 1992.

Hughes, Winifred, *The Maniac in the Cellar: Sensation Novels of the 1860s*. Princeton University Press, 1980.

Law, Graham and Andrew Mauder, *Wilkie Collins: A Literary Life*. Basingstoke: Palgrave Macmillan, 2008.

Loesberg, Jonathan, 'The Ideology of Narrative Form in Sensation Fiction'. *Representations* 13 (1986), 115–38.

Mangham, Andrew, *Violent Women and Sensation Fiction: Crime, Medicine and Victorian Popular Fiction*. Basingstoke: Palgrave Macmillan, 2007.

Mangham, Andrew (ed.), *Wilkie Collins: Interdisciplinary Essays*. Newcastle: Cambridge Scholars Publishing, 2007.

Maunder, Andrew and Grace Moore, *Victorian Crime, Madness and Sensation*. Farnham: Ashgate, 2004.

Maunder, Andrew (ed.), *Varieties of Women's Sensation Fiction, 1855–1890*. 6 vols. London: Pickering and Chatto, 2004.

Nayder, Lillian, *Unequal Partners: Charles Dickens, Wilkie Collins and Victorian Authorship*. London: Cornell University Press, 2002.

Wilkie Collins. New York: Twayne Publishers, 1997.

Nemesvari, Richard, 'Robert Audley's Secret: Male Homosocial Desire in *Lady Audley's Secret*'. *Studies in the Novel* 27:4 (1995), 515–28.

O'Neill, Philip, *Wilkie Collins: Women, Property and Propriety*. London: Macmillan Press, 1988.

Page, Norman (ed.), *Wilkie Collins: The Critical Heritage*. London: Routledge and Kegan Paul, 1974.

Palmer, Beth, *Women's Authorship and Editorship in Victorian Culture: Sensational Strategies*. Oxford University Press, 2011.

Peters, Catherine. *The King of Inventors: A Life of Wilkie Collins*. London: Secker and Warburg, 1991.

Pykett, Lyn, *The Improper Feminine: The Sensation Novel and the New Woman Writing*. London and New York: Routledge, 1992.

The Sensation Novel: From The Woman in White to The Moonstone. Plymouth: Northcote House, 1994 and 2012.

Wilkie Collins. Oxford University Press, 2005.

Pykett, Lyn (ed.), *Wilkie Collins*. Basingstoke: Macmillan, 1998.

Radford, Andrew, *Victorian Sensation Fiction: A Reader's Guide to Essential Criticism*. Basingstoke: Palgrave Macmillan, 2009.

Smith, Nelson C. and R. C. Terry (eds.), *Wilkie Collins to the Forefront: Some Reassessments*. New York: AMS Press, 1995.

Talairach-Vielmas, Laurence, *Wilkie Collins, Medicine and the Gothic*. Cardiff: University of Wales Press, 2009.

Taylor, Jenny Bourne, *The Cambridge Companion to Wilkie Collins*. Cambridge University Press, 2006.

'In the Secret Theatre of Home': Wilkie Collins, Sensation Narrative, and Nineteenth-Century Psychology. London: Routledge, 1988.

Tomaiuolo, Saverio, *In Lady Audley's Shadow: Mary Elizabeth Braddon, and Victorian Literary Genres*. Edinburgh University Press, 2010.

Tromp, Marlene, Pamela K. Gilbert and Aeron Haynie (eds.), *Beyond Sensation: Mary Elizabeth Braddon in Context*. Albany: State University of New York Press, 2000.

Wolff, Robert Lee, *Sensational Victorian: The Life and Fiction of Mary Elizabeth Braddon*. New York and London: Garland, 1979.

Wood, Charles W., *Memorials of Mrs Henry Wood*. London: Richard Bentley and Son, 1894.

Wynne, Deborah, *The Sensation Novel and the Victorian Family Magazine*. Basingstoke and New York: Palgrave, 2001.

INDEX

226

asylum, 16, 26, 32, 60, 73, 82, 102, 111, 118, 125, 133, 136, 137, 158, 159, 164, 191, 194, 218, 221, 222
heredity, 82, 185
hysteria, 164, 186, 193, 197
monomania, 185, 189
psychology, 15, 23, 129, 184, 192, 212
Malet, H. P.
Lost Links in the Indian Mutiny, 116
Mann, Jessica, 207
Mansel, H. L., 8, 9, 18, 37, 87, 93, 99, 101, 129, 146, 147, 168, 169, 173, 174, 175, 176, 177, 178–9, 184
'Sensation Novels', 168
marriage, 11, 13, 17, 21, 22, 23, 26, 27, 31, 37, 44–5, 63, 73, 74, 76, 77, 81, 82, 102, 103, 107, 120, 125, 137, 156, 157, 158–60, 161, 187, 193, 196–8, 199–201, 203, 204, 206, 207, 208, 211, 212, 216, 221
divorce, 17, 18, 93, 143, 156, 159, 160, 162, 203
Married Women's Property Act (1870), 157
Married Women's Property Act (1882), 163
Marryat, Florence, 3, 54, 142, 145, 148–50, 197–9, 204, 205–7
In Her Father's Name, 197
In the Name of Liberty, 197, 204
Open! Sesame!, 148
The Spirit World, 150
There is No Death, 148
Martin, R. Montgomery, 115
Masson, David, 52
Master Humphrey's Clock, 177
Matrimonial Causes Act (1857), 17, 119, 157, 162
Matus, Jill, 188
Maunder, Andrew, 2, 3, 7, 52, 218
Meade, L. T.
The Detections of Miss Cusack, 215
medicine, 4, 5, 27, 106, 109, 111, 182, 183, 184, 187, 189, 194
vivisection, 5, 156, 163, 164, 165, 196
melodrama, 2, 3, 5, 8, 11, 57, 59, 62, 66, 92, 101, 171, 218
Menke, Richard, 163
Meredith, George, 212
Evan Harrington, 212
Rhoda Fleming, 212
mesmerism, 142
Michie, Helena, 79
Millais, John Everett, 23, 36, 41
The Bridesmaid, 23

Miller, D. A., 215
modernity, 5, 10, 12, 184, 204, 215
Money, Edward
The Wife and the Ward, 116
Montcrieff, William Thomas, 56
Moore, George, 176
Moore, Louisa, 61
Morley, Henry, 52, 55, 169
Morning Advertiser, 61
Morning Post, 64
Mosenthal, Salomon Herman von
Deborah, 62
Muddock, Jack
The Great White Hand or the Tiger of Cawnpore, 116
Mudie, Charles, 176, 178
Mudie's Select Library, 132, 175, 176
murder, 12–16, 25, 28, 34, 46, 60, 63, 64, 123, 127, 137, 143, 156, 159, 160, 173, 189, 191, 192, 194, 197, 200–1, 202, 204, 211
Musical Standard, 62
My Lady (anon.), 17–18

Nation, 217
Neilson, Julia, 65
Neo-Victorianism, 6, 210, 221
New Monthly Magazine, 16, 88
New Woman fiction, 1, 6, 190, 196–7, 200, 201, 202, 203, 204, 205, 208, 215, 216, 219
New York Herald, 170
New York Times, 170
Newby, Mrs C. J./Warburton, Emma, 18, 171
Wondrous Strange, 171
Newby, T. C., 171
Newgate novel, 7, 15, 59, 214
newspapers, 4, 15, 17, 44, 60, 85, 93, 114, 169, 176, 178, 214
Nicoll, Allardyce, 54
North British Review, 85, 173
Norton, Caroline
English Laws for Women in the Nineteenth Century, 157
Nunn, Trevor, 218

Observer, 58
Old Bailey, the, 52
Oliphant, Margaret, 7, 8, 9, 11, 37, 87, 95, 96, 108, 129, 131, 132, 138, 147–8, 211, 213
Salem Chapel, 131, 138, 211
Olympic Theatre, 39

Cambridge companions to...

AUTHORS

TOPICS